HEGEL'S THEORY
OF MENTAL ACTIVITY

HEGEL'S THEORY
OF MENTAL ACTIVITY

An Introduction to Theoretical Spirit

WILLEM A. deVRIES

CORNELL UNIVERSITY PRESS

ITHACA AND LONDON

To Dianne

Contents

Preface   xi
A Note on the Texts   xvii
The Structure of Subjective Spirit   xxi

1   Science, Teleology, and Interpretation   1
   Physicalism and Causalism   1
   Our Relationship to Nature   4
     Two Approaches to Nature   4
     Objective Purpose   7
     Universal Purpose   10
   The Need for Philosophy   13

2   Hegel's Reconception of the Philosophy of Mind   18
   Philosophical Psychology: Hegel's Predecessors   18
     Against Rational Psychology   19
     Against Empiricist Psychology   22
   Philosophical Psychology: Hegel's Methodology   24
     From Soul to Spirit   25
     Subjective Spirit   26
     Philosophy and Psychology   28
   The Philosophy of Spirit   31

3   Nature and Spirit   33
   Metaphysics and the Structure of the Sciences   33
     The Languages of Nature and Spirit   35
     Hegel as a Weak Monist   41

Distinguishing Nature and Spirit   46
   Externality and Self-determination   46
   The Nature of Spirit   49

4   Sensation: Mind's Material   53
   The Sentient and the Nonsentient   54
      The Nature of the Animal Organism   55
      The Sentient Organism   56
   The Object of Sensation   60
      Inner and Outer Sense   61
      Mediate and Immediate Objects of Sense   63
   Sensation as Noncognitive   67

5   Feeling   71
   The Role of Feeling   72
   Feeling and the Self   74
   The Soul's Relation to Reality   78
   The Liberation of the Soul   84

6   Phenomenology: The I Emerges   87
   Consciousness and the I   89
      Does "I" Refer?   90
      The Sense of "I"   92
      The Reference of "I"   97
   The Thinking Subject   99
      Universality and Self-relation   99
      Thinking as a Subject   104

7   Intuition   108
   The Role of Intuition in the Psychology   108
   Attention, Space, and Time   111
   Intuition Proper   116

8   Representation and Recollection   119
   The Role of Representation   119
   Recollection   125

9   Imagination: Universality and Signification   135
   Associative or Reproductive Imagination   135
   Symbolic Imagination   141
   Sign-making Imagination   143

10   Memory: Language as the Material of Thought   149
     Signification and Language   149
     The Stages of Memory   153
        Recollective Memory   153
        Reproductive Memory   154
        Mechanical Memory   157

11   Representing versus Thinking   164
     Traditional Accounts of Thought   164
        The Classical and Symbolist Theories of Mind   164
        Problems with Symbolism   167
        Problems with the Classical Theory   169
        Problems with Representationalism   170
     Hegel's Response to the Traditions   171
        The Active Concrete Universal   171
        The Rejection of Inspectivism   174

12   Thought   176
     The Immediacy of Thought   176
     The Nature of Thought   178
        The Formal Structure of Thought   179
           Concepts   179
           Judgments   180
           Inferences   190
        The Nature of Thinking Activity   195
     The Transition to Practical Spirit   198
     Conclusion   200

References   203
Index   207

Preface

I have high hopes for this book. First, it should fill a conspicuous gap in the Hegel literature, for the *Philosophy of Subjective Spirit* is—unjustly—second only to the *Philosophy of Nature* in the lack of attention it receives.

The book should also help stir up a bit more interest in Hegel in Anglo-American philosophical circles, where the philosophy of mind is currently one of the most active and exciting fields. It is in the *Philosophy of Subjective Spirit* that Hegel confronts the questions about the nature of human understanding and thought so central to the British tradition after Locke. I think I show here that Hegel's appreciation of the complexity of our minds and the peculiarities of our discourse about them is quite sophisticated—more so than that of his major contemporary rivals.

My own philosophical language is that of the Anglo-American tradition, but few of my comrades have devoted enough time to Hegel's works to appreciate him. There is surely no excuse for Hegel's writing style; it is simply abominable. But the stylistic difficulties of Aristotle's *Metaphysics* or Wittgenstein's *Tractatus* have not prevented them from being read carefully and often. Hegel's technical language cannot be the only way to express his insights, so I have tried to make Hegel speak Anglo-American here (I say "Anglo-American" rather than "English" because I am not just translating into my native language). No doubt my efforts will distress many readers, both because I have made Hegel too Anglo-American and because I have not done the job thoroughly enough. If opinion on this matter is roughly split, I will be content.

Third, I hope that the book is controversial. A fight has been brewing among Hegel scholars, one that has been kept relatively quiet because the field is small. It is not quite the old battle between left and right Hegelians, which centered on religious and social issues, but a new (though related) battle centered on the correct Hegelian treatment of the empirical sciences. Everyone has to admit that Hegel paid close attention to the empirical sciences. The disagreement is over whether philosophy itself emerges out of them and depends on them in some real sense (this would be the position of the Hegelian left, I suppose) or comes to the empirical sciences from outside, with a fund of knowledge both independent of and superior to that of the empirical sciences (the position of the right). Neither extreme position is correct (of course), but on the whole readers will find this book constantly straining toward the left, despite the many right-wing pronouncements of Hegel himself. The Hegelian system can be equally consistently developed toward the left—and it is so much more vital and interesting when it is.

Thus I read Hegel as a great naturalist, as one who saw man as arising out of and continuous with nature and capable of being understood only in this natural context. He was certainly not a total naturalist, but no ultimate break is to be found between nature and spirit in Hegel's system. In his dislike of absolute dichotomies Hegel shares an important trait with his (to me most congenial) successors, the pragmatists.

I must point out right away that this is not a book about the *Phenomenology of Spirit*. There are plenty of those (new ones, too) already. I have focused almost exclusively on Hegel's mature system as it is found in his *Encyclopedia of the Philosophical Sciences*. This work, supplemented by his lecture notes, constitutes his considered and final opinions in the philosophy of mind. The early *Phenomenology*, as fascinating as it is, is by Hegel's own admission a "peculiar early work." In particular, as even a cursory glance shows, it lacks precisely those parts of the system which are most important for the philosophy of mind, the Anthropology and the Psychology. The attention lavished on the early *Phenomenology* has probably been the major reason the *Philosophy of Subjective Spirit* has been slighted. It would be easy to think that the early *Phenomenology*, like the greater

Logic, contains the full version of something that the *Encyclopedia* has only in outline. I think such a view is simply wrong; Hegel did a great deal of rethinking while he was in Nürnberg, but I cannot argue that point here. I hope that this book will spur a greater interest in the relation between the early *Phenomenology* and the *Encyclopedia.*

One more word of caution. I have often used material from the *Zusätze* in the *Encyclopedia,* the additions based on Hegel's and his students' lecture notes inserted as clarificatory material by Hegel's posthumous editors. Because this material does not always stem directly from Hegel's hand and because some of the original sources have disappeared and cannot be checked, the *Zusätze* arouse suspicion among many Hegel scholars, especially now that, thanks to the editors of the new critical edition of the corpus, we are finally becoming accustomed to reliable texts. In the case of the *Philosophy of Subjective Spirit,* however, where no complete collateral texts are available, and where the *Zusätze* comprise the bulk of what material we have, using these notes is almost unavoidable if the interpretation is going to have any real meat on its bones. To think that the *Encyclopedia* could be interpreted adequately without the *Zusätze* is simply to ignore the fact that our background understanding of Hegel and his project—a background on which any further or new interpretation must draw—has already been deeply affected by the *Zusätze,* which have been part of the corpus since Hegel's death. Our understanding of Hegel has already been influenced by this material; we probably cannot extirpate its influence, so it is best to make it explicit. Sufficient amounts of the annotation can be traced to independent sources (especially the Kehler and Griesheim manuscripts) to attest to its pedigree. Judicious use of this material is possible, justifiable, and certainly helpful. I have been careful, though, to indicate whenever a quotation comes from a *Zusatz.*

The first chapter of the book is an account of Hegel's most important systematic commitments that bear on the philosophy of mind. It is quite general and should help orient the reader who has had little contact with Hegel's texts. The second chapter narrows the view to Hegel's philosophy of mind, emphasizing its relations to its well-known predecessors. Again, no familiarity with Hegel's texts should be necessary. In the opening chapters I have sought to avoid "front-loading" the book with explanations of Hegelian terminology. People very familiar with Hegel will find that a bit frustrating, for they are used to discussing Hegel in Hegel's terms. I can only ask that such readers bear with me. Several non-Hegelian readers have told me that these chapters do a good job of getting Hegel across precisely because they do not try first to get the terminology across and only later to fill in the position.

In the third chapter the view widens again temporarily in order to make the Hegelian distinction between Nature and Spirit clearer. I argue that this distinction is not an absolute dichotomy, that there is a vague gray area between the two polar concepts. I also propose an interpretation of the relation between the natural (bodily) and spiritual (mental) aspect of a person that, if correct, shows Hegel's sophistication as a philosopher. Although no detailed knowledge of Hegel's texts is required in this chapter, without a general familiarity with the system the larger picture I am trying to make sense of will not be clear.

From the fourth chapter onward we are in the thick of Hegel's philosophy of mind. At this point real textual exegesis is unavoidable. I have cited much of the relevant material, which is often quite skimpy, since the *Encyclopedia* is only an outline of the system, and have tried to make the essential points as clear as possible in my interpretations. The order of the chapters basically follows Hegel's own ordering of the topics: sensation, feeling, the I, intuition, the varieties of representation, and, finally, thought. Chapter 6, on the I, serves as a timely centerpiece, recapitulating the previous chapters and foreshadowing what follows. Chapter 11, on the distinction between representation and thought, sets off the last chapter, on thinking, by showing how this most Hegelian part of Hegel's system relates to a long-standing, fundamental disagreement in the philosophy of mind; it is really only at this point that the full scope of Hegel's philosophy of mind comes into view.

In many ways this book is only an introduction to Hegel's philosophy of mind. The issues are extremely complex; questions of textual interpretation are very thorny. But work on this important part of Hegel's system has to begin somewhere; the reading of his philosophy offered here will have served well if it prompts others to challenge it, rebut it, and dig still deeper into Hegel's philosophy of mind.

As I near the end of this project, I realize humbly how much help I have received. I have been fortunate to have been generously supported by the German Fulbright Commission; without their support I could not have attempted to write about Hegel. Chapter 6 was written while I attended an NEH Summer Seminar for College Teachers given at Cornell University by Sidney Shoemaker; I am grateful to everyone involved, especially Professor Shoemaker. Amherst College provided funds for research expenses, and the final revisions of the manuscript were undertaken while I enjoyed an Andrew W. Mellon Faculty Fellowship at Harvard University.

Though financial support was a sine qua non for this project, the people who helped me were its lifeblood. Starting with my work on Hegel in graduate school at the University of Pittsburgh, a setting not known for cultivating Hegel scholars, I have received helpful advice and searching criticism from Wilfrid Sellars, Paul Guyer, Annette Baier, and Nicholas Rescher. The time I spent at the Hegel Archive of the Ruhr University in Bochum was crucial to this enterprise, and I am beholden to Walter Jaeschke, Hans-Christian Lucas, Kurt Meist, Friedrich Hogemann, Manfred Baum, Wolfgang Bonsiepen, Annemarie Gethmann-Siefert, and Klaus Düsing for their assistance. A special word of thanks is due to Frau Exner, who made extra efforts to make both research and life in Germany easier.

My former colleagues at Amherst College were sometimes amused by my interest in Hegel but always supportive; William E. Kennick, however, went beyond the call of duty to read and comment on the entire manuscript in an earlier draft. His constant encouragement was very important to me. Contacts among a small but growing group of "young Hegelians" also provided needed comment and support. Harold Kincaid, Crawford Elder, R. C. Solomon, and Kenneth Westphal all deserve my thanks. Michael Hardimon is another brave soul who dared a large chunk of the manuscript and thereby made it better.

My final scholarly thanks also go well beyond the scholarly. The philosophical discussion group I participated in for six years in the Pioneer Valley, the infamous Propositional Attitudes Task Force, has been a constant source of philosophical and personal support. What philosophy of mind I know I owe to them. My thanks and more to the PATF and the visitors who have joined us: Murray

Kiteley, John Connelly, Thomas Tymoczko, Janice Moulton, Thomas Wartenburg, Meredith Michaels, Lee Bowie, Herbert Heidelberger, Bruce Aune, William Lycan, Lynne Baker, Christopher Witherspoon, Steven Weisler, and an extra thanks to Jay Garfield, a colleague in graduate school and in the Valley, perhaps the closest member of my philosophical family. An honorary member of the PATF and a Mellon fellow at Harvard, Daniel Lloyd, has endured the entire manuscript and yet become a close friend. I spent a wonderful year at Tufts University while the manuscript was being turned into a book. I'd like to thank my colleagues there, as well as my student Daniel Mullen, who scoured page proofs for me.

Cornell University Press has been a pleasure to work with. At every turn the press has proved itself efficient and gracious; I could not have dreamed of more. My thanks to John Ackerman, Barbara Salazar, John Thomas, and all the others who have made this manuscript into a book.

I am grateful to Kluwer Academic Publishers for permission to quote from M. J. Petry's translation of _The Philosophy of Subjective Spirit_ (copyright © 1978 Kluwer Academic Publishers, Dordrecht, Holland), and to _Idealistic Studies_ for permission to use segments of my article "Hegel on Representation and Thought," published in vol. 15 (May 1987).

Finally, to thank my family—both the greatest inspiration and (as we all know) the greatest impediment to work—seems fatuous: how can one presume to thank a raison d'être? My wife, Dianne, has the uncanny ability to make me write clearer, better prose, even though she claims to understand Hegel neither before nor afterward. My respect for her intellect and my reliance on her love have never stopped growing. I hope my children look at the book someday; I am not sure I wish that fate on the rest of my family, but I thank them for their unfailing support. My mother, Dr. Jenny B. deVries, helped as both a supportive parent and an expert in the German language; I owe her too much to catalog.

WILLEM A. DEVRIES

Ashland, Massachusetts

A Note on the Texts

Readers who are new to Hegel often find the references to his works confusing. There is no standard citation format for his books, and it is not even clear from the titles to the translations just how they correspond to the German editions. Let me take a moment to review the status of the texts for the neophyte Hegelian. Hegel published only four books in his life: *The Phenomenology of Spirit*, published in 1807; *The Science of Logic*, in three volumes, published in 1811, 1812, and 1816; *Encyclopedia of the Philosophical Sciences*, which was originally published in 1816 and revised in 1827 and 1830; and *The Philosophy of Right*, published in 1822. He also published some articles early in his career and during his Berlin period in the 1820s. After Hegel died, his students and admirers (they called themselves the "society of the friends of the eternalized") decided to publish a collected edition of his works. Besides collecting the pieces Hegel had published himself, they assigned various members of the group to collect and edit texts of Hegel's lectures on art, religion, the history of philosophy, and the philosophy of history. The editors used Hegel's own lecture notes (often several sets from different years) and student notes as well in reconstructing a single text for each topic. This posthumous edition became the basis for all subsequent editions of Hegel; only now, with the new critical edition being assembled in Germany, is a serious effort being made to reconstruct the Hegelian corpus on the basis of the original texts.

Of particular interest to us is the fate of Hegel's *Encyclopedia of the Philosophical Sciences*. This is not quite (though almost) the hubristic adventure that its title makes it seem; it was written to be a lecture guide for Hegel's students. By the time Hegel wrote the *Encyclopedia*, he thought he had developed a unitary, coherent system within which each philosophical topic, from logic through political theory to aesthetics and beyond, could be treated. The *Encyclopedia* is the outline of this system, made available primarily so that his students could locate his lectures in their broader context. The sections of the *Encyclopedia* offer mere summaries of what sometimes took Hegel several lectures to get across. (For readers unfamiliar with the overall structure of the Hegelian system, W. T. Stace's book *The Philosophy of Hegel* contains a fold-out synopsis of the ordering and subordination of all the concepts in the system. It is, in fact, a properly laid-out table of contents for the *Encyclopedia*. For Hegel even more than for Kant, the architectonic of his system is a major element of the system, perhaps even the single most important aspect of it. I have included an outline of the part of Hegel's system dealt with here—the structure of subjective spirit—following this note.)

When the *Encyclopedia* was included in the posthumous edition of Hegel's works, the editors, cognizant of the fact that its extreme compression makes for very obscure and difficult reading, added supplementary material taken from Hegel's lectures (both Hegel's notes and his students') to the relevant sections. This procedure undoubtedly made the *Encyclopedia* easier to read, but it has raised numerous worries about the authenticity of the supplementary texts—called *Zusätze* in German. I have defended in the Preface my use of the *Zusätze*.

The *Encyclopedia* is divided into three major sections—Logic, Philosophy of Nature, and Philosophy of Spirit—and German publishers usually issue them as separate volumes of the *Encyclopedia* (the one-volume Pöggeler-Nicolin edition omits the *Zusätze*). The English translations have been published as separate titles—*The Logic of Hegel*, *Hegel's Philosophy of Nature*, and *Hegel's Philosophy of Mind*—with no indication that they are parts of a larger work. The *Encyclopedia* consists of consecutively numbered paragraphs (demarcated by the symbol §), and the English translations preserve the paragraph numbers. Because the paragraphs are generally quite short, even with the *Zusätze*, I have used them as my citation markers in all references to the *Encyclopedia*; thus readers may use any edition, English or German, to track the references.

Recently Michael J. Petry, noting the shameful lack of attention that the *Philosophy of Subjective Spirit* has received, published a very scholarly bilingual edition of this portion of the *Encyclopedia*. Appearing under the title *Hegel's Philosophy of Subjective Spirit*, this is not a separate book but simply a new and scholarly edition of the first third of the last third (the philosophy of spirit) of Hegel's *Encyclopedia*. Petry does, however, include new material beyond that included in the original posthumous edition: he traces some of the *Zusätze* back to the two remaining sets of lecture notes available, and he also includes an unfinished work in which Hegel hoped to expand this part of the *Encyclopedia*. Hegel's *Philosophy of Right* is an expansion of the material contained in the philosophy of objective spirit, the part of the *Encyclopedia* that follows the philosophy of subjective spirit. After publishing the *Philosophy of Right*, Hegel started work on a similar expansion of the earlier part of the *Encyclopedia*, but he never finished it.

I have put citations in the text whenever possible. Standardized citations have been used when they were available. Full bibliographic details are given in the bibliography. To keep the Hegel citations in the text short, I have indicated their sources by the following abbreviations:

PhG G. W. F. Hegel. *Phänomenologie des Geistes*. Edited by J. Hoffmeister. 6th ed. Hamburg: F. Meiner, 1952.

PhS G. W. F. Hegel. *Hegel's Phenomenology of Spirit*. Translated by A. V. Miller. New York: Oxford University Press, 1977.

SL G. W. F. Hegel. *Hegel's Science of Logic*. Translated by A. V. Miller. London: George Allen & Unwin, 1969.

WdL G. W. F. Hegel. *Wissenschaft der Logik*. Edited by G. Lasson. Hamburg: F. Meiner, 1934.

All references to the *Encyclopedia of the Philosophical Sciences* are by section numbers (§). If the citation is to textual material added by the editors of the posthumous edition of Hegel's works, I indicate it as a *Zusatz*. The current standard edition of the *Encyclopedia* in German (*Enzyklopedie der philosophischen Wissenschaften*, edited by F. Nicolin and O. Pöggeler [Hamburg: F. Meiner, 1959]) does not contain the *Zusätze*, so I have worked principally with the Suhrkamp *Theorie Werkausgabe* (G. W. F. Hegel, *Enzyklopedie der phi-*

losophischen Wissenschaften, vols. 8–10 of G. W. F. Hegel, *Werke*, edited by Eva Moldenhauer and Karl Markus Michel [Frankfurt am Main: Suhrkamp, 1970]). When the provenance is not clear from the context, I distinguish references to sections in the *Encyclopedia Logic* and the *Philosophy of Nature* by marking them *EL* and *PN*, respectively. Most references are to the *Philosophy of Subjective Spirit* (*PSS*). I have worked largely with the available English translations of the *Encyclopedia*, especially Petry's, but I have not hesitated to supply my own translations for greater accuracy. Unless I have noted otherwise, translations of substantial quotations are Petry's. The English editions are:

Hegel's Philosophy of Mind. Translated by W. Wallace and A. V. Miller. New York: Oxford University Press, 1971.

Hegel's Philosophy of Nature. Translated by W. Wallace and A. V. Miller. New York: Oxford University Press, 1970.

Hegel's Philosophy of Nature. 3 vols. Translated and edited by M. J. Petry. London: George Allen & Unwin, 1970.

Hegel's Philosophy of Subjective Spirit. 3 vols. Edited and translated by M. J. Petry. Boston: D. Reidel, 1978.

The Logic of Hegel. Translated by W. Wallace. New York: Oxford University Press, 1892.

The Structure of
Subjective Spirit

I. Anthropology—The Soul
  A. The Natural Soul
     1. Natural Qualities
     2. Natural Changes
     3. Sensibility
  B. The Feeling Soul
     1. The Feeling Soul in Its Immediacy
     2. Self-feeling
     3. Habit
  C. The Actual Soul
II. The Phenomenology of Spirit—Consciousness
  A. Consciousness as Such
     1. Sensuous Consciousness
     2. Perception
     3. Understanding
  B. Self-consciousness
     1. Desire
     2. Recognitive Self-consciousness
     3. Universal Self-consciousness
  C. Reason
III. Psychology—Spirit
  A. Theoretical Spirit
     1. Intuition
        a. Feeling
        b. Attention

       c. Intuition Proper
    2. Representation
       a. Recollection
          i. The Image
          ii. The Unconsciously Preserved Image
          iii. Recollection Proper
       b. Imagination
          i. Associative, Reproductive Imagination
          ii. Symbolic Imagination
          iii. Sign-Making Imagination
       c. Memory
          i. Name-Retaining Memory
          ii. Reproductive Memory
          iii. Mechanical Memory
   3. Thinking
       a. Understanding
       b. Judgment
       c. Formal Reason
B. Practical Spirit
   1. Practical Feeling
   2. Impulses and Willfulness
   3. Happiness
C. Free Spirit

HEGEL'S THEORY
OF MENTAL ACTIVITY

Science, Teleology, and Interpretation

PHYSICALISM AND CAUSALISM

A philosophy of mind is supposed to tell us, among other things, the nature of the concepts we use in our descriptions and explanations of mental phenomena. Behaviorism, as a philosophy of mind, tells us that concepts of the mental are really concepts of complicated complexes of dispositions to overt behavior. Functionalism maintains that concepts of the mental are functionally defined concepts of states of the individual differentiated by their typical causal role in the overall (internal and external) behavior of that individual. Both of these modern philosophies of mind tell us that mental concepts are not concepts of occurrent properties of mental substances but concepts of complex *causal* properties.[1] Fundamental to both philosophies is a commitment to the priority of the causal, physical order; our concepts of the mental are to be made sense of by showing how the mental fits into the causal order of nature.

The associationist psychology of the Enlightenment that Hegel was so familiar with is a bit harder to specify exactly, since mental states tended to be reified into entity-like *ideas*. Nonetheless, it is clear that the associationists share the commitment to the priority of the causal with their present-day counterparts. This is clearly confessed at the very inception of associationism, when Hume com-

---

1. Functionalism itself is actually mute about whether the functionally defined concepts of the mental are instantiated in a mental or a material substance—but they are not, in any case, concepts of purely occurrent states.

pares his own project with Newton's and his principles of association with Newton's law of gravitation.

In this chapter I argue that Hegel offers us a significantly different understanding of the basic nature of our concepts of the mental and that, unless we recognize this, his entire project will remain opaque to us. Hegel's disagreement with the standard reading of our concepts is not confined to our concepts of the mental, however; Hegel gives us a thorough reinterpretation of the systematic interrelations among all our concepts, though we confine our argument here to his view of the mental.

Since Descartes (certainly at least since Newton), the natural sciences (especially physics) have provided the model of empirical knowledge that has dominated philosophical reflection. But the natural sciences have served as a model in different ways. Some philosophers have tried to mimic in their own philosophies of mind what they took the structure of physics to be. Thus the resemblance Hume apparently saw between his philosophy and Newtonian mechanics was the postulation of elementary atoms with the primitive property of attracting other atoms and complexes thereof. Other philosophers have taken physics to be the *sole* exemplar of empirical knowledge and have therefore sought to *reduce* the mental to the physical. For many philosophers, though, physics and the natural sciences provided a model, not through the particular claims physics makes, but as an example of proper scientific methodology. To such philosophers physics is exemplary because of the clearly intersubjective, repeatable nature of the evidence employed, the rigorous formulation and generality of its laws, and so forth. If there is a science of the mind, according to this group of philosophers, it must be consistent with physics and the other natural sciences and like them in these general, methodological respects, even if it does not ultimately reduce to physics or physiology. And if our present concepts of the mental cannot find a place in such a science of the mind—well, so much the worse for them.

We could try to understand Hegel's project in the philosophy of subjective spirit, indeed in the *Encyclopedia* as a whole, along these lines, but with little hope of success. In some sense, surely, Hegel is committed to psychology's being consistent with physics, for they are both aspects of *one* world; but "naturalizing" psychology is not the way to understand their consistency, according to Hegel.

The scientistic philosophers share the assumptions that all objects and events arise within one causal order and that physics is the most general and complete description of that causal order. The principle of these philosophical physicalists is that to understand something fully (i.e., scientifically) is to locate it within the causal order, showing how it depends on the objects and events physics deals with. These assumptions are not shared by Hegel; he offers us a very different picture of how the world hangs together. It is not that Hegel denies that there is a sense in which all the other objects and events of the world depend on those dealt with in physics—the existence of the physical is a necessary condition of the existence of biological and spiritual phenomena in his system as well. But this dependency relation is not the right one to be concerned with; that is, Hegel denies the conceptual and ontological *priority* of the causal, physical order. In particular, truly understanding something is not, according to Hegel, a matter of locating it within the causal order, but a matter of locating it within the self-realization of the Absolute, a teleological structure that transcends the physical. The teleological order, not the causal order of efficient causes, is the ultimate touchstone. This change (which leaves untouched a great deal of the hierarchical ordering of disciplines on which both Hegel and the physicalist can agree) means that Hegel's philosophical enterprise is quite different from that of the philosophical physicalist.

Philosophical physicalism is very familiar, perhaps even the dominant view in contemporary philosophy. Its most venerable opponent is straightforward dualism—the claim that some of our concepts (usually our concepts of the mental) have nothing in particular to do with the causal, physical order but are about a disjoint order of things. The mental order is usually conceived to be itself a causal order, but mental and physical causation are held to be different species of the same genus. Cartesian dualism is thus as committed to the priority of the causal order as philosophical physicalism; unable to fit everything into the physical order, it accepts the existence of another, disjoint causal order to account for the leftovers.

Hegel does not want to accept either position, so he rejects their common assumption, the priority of the causal. What he proposes in its place is the priority of the teleological. To support this position

Hegel breaks with his predecessors in proposing a different analysis of the concept of teleology and a different approach to legitimating the concepts we use.

OUR RELATIONSHIP TO NATURE

Two Approaches to Nature

Hegel's strategy for arguing the priority of the teleological order set forth in his system is basically straightforward: he claims that the approach of the physicalistic philosopher is really a one-sided abstraction from a more adequate, integrated, teleological approach. Since the physicalistic approach is only an abstraction from this more adequate approach, it must also be thought of as posterior to it.

Hegel differentiates two relationships we can have to nature, the practical and the theoretical. Neither is adequate in isolation; both point beyond themselves to an integrated view of nature which sublates them (that is, preserves in a unified view what is true and valuable in both while abandoning their individual weak points).

In our practical relationship to nature we behave as individual beings for whom nature is a means, an instrument for our purposes. Natural things themselves are (correctly) treated by us as devoid of intrinsic purpose, but we (incorrectly) treat them as if we can impose our purposes on them without resistance, as if their purpose is to serve us. In this practical relationship to nature we are concerned, not with the universal characteristics of things, but with turning the individual things immediately at hand to our own individual purposes:

> Two further determinations are immediately apparent here. (a) The practical approach is only concerned with the individual products of nature, or with certain aspects of these products. . . . Nature itself, as it is in its universality, cannot be mastered in this manner however, nor bent to the purposes of man. (b) The other aspect of the practical approach is that our purpose overrides the objects of nature, so that they become means, the determination of which lies not in themselves but in us. (*PN* §245, *Zusatz*)

The practical relationship to nature affords us only a thoroughly subjective, highly limited point of view which, when generalized, quickly leads to absurdity. To believe, for instance, that cork trees exist in order to provide us with bottle stoppers is just "silly" (*PN* §245, *Zusatz*).

The second relationship to nature we commonly adopt, the theoretical relationship, is equally inadequate.

> In the theoretical approach (a) the initial factor is our withdrawing from natural things, leaving them as they are, and adjusting to them. In doing this we start from our sense-knowledge of nature. If physics were based only on perception however, and perceptions were nothing but the evidence of the senses, the activity of a natural scientist would consist only of seeing, smelling, hearing, etc., so that animals would also be physicists. . . . (b) In the second relation of things to us, they either acquire the determination of universality for us, or we transform them into something universal. The more thought predominates in ordinary perceptiveness, so much the more does the naturalness, individuality, and immediacy of things vanish away. As thoughts invade the limitless multiformity of nature, its richness is impoverished, its springtimes die, and there is a fading in the play of its colours. That which in nature was noisy with life, falls silent in the quietude of thought; its warm abundance, which shaped itself in a thousand intriguing wonders, withers into arid forms and shapeless generalities, which resemble a dull northern fog. (*PN* §246, *Zusatz*)

The theoretical approach to nature is intended to capture nature as it is in itself, but it can grasp nature only by transforming it into an abstract structure of forces, laws, and genera (see *PN* §246, as well as *EL* §20ff.). The theoretical approach to nature therefore cannot fully succeed in its intention to grasp nature as it is.

The practical approach to nature is concerned only with the immediate individuality confronting it, and the theoretical approach is concerned only with the abstract universality of nature. Neither approach is adequate for understanding our actual intercourse with nature or for understanding nature itself. We act within nature understandingly, rationally. We do not normally combine the practical and theoretical approaches by alternating between them; rather, they are more properly conceived of as abstractions from a total and fundamentally sound relation that we normally bear to nature.

Constructing a balanced and adequate approach to nature is a problem, a problem contemporary philosophers must face as well. I shall bow to contemporary practice and put the point in a linguistic mode. The pure language of science contains no practical vocabulary; it is not a language in which one can deliberate and formulate intentions. The language of science can be used within such deliberations to formulate some of the premises of our practical reasoning, but it is not itself sufficient for deliberation. It is, as well, a thoroughly objectifying language, without resources for the expression of the subjective. Theory aims, apparently, at a thoroughly objective, impersonal comprehension of the world; practice, however, seems essentially tied to the subjective, personal agent. The language of science cannot, therefore, be the sole language we use in confronting the world unless we abandon our humanity and subjectivity.

The language of practice, however, is not complete either. Practical reasoning and the proper formulation of intentions require an understanding of the world's independence of us, of its universal patterns. Our subjective intentions make sense only against an independent, objective world. But this means that a language of pure practice is impossible; it must be conjoined with a theoretical language. A language of pure theory may seem to be still a viable possibility—but it is not hard to see that it must also be conjoined with a language of practice if it is to function in the practice of science.

As I have already intimated, this distinction between the theoretical and the practical is connected to the equally important distinction between the objective and the subjective. Statements from the theoretical point of view are in the objective mode: "Unsupported bodies near the surface of the earth fall at $\frac{1}{2}gt^2$." Although there can be no theories without theorizers, the theorist per se never shows up *within* the theory (at least outside quantum mechanics). The fact that the objectivity of the theory emerges from the subjectivity of the theorist is an *extratheoretical* fact. The theoretical and the objective approaches to the world go hand in hand.

Statements from the practical point of view usually wear their subjective origin on their sleeve, for they point to human purposes, often explicitly. Even the "objective practice" enjoined by ethics has to root in our personal motivational structures in order to be realized. Unlike theory, practice cannot even superficially ignore the subjectivity of the agent without obvious incoherence.

This general conflict between subjective and objective, theoretical and practical approaches to the world has been addressed in different shapes by various present-day philosophers. Thomas Nagel has spent a great deal of time exploring the conflict between the subjective and the objective points of view.[2] Wilfrid Sellars has noted the distinction between the theoretical and the practical languages with which we engage the world and has suggested that they must be conjoined into a "synoptic vision" of the world.[3] Hegel, however, would strongly disagree with the idea that the two can be simply conjoined—a deeper synthesis must be reached, one in which the two approaches or languages do not simply coexist alongside each other but inform each other and meld into a complete and unified vision of the world.

Objective Purpose

According to Hegel's diagnosis of the tension between the practical and theoretical approaches to nature, the proper resolution of that tension calls for a concept of *objective purpose*. The practical approach to nature is overly subjective, considering nature only in relation to practical, subjective purposes. Any attempt to adapt the subjective, practical approach to the universality and objectivity of nature must involve a significant revision of the concept of purpose, however; simply extending the concept of purpose applicable to individual subjectivities to cover the whole world (say, by taking nature to be God's instrument) cannot prove satisfactory. An objective purpose cannot be just a very big subjective purpose.

Hegel has provided us with a relatively detailed analysis of the concept of purpose in his two *Logics*. I summarize his analysis here.[4] In Hegel's time, purposes were standardly treated as arising from the beliefs and desires of some subjectivity. Knives are sharp in order to cut (or knives are for cutting) because someone has created

2. Thomas Nagel, *The View from Nowhere.*

3. Wilfrid Sellars, "Philosophy and the Scientific Image of Man," in *Science, Perception, and Reality*, pp. 1–40.

4. For details see, W. deVries, "The Dialectic of Teleology," Proceedings of the Hegel Society of America, 1980.

them with the intention that they serve as cutting devices. A subjectivity suffuses its own purposes into a distinct and often recalcitrant objectivity in all such cases. Such a conception of teleology, however, can account for the purposiveness of natural things only with difficulty. If the heart beats in order to pump blood (or the heart is for pumping blood), then there must be someone who created hearts with the intention that they serve as pumps. But that someone is clearly not any particular, finite subjectivity. There must be some subjectivity that stands outside the finite and objective realm and works its will upon it, namely God. Hegel thinks that this line of thought presupposes a completely unsupportable conception of a transcendent God. If there is natural teleology, Hegel realizes that it cannot be understood by any extension of the subjective model.

Indeed, reflection on the subjective or intentional model of teleology is sufficient to demonstrate the need for a concept of natural or objective teleology, Hegel believes, for intentional teleology actually *presupposes* natural teleology. In the intentional model of teleology a subjectivity works its will upon a distinct objectivity; normally it does so by employing an instrument, a means for its end. But since the instrument is itself in the objective order, how is the subjectivity to work its will upon it? There must be something that bridges the gap between the subjective and objective realms, normally the body. The possession of a body, a single, unified entity with both subjective and objective aspects, is the necessary presupposition of intentional teleology. But the body itself is teleologically saturated: the heart beats in order to pump blood; the body moves in order to nourish itself. Intentional or subjective teleology is built on the natural, objective teleology of the organism.

In all teleology there is at least implicit reference to the good. In intentional teleology this reference is itself intentional; intentional action aims at a subjectively valued end. In natural, objective teleology activity aims at the objective good of the organism. But Hegel does not conceive of the natural good of an organism as a matter of its mere survival or even the survival of its species; rather, Hegel believes that for each thing-kind there is an ideal paradigm of that thing-kind of which all the individuals of the kind can be seen as approximations. Natural organisms (unlike artifacts) seek to realize their ideal on their own, with more or less success in individual cases. All natural teleology, including the beating of the heart in order to pump blood, is subordinate to the striving of the individual to realize as best it can its ideal type. According to Hegel's analysis, all natural teleology is at heart self-realization.

Hegel accepts Kant's second criterion for a *Naturzweck*, namely, "that its parts should so combine in the unity of the whole that they are reciprocally cause and effect of each other's form" (Kant, *Critique of Judgment* §65, Bernard p. 219, Ak. p. 291). But while Kant admits that the whole is there *because* of its parts and the parts there *because* of the whole, Kant also believes that these two "becauses" are radically different. The first is objective, capable of clear justification; the second "because" is at best subjective, regulative, useful in spurring further scientific research. But in Hegel's view both "becauses" are equally objective. Teleological explanations appeal to the paradigm of the relevant thing-kind, but this ideal is not subjective, it is what defines that thing-kind. (Think of the Aristotelian dictum that to know something as it is "by nature" is to know it at its best.) It is not something we dream up; it is there, objectively present and explanatorily unavoidable. To say that such an ideal is merely subjective is to subjectivize the world entirely, to make the ontological structure of the world an artifact of our point of view alone. Hegel refuses to do this.

The ontological structure of the world, its articulation into natural kinds, is intrinsically teleological, according to Hegel. The behavior of organisms must be understood as a striving to realize the organism's ideal and thereby to realize itself fully. And even the articulation of the inorganic realm, as devoid of internally active purpose as the inorganic is, must still be viewed as a structure contributing to the realization of a higher end, the self-realization of the Absolute.

But even if we grant Hegel's argument that intentional teleology presupposes natural teleology, and thus grant that there are some objective purposes aimed at by organisms capable of intentional action, it certainly does not follow that there must be *an* objective purpose for the whole world. Hegel's analysis of teleology might establish the possibility of objective purpose and even the reality of some objective purposes, given the reality of subjective purposes, but it cannot justify belief in the existence of one universal objective purpose for the whole of nature. Hegel was, I believe, cognizant of this shortcoming and argued for the existence of an ultimate objective purpose from a different angle, namely, from the inadequacy of the theoretical approach to nature. In other words, the inadequacy of the practical approach to nature justifies employment of the concept of objective purpose, and, as we shall see, the inadequacy of the theoretical approach justifies belief in the existence of a universal objective purpose.

Universal Purpose

Like most post-Cartesian philosophers, Hegel recognizes the importance and generality of physics. Nevertheless, he believes that it does not even potentially provide a complete understanding of the world. "The inadequacy of the thought determinations used in physics may be traced to two very closely connected points. (a) The universal of physics is abstract or simply formal; its determination is not immanent within it, and does not pass over into particularity. (b) This is precisely the reason why its determinate content is external to the universal, and is therefore split up, dismembered, particularized, separated and lacking in any necessary connection within itself; why it is in fact merely finite" (*PN* §246, *Zusatz*).

Hegel's complaint against the concepts used in theoretical physics is not very clear in any of his writings, partly because it is a complaint quite foreign to our modern scientistic consciousness. But the basic thrust of his objection can be made sufficiently clear. The "universal" of physics is, first of all, some explanatory posit, such as a force or a law. Part of its being abstract has surely to do with the fact that it is supposedly reached by abstraction from the rich world of ordinary experience, but that is not all that is carried by the term "abstract." It is also abstract in that the various forces and laws governing the behavior of things are all independent of each other, without any intrinsic connection; whatever the ultimate laws are, they are simply primitive givens, each independent of the others. This is supposed to be a further fault with the abstract universals of the theoretical approach, but it is not immediately obvious why.

I think that Hegel is worried about two different things when he complains about the way the theoretical approach (or what he calls "the attitude of the understanding," which comes to much the same thing) divides and analyzes things into disparate and unconnected elements. First, Hegel is bothered by the idea that the ultimate structure of the world might not have a unitary principle, that we might have to accept a plurality of principles as ultimate. Such a situation would always leave questions about why just those principles were ultimate givens and whether they in turn depended on some unitary and still more fundamental principle. The desire for unity and completeness seems overwhelming in Hegel, although I can see no irrefutable argument that the world ultimately must be unitary. Second, Hegel often complains that the analytic approach of the theoretical attitude loses the inner unity of the things it dissects, killing them: "Take a flower for example. The understanding can note its particular qualities, and chemistry can break it down and analyse it. Its color, the shape of its leaves, citric acid, volatile oil, carbon, hydrogen etc., can be distinguished; and we then say that the flower is made up of all these parts" (*PN* §246, *Zusatz*). He goes on to agree with Goethe that such an analysis "holds the parts within its hand,/But lacks, alas, the spiritual band." But Hegel does not want to suggest that philosophy is necessary because it can find something else, something above and beyond the elements isolated by the sciences, namely, the spiritual band; rather, Hegel's complaint, I believe, must be read as a complaint about the inability of the sciences to supply adequate analyses of our concepts of natural kinds. A proper understanding of the nature of a thing-kind, which is more than a mere assemblage of parts, shows that the "spiritual band" is immanent within the thing, the ideal toward which the thing strives.

The scientific, empirical analysis of a flower can show us how the flower works, how its elements interact, but it does not by itself show us why those elements together constitute a natural kind. Natural, as opposed to artificial or artifactual, kinds, are *natural* (and therefore, Hegel believes, nonarbitrary) unities. Natural kind concepts play an extremely important explanatory role for Hegel, because every chain of explanations must ultimately come to a close, and explanations end in proper classifications. Every explanatory enterprise presupposes some basic set of entities with certain primitive powers; when an explanation has been pursued down to this basic level, any further questions about the basic entities or primitive powers can only be answered by saying that they are that kind of thing. Every explanatory enterprise takes certain kinds to be natural; seeking further explanation of those natural kinds opts out of that explanatory enterprise in favor of another, perhaps more general form of explanation. The natural kinds articulate the primitive structures of the world.

The paradigmatic natural kinds for Hegel, biological genera, consist of self-developing, self-maintaining organisms with common structures and behaviors and, most important, a common ideal type toward which the individuals strive. But the theoretical attitude analyzes the natural kinds of our world away, Hegel believes, decomposing them into an ungainly conglomeration of properties with no clear unity to them. The theoretical attitude thus constructs a world bled of all internal structure into which any organization is introduced by *us*—which contradicts the essential goal of the theoretical attitude, namely, the grasping of the world as it really is. The only remedy, as Hegel sees it, is to admit the insufficiency of the analytic tendencies of theory and, indeed, to counter them by taking nature, the world itself, to be a natural kind—that is, to be determined by an objective ideal.

This is a large mouthful to swallow. It is unclear that the inner cohesion of a natural kind must be sold short by analysis. True, in Hegel's time the organic realm did still seem quite separate from the inorganic, and impervious to chemical or physical analysis, but this barrier was initially overcome in Hegel's own lifetime and has been totally done away with in the modern development of biology, through both evolutionary theory and molecular biology. Yet even in the progress of the biological sciences the conception of teleology has not completely vanished. There are properties of organs and organisms that are still best explained by reference to the larger organic or environmental context. According to Hegel, this would signal defeat for the strictly analytic strategy of the understanding.

The notion of a natural kind is perhaps no clearer now than it was in Hegel's day, but it is certainly not evident that all natural kinds must be like biological kinds. It may be the case that through scientific research certain natural kinds, or what were taken to be such, are indeed analyzed away, but it is more important to realize that science is really offering us a new and even more powerful set of natural kinds with much broader and better defined explanatory powers. Hegel's instrumental interpretation of the empirical sciences is not by any means the only one possible.

Hegel strains the boundaries of the concept of a natural kind when he, in effect, takes the world-whole to be a natural kind with the structure appropriate to his paradigmatic natural kinds. Perhaps the strongest thing that can be said in favor of this assimilation is that the nature of the world-whole is the ultimate explanatory dead end. If natural kinds are explanatory resting places, then, since the nature of the world-whole is the final and ultimate resting place, it must be the highest natural kind. But totalizing concepts are notoriously dangerous: the totality of finite numbers is not a finite number; the set of all sets is impossible. We have to be extremely suspicious of Hegel's rather dogmatic belief that the world-whole does form a unitary totality.

THE NEED FOR PHILOSOPHY

We are now in a position to say why, according to Hegel, the empirical sciences cannot deliver a complete understanding of the world, why philosophy itself must rework the results of the empirical sciences in order to complete the task. Even if Hegel's arguments were sufficient to justify our use of the concept of objective purpose, why would this be a matter for philosophy, rather than for a slightly revised empirical science? It is surely the case that we discover empirically what the purpose of the heart or brain is; why not believe that particular teleological connections, like particular causal connections, must be discovered by observation and experiment?

It is undoubtedly right that particular teleological connections must be ascertained experientially. Such particular connections, however, are not the ones that the Hegelian philosopher claims to be able to supply. His concern, rather, is with the *ultimate* end, the self-realization of the Absolute, the world-whole's fulfillment of its potential. As we have seen, Hegel believes that the world-whole, like every natural kind, has an ideal to live up to. But there are certain peculiarities about the world-whole kind: there can be only one world-whole according to Hegel, so it can in principle have only one instance; because the universal and ideal is what is substantial about the world, according to Hegel, the world-whole cannot in the long run fall short of the ideal, as every finite being does; because there is nothing else it could depend on, the world-whole must be absolutely independent and self-contained, even to the point of being self-explanatory. We have questioned Hegel's right to this concept of the world-whole, but he undeniably employs it, and a full examination of his arguments to justify it would be a complete examination of virtually his entire philosophical system. Since our primary purpose here is to understand Hegel's philosophy of mind, I do not question this assumption further. Let us rather examine its role in the system.

Hegel easily grants that particular teleological connections are available to empirical discovery and confirmation, but the case is not the same with the ultimate goal. Because there are strong constraints on an ultimate goal, Hegel thinks that the nature of such a telos is not merely de facto but can be established a priori and shown to be necessary.[5] Absolute teleology, then, is not an empirical matter. But if the world as a whole must be seen as a unity striving to realize its own particular intrinsic end, then this must affect the way we understand the empirical detail of the world as well. There is then an added dimension to the finite things of the world, for we must understand whether and how they contribute to the realization of the Absolute.

Hegel is not committed to being able to say of any individual finite thing how it contributes to the realization of the Absolute, any more than a thorough comprehension of any natural kind by itself gives one knowledge of any particular member of that kind. Hegel, as he claimed, cannot deduce Krug's pen.[6] But there are a priori constraints on the totality, the Absolute, simply by virtue of the fact

5. For convenience I write as if the a priori–a posteriori distinction were unproblematic. In fact, though, Hegel does not believe that there is a clear distinction between the a priori and the a posteriori—not because the distinction itself is unclear, but because it is really a matter of degree. In order to do Hegel full justice, we need to abandon the a priori–a posteriori dichotomy and employ instead the notion of degrees of empirical sensitivity. I develop this notion in more detail in Chapters 2 and 3.

6. Wilhelm Traugott Krug attacked the grand systems of German idealism—Fichte was his particular target—by demanding that they deduce even something minor, such as his pen, from the system. Hegel first attacked Krug in a review article in the *Critical Journal of Philosophy*, which he edited with Schelling in Jena in 1802–3; G. W. F. Hegel, *Jenaer Schriften, 1801–07: Werke in 20 Bänden*, pp. 188–207. He returned to the problem of Krug's pen in a footnote to *Encyclopedia* (PN) §250. Hegel's answers to Krug are not consistently satisfying. A classic modern essay is D. Henrich, "Hegels Theorie über den Zufall," in *Hegel im Context*, pp. 157–86.

that it is the ultimate totality. It must be self-sufficient and independent (since there is nothing else it could depend on), capable of
encompassing the variety and the conflicts of the world, unifying
them without nullifying them. Perhaps most important, in Hegel's
view the Absolute must also be explanatorily closed. This means,
essentially, that philosophical explanations must form a neat curve
in which nothing is accepted as a brute primitive. Although explanation in some of the world's dimensions may run off into infinity
(this is notably the case for causal explanation), philosophical, that
is, teleological explanation does not proceed into infinity. Philosophical reflection exposes the world to be a self-developing, self-
realizing structure, and no further demands can be made for explanation when we have seen what kind of thing the world is. The only
further demands that can be made are for further detail and deeper
insight into the structure thus realizing itself. Since the concept of
the world-whole as the highest kind can be constrained a priori, and
since in this instance alone concept and reality, kind and instance
must fully coincide, we do have considerable a priori knowledge of
the structure of the world.

Hegel's argument that philosophy is an essential element in our
knowledge of the world has two parallel forms, one to the effect that
the sort of thing philosophy can tell us is metaphysically fundamental, the other to the effect that it is also epistemologically fundamental. These arguments can be summarized as follows:

1. Individuation and classification are both metaphysically and epistemologically fundamental. From the metaphysical point of view, there
   is no entity without identity, and crucial to anything's identity is what
   kind of thing it is. Epistemologically, one knows nothing about a
   thing unless one can subsume it under some thing-kind, and the most
   important piece of knowledge one can normally have about something is what kind of thing it is.[7]
2. Natural kinds are teleologically determined and must be understood
   teleologically as ideals, objective purposes of natural things.
3. Purposes can be subordinated to each other; for example, the objective purpose of the heart is to pump blood, but its pumping blood

---

7. Hegel still thinks of knowledge as primarily of "objects" rather than of facts or
propositions. Some of the complex reasons for this tendency are explored in Chapter
12.

subserves the purpose of keeping the organism alive, which itself might subserve the purpose of keeping the species alive.

4. What something is, its kind, is determined not only by its immediate objective purpose but by its superordinate purposes as well. Similarly, understanding (completely) what something is entails understanding all the objective purposes defining it.

5. The world-whole is a kind, the ultimate kind; it is the universal objective purpose. Because it is the universal objective purpose, all other purposes are subordinated to it.

6. What anything really is depends on how it subserves the universal objective purpose, the self-realization of the Absolute. Understanding anything completely entails understanding how it helps realize the Absolute.

Given the role philosophy plays in Hegel's understanding of our world, we can see that philosophy must accordingly be essentially interpretive. We have to be a little careful with the notion of "interpretation," for the word is often used quite broadly and in such uses does not have the special meaning I reserve for it here. As I use the term, an interpretation is an attempt to understand a set of complex relations among a group of items, including part-whole relations and means-ends relations. This much is common to all uses of "interpretation," including a statistician's interpretation of a set of data. Interpretation in my special sense, however, is singled out by being explicitly holistic and making sense of the individuals and the relations in the group in terms of a projected whole with certain normative characteristics to which they are assumed to belong. The whole to which they belong must impose some real constraints on the interpretation, constraints derivative from the fact that the projected whole is assumed to have certain valuable traits. Interpretation has an essential axiological component. Furthermore, the value to be realized in the whole must in some sense have a constitutive tie to the individuals within the whole, as truth does to meaning.

I believe that this characterization separates linguistic or literary interpretation from statistical interpretation, because the statistician does not (on my purified picture of statistical endeavors) rely on an antecedent (much less a priori) projection of an axiologically characterized whole. (To the extent that statisticians do do something like that, e.g., assume that their populations have certain valuable traits, they are involved in interpretation in my sense.) Linguistic interpretation is constrained by the principle of charity, for instance, which projects an essentially truthful belief set for each speaker or community. The whole projected in literary interpretation is much vaguer and harder to characterize, but the literary work must be interpreted, for example, as having some thematic structure and as portraying a not fully determinate but still coherent world. (Note that on this reading much of the actual procedure even in the sciences could be taken to be interpretive, if principles of conservation or least action or theoretical desiderata such as economy and simplicity were considered axiological.)

A complete understanding of the world, according to Hegel, involves comprehending a projected whole—the Absolute—and then constraining one's understanding of the particularities of the world in the light of that projected whole. Furthermore, the true character of the individuals depends on their connection to the whole; their potential contribution to the realization of the ultimate value is what makes them what they really are. Such an interpretive methodology is quite different from either a deductive or an (enumerative) inductive strategy. Yet these latter were still the dominant paradigms in Hegel's era. Kant realized the necessity of employing an interpretive strategy but relegated it to a merely regulative role in our construction of knowledge. Hegel insists that an interpretive approach to the world is an unavoidable and essential feature of a proper relation to the world.

2

Hegel's Reconception of the Philosophy of Mind

PHILOSOPHICAL PSYCHOLOGY: HEGEL'S PREDECESSORS

Many histories of philosophy attempt to classify Hegel as a latter-day rationalist. While there is much to be said for such a classification, in the philosophy of mind[1] it can be misleading. For however much Hegel may share with his rationalist predecessors, his philosophy of mind is dominated by very different concerns.

The central questions in the rationalist philosophy of mind concern the substantiality, simplicity, immortality, immateriality, and freedom of the soul. The doctrines of concept acquisition, judgment, the nature of sensation and perception, and so forth are developed to support the metaphysical positions at the center of rationalist concern. Despite their interest in concept acquisition, the empiricists, in their reaction against rationalism, retain a strong, though critical, interest in the search for the attributes of the soul. Even in Kant we find that, alongside his revolutionary doctrines of concept acquisition, judgment, and the nature of sensation and perception, the attributes of the soul receive careful attention in the first *Critique*.[2] But virtually all of these questions simply disappear

1. I am using "philosophy of mind" in its contemporary sense, where "mind" is not a translation of the Hegelian term *Geist*. In extension, the contemporary "philosophy of mind" is closer to Hegel's "subjective spirit."
2. Karl Ameriks, in *Kant's Theory of Mind*, has recently argued that Kant is not simply critical of rational psychology but also holds positive doctrines about the attributes of the soul.

when we turn to Hegel. He gives the term "soul" a quite restricted meaning and place in his system and claims that his predecessors asked the wrong questions about the soul. McTaggart remarks, for instance, that Hegel just does not seem interested in the immortality of the soul.[3] In *Encyclopedia* §389 Hegel claims immateriality for the soul but then turns right around and says that this is of no real interest unless one makes some faulty presuppositions (we analyze this passage more closely below). The attributes of the soul posed a central philosophical tangle for his predecessors; in Hegel's philosophy this tangle has dissolved, leaving but few residual questions scattered around the system.

Against Rational Psychology

In his introduction to the *Philosophy of Spirit*, Hegel makes it quite clear that he thinks that both the rationalists and empiricists had the wrong approach to philosophical thinking about spirit and the mental (§378). He gives Kant credit for having freed all subsequent philosophers from the need to do rational psychology (§47). But on a closer look at §47, it is not clear why Hegel lauds Kant for freeing us from rational psychology, for he claims both that Kant's criticisms are not essentially different from the criticims of the empiricists, in particular Hume's, and that they are faulty. Why, then, should the destruction of rational psychology be credited to Kant? Perhaps the answer is simply that the power of the Kantian system and its greater acceptance (at least in Germany) made rational psychology impossible in a way that Hume's philosophy did not. The destruction of rational psychology would then be attributed to Kant as a matter of historical fact.

In any case, Hegel disagrees with Kant's (and therefore Hume's) reasons for rejecting rational psychology. In both cases, according to Hegel, their objection amounts to pointing out that the properties that rational psychology seeks to attribute to the soul are not sensible, cannot be found in sense experience. For both Hume and Kant this entails that we do not have and cannot employ any meaningful concept of them. But this objection does not bother Hegel in the least; he replies that the whole point of thinking, of theorizing, is

3. J. M. E. McTaggart, *Studies in Hegelian Cosmology,* p. 5.

the construction or development of concepts that go beyond what can be found in sense experience, so that the use of such concepts cannot be what is wrong with rational psychology.[4]

When he intimates what *is* wrong with rational psychology, Hegel criticizes the rationalists for having treated the soul as a *thing;* for having used abstract categories of the understanding which are, properly speaking, too lowly to grasp the nature of spirit; and, last but not least, for having misconceived the very nature of philosophical truth and the nature of predication. These charges are all connected, each cutting a little deeper than the preceding one.

In accusing rationalists of treating the soul as a thing, Hegel argues that they use "merely abstract categories of the understanding":

> The old metaphysics considers the soul as a thing. "Thing" is, however, a very ambiguous expression. As a thing we primarily understand something immediately existing, something we represent sensibly, and this is the sense in which the soul has to be spoken of. It has accordingly been asked where the soul has its seat. As possessing a seat the soul is in space and is represented sensibly. Similarly it is appropriate to the conception of the soul as a thing to ask whether it is simple or composite. The question is particularly interesting in relation to the soul's immortality, insofar as this is thought to be conditioned by the soul's simplicity. But in fact abstract simplicity is a determination which corresponds to the essence of the soul as little as composition does. (§34, *Zusatz,* my tr.)

It is clear in this passage that Hegel is charging the rationalists with something like a category mistake. Their notion of the soul mislocates the heart of the matter, and when one sees this, many of the earlier troublesome questions about the soul's attributes simply fall away. Yet Hegel's critique is more radical than the mere accusation of a category mistake about the soul, for he believes that a similar confusion occurs in other central concepts:

4. Hegel does not think that concepts can be simply divided into the sensible and the nonsensible. While some concepts—e.g., red or sweet—are clearly sensible, there is a wide range of progressively less sensible concepts, from such as fragility through such as electromagnetic radiation to even the concept of spirit itself. Concepts vary in their degree of empirical sensitivity.

The question of the immateriality of the soul can still be of interest only if a distinction is drawn in which matter is presented as *true* and spirit as a *thing*. Even in the hand of the physicists, however, matter has become subtler in more recent times, for they have hit upon *imponderable* materials such as heat, light, etc., to which they have found no difficulty in adding space and time. Although these imponderables have lost not only gravity, the property peculiar to matter, but also to a certain extent the capacity of offering resistance, they still have a sensuous determinate being, a self-externality. *Vital matter* however, which can also be found included among them, lacks not only gravity but every other determinate being which might justify its being regarded as *material*. (§389)

Here Hegel dismisses the question of the immateriality of the soul, not as senseless, but as simply uninteresting. What interest it may have is founded on a set of confusions. Noteworthy in this passage is that Hegel does not attack the confusion of treating the soul as a thing but rather points to the difficulties and confusion surrounding the concept of matter. The scientists of his day were busy extending Newtonian physics, or trying to, by discovering new forms of "matter" which were successively more divorced from their original model. The notion of "vital matter" takes this development to a ridiculous extreme, for it would share none of the essential properties of matter. The soul is clearly not a Newtonian particle, but if we let the notion of matter wander too far from this paradigm, Hegel believes, the question of the immateriality of the soul becomes empty and loses interest. Those who ask about the immateriality of the soul, then, are subject to a double confusion. They commit a category mistake in treating the soul as a thing and exhibit as well a lack of real understanding of the notion of matter. They are, as it were, in the wrong categorial ballpark.

A standing fault of rationalistic dogmatism, according to Hegel, is the tendency to elevate commonsense, everyday concepts abstracted from sense experience into universal and necessary metaphysical principles or categories. But the kind of concepts we use in our everyday encounters with the finite world are quite insufficient to express the universal and necessary truths that are the content of metaphysics:

The thinking of the old metaphysics was finite thinking, for it moved along thought determinations, the limits of which were supposed to be fixed and not further negatable. It was asked, for example, does God exist? [*Hat Gott Dasein?*] And existence is considered something purely positive, something final and excellent. We will see later that existence is in no way a pure positive, but is rather a determination which is too base for the Idea and not worthy of God. . . . In the same way one asked whether the soul is simple or composite. Thus simplicity as well counted as a final determination, capable of grasping the True. *Simple* is, however, as poor, abstract and one-sided a determination as existence, a determination which we will later see is, as untrue, incapable of grasping the True. If the soul is treated as only simple, it is determined by such an abstraction as one-sided and finite. (§28, *Zusatz*, my tr.)

Rational psychology tries to capture the soul in simple and abstract concepts that cannot do justice to the actuality of the soul, and it proceeds by trying to assign these predicates in a thoroughly external fashion.[5]

Against Empiricist Psychology

Hegel is quite aware that there is a perfectly legitimate enterprise called empirical psychology. This is as much a science as physics or chemistry, although its practitioners, according to Hegel, tend not to be very clearheaded about their enterprise. Insofar as it is purely empirical, it is limited to gathering and classifying the empirical phenomena of mind. But many psychologists also attempt to philosophize about the mind on this empirical basis, or worse, to claim that empirical psychology is already philosophy—an idea Hegel completely rejects. While philosophy can never let the empirical realm out of its sight, empiric*ism* is a deadly antiphilosophical disease.

According to Hegel, empiricism is methodologically no better off than rationalism, and perhaps worse. In both cases abstract con-

5. A discussion of Hegel's theory of predication, however central to his metaphysics, would take us too far afield. A good introduction to this topic is provided by Richard Aquila, "Predication and Hegel's Metaphysics," in *Hegel*, ed. M. J. Inwood, pp. 67–84.

cepts are assigned externally to the subject; both have faulty views of predication. But since empiricism restricts its view to the sensible, it is blinded entirely to the metaphysical and incapable of dealing at all with the universal and necessary: "An empiricism that is consistently carried out, insofar as it restricts its content to the finite, rejects the supersensible in general, or at least the knowledge and determination of it, and leaves to thought only abstraction and formal universality and identity" (§38, my tr.). Hegel clearly has an extreme "ideal type" of empiricism in mind here, one that allows only the collection and classification of empirical data without permitting the essential theoretical move to nonsensible predicates or modal qualifiers; as such, it makes science and philosophy impossible: "The fundamental deception in scientific empiricism is that it uses the metaphysical categories of matter, force, and certainly also of one, many, universality and infinitude, etc.; infers in accordance with such categories, and thereby presupposes and applies the forms of inference, all the while not knowing that it thus contains and practices metaphysics itself; and uses these categories and their connections in a completely uncritical and unconscious way" (§38, my tr.).

Hegel also has a particular objection to the empiricist's practice of "philosophical" psychology: "In empirical psychology, it is the particularizations into which spirit is divided which are regarded as being rigidly distinct, so that spirit is treated as a mere aggregate of independent powers, each of which stands only in reciprocal and therefore external relation to the other" (§378, *Zusatz*). The empiricist collects various phenomena and tries to sort them under different classifications. The different kinds of mental phenomena are then attributed to various different mental faculties. But, Hegel complains, there is no principle behind this division of faculties; they are thought up ad hoc, and there is no way to show their intrinsic unity. Only someone with an independent (philosophical) conception of the whole can be proof against this danger. This conception of the whole must be validated independently of the particular empirical phenomena and must be capable of (at least partially) justifying the classifications employed by the working empirical psychologist. But the empiricist, who has no such conception, cannot but remain captured in empirical detail, unable to find the key to the underlying unity in the phenomena precisely because it is underlying and supersensible. The empiricist is like a builder with all the raw materials but no plans or idea of what is to be built.

The problem for both rationalism and empiricism, then, is that they treat the soul as a supersensible thing. Thinking of the soul as a *thing*, rationalism tries to conceive of it using only the concepts that are appropriate to finite objects and thus necessarily falls short of its goal. Empiricism, on the other hand, noting that the soul is *supersensible*, refuses to try to say anything interesting about it and restricts itself to botanizing the empirical phenomena of mind uncritically. Empiricism is correct in holding that one cannot use concepts compounded from sense experience to describe or conceive the supersensible; it is wrong in thinking that therefore the supersensible cannot be conceived. Rationalism is correct in trying to conceive the supersensible; it is mistaken in attempting to do so by simply assigning it predicates constructed from sense experience uncritically.

PHILOSOPHICAL PSYCHOLOGY: HEGEL'S METHODOLOGY

Having seen what Hegel thinks is wrong with the philosophical psychology of his predecessors, we now face the more difficult task of figuring out what he believes to be the right way to do philosophy of mind. When Hegel attempts to state the proper method in philosophy, he often describes it as being basically passive. One needs merely to watch the appropriate concept (in our case the concept of spirit) develop or unfold itself. Even more frequently Hegel drops all reference to the philosopher and claims that philosophy deals only with the self-development of the concept. Today we find such a description of philosophical method quite unilluminating, and to understand what Hegel means by such talk one has to work out in some detail his theory of the nature of thought. By the end of this book, Hegel's descriptions of a passive philosophical method will make sense, but for now let us approach the task from another angle. Let us try to reconstruct Hegel's intentions in his philosophy of mind without relying explicitly on his own methodological pronouncements. How does the content and practice of his philosophical psychology distinguish his enterprise from the unsuccessful attempts of his predecessors?

From Soul to Spirit

The first difference between Hegel and his predecessors, one notices immediately, is a shift from a focus on the soul to a focus on spirit. The word "soul" is reserved by Hegel for the lowest level of spirit: "Spirit is distinguished from the soul, which is both the middle between corporeality and spirit and the tie between them. Spirit as soul is sunken into corporeality and the soul is what animates [*das Belebende*] the body" (§34, *Zusatz*, my tr.). Thus "soul" acquires a restricted meaning, namely, spirit at its most thinglike level—a meaning Hegel probably adopts because of his predecessors' predilection for treating soul as a thing. Its successor concept, spirit, is not thinglike at all: rather, spirit is thought to be a pure, self-generating activity.[6] Rather than being thought of as a particular kind of thing with specific properties and interactions with other things, spirit has to be thought of as a particular pattern of activity, a special kind of organization which interactions among things can exhibit. Spirit cannot be adequately grasped through categories or concepts abstracted from finite things, much less from sensible things, because it is not a thing or even like a thing.

And "spirit" has a much broader use than "soul," for it denotes the underlying activity informing and accounting for not only the mental activity of the individual but also the social and historical activity of a community. Hegel's shift from "soul" to "spirit" emphasizes the nonthingishness, the active nature of the human essence as well as its communal or social nature. Hegel thereby emphasizes that he is investigating what is universal to us all, one and the same in us all, something in which we each participate rather than an entity we each individually possess (or are) independently of all others.

As comprehension of the nature of spirit, which informs not only the intellectual and practical life of the individual but of the whole of

6. For a good introduction to the concept of spirit, see R. C. Solomon, "Hegel's Concept of *Geist*," in *Hegel: A Collection of Critical Essays*, ed. A. MacIntyre, pp. 125–49. The concept of spirit is treated again in more detail in Chapter 3.

humanity as well, the philosophy of spirit must be seen as a much broader discipline than the philosphy of soul. Describing something as a spiritual phenomenon presupposes for its individuation as well as its explanation a certain set of explanatory principles not applicable to the merely mechanical, chemical, or organic but pervasive throughout the psychological, anthropological, and sociological.

Hegel characterizes the spiritual as the internal, in contrast to the externality of material objects (see, for example, §381). This contrast between internal and external is best understood, I believe, in terms of self- and other-determination. Spirit is what is self-determined; that is, spiritual phenomena are to be construed as manifestations of a self-productive activity. A self-productive activity is a special form of teleological activity, namely, one in which the telos is itself such self-productive activity.[7] To describe something as spiritual, then, is to commit oneself to the notion that it can be adequately explained only by showing how it is the manifestation of such a self-producing activity.

This explanatory schema has a broad-ranging field of application. Mechanical interactions, such as those studied by Newton, are not themselves to be explained in terms of manifesting a self-producing activity, but the very existence of mechanical interactions in the world is to be explained in those terms, for their existence is itself a spiritual phenomenon. Virtually all forms of human activity— whether individual or social—are to be understood as manifestations of a self-productive activity. The philosophy of spirit is devoted to showing how human activity embodies the defining structure of spirit.

Subjective Spirit

With this introductory understanding of Hegel's general conception of the philosophy of spirit[8], we can also see what a philosophy of subjective spirit—what we today call the philosophy of mind—

7. See Crawford Elder, *Appropriating Hegel,* for more discussion of this form of teleology.

8. I return to a fuller description of spirit in Chapter 3.

should be. A philosophy of subjective spirit is devoted to showing how the psychology of individual humans embodies the defining structure of spirit. Particular explanations of particular human actions are not, of course, in the purview of the philosopher, but discovering and explicating the form such explanations must take, as well as relating these forms to their counterparts in other disciplines, including logic and philosophy, are. The philosopher has a dual relation to empirical psychology; the philosophical understanding of the specifications of the general concept of spirit must be tested against the empirical facts, and the results and methods of empirical psychologists must be tested against the a priori analysis of the concept of the spiritual.

We must think of Hegel as directing his efforts inter alia toward the constitution of a more adequate empirical psychology. That this is indeed the case has recently been heavily emphasized by M. J. Petry's work in translating and editing the *Philosophy of Nature* and the *Philosophy of Subjective Spirit*. Hegel shows throughout his work a good knowledge of the contemporary state of the sciences, and it is constantly his concern to show how the empirical disciplines and his own system coalesce. Perhaps the most convincing evidence that his psychology was practiced with one eye on the state of the empirical disciplines is that in his manuscript of 1822 the second main factor said to contribute to the demise of the older philosophies of mind is itself an empirical one, namely, the discovery of hypnotism (called in Hegel's time animal magnetism) (*PSS*, vol. 1, p. 99). Here, Hegel thinks, is an empirical phenomenon that resists explanation by any of the old methods; it confounds the categories of the understanding.

Hypnotism prompted an understandable fascination in Hegel's time. Besides being good for parlor games, it was also seen to provide a serious challenge to the psychological theories of the day. Familiarity has perhaps bred contempt in contemporary psychological theorizing for the still amazing features of hypnotism. We have today a fairly divided stance toward it: we regularly turn to it to help in police work, psychotherapy, and self-development programs, but we also regard its results skeptically, since no theory has yet explained or accommodated it. Hypnotism attracted considerable attention in early nineteenth-century Berlin, including special studies by committees of the Berlin Akademie.[9] Hegel's interest in the phenomenon mirrors the importance it played in all psychological speculation of the era.

Hegel does not cite the phenomenon of hypnotism as itself revealing a higher point of view; that is, he certainly does not believe that the hypnotic subject or the hypnotist has special access to an epistemologically privileged position—quite the contrary. Nor does he claim that hypnotism is incomprehensible, miraculous, or mystical and therefore overcomes the philosophies of mind of the rationalists and empiricists. Rather, he claims that hypnotism presents us with a phenomenon that cannot be explained using the abstract thing-based concepts common to rationalist and empiricist philosophies of mind. If we go beyond these concepts, however, we can understand hypnotic phenomena, and Hegel takes it as one of the strong points of his philosophy of subjective spirit that it can accommodate hypnotic phenomena, whereas its competitors cannot. Here, then, is a clear case in which Hegel calls on empirical phenomena to support his philosophical doctrine, and in which he shows a clear expectation that philosophical doctrine will make contact with the empirical sphere.

Philosophy and Psychology

We can refine our idea of what Hegel thinks the relation between philosophy and the empirical sciences ought to be from a remark in his text of 1822 about Eschenmayer's psychology:[10]

> The first part, psychology, as empirical, makes no claim to being scientific; the second part, pure psychology, ought to have the determination of exposing the principles of this empirical material and of discovering the structure of the schema simply presupposed thereby and indicating its derivation. Eschenmayer, however, without further

9. For an account of the controversies surrounding hypnotism in nineteenth-century Berlin, see Walter Artelt, *Der Mesmerismus in Berlin*.

10. A. C. A. Eschenmayer (1768–1852) was a practicing physician who in 1811 became professor *extraordinarius* of medicine and philosophy at Tübingen (Hegel's alma mater), where later (1818) he also held the chair of practical philosophy. He was influenced by Schelling in his early career and thus shared common roots with Hegel. His fascination with hypnotism was often satirized, but his psychology textbook is not particularly distinguished.

ado simply puts the speculative knowledge that should come in here into (1) reflections by means of concepts, judgments, and inferences, and (2) ideal intuitions, (*PSS*, vol. 1, p. 101, my tr.).

Hegel subsequently castigates Eschenmayer for the all-too-common fault of discussing the material in an empirical and, in the end, arbitrary fashion. And Hegel dismisses any possible call on ideal intuition out of hand; intuition is a fickle lady on whom anyone can call.

What emerges from this passage is a characterization of what a pure psychology is supposed to accomplish and a warning about how not to do it. A pure psychology is dedicated to "exposing the principles of this empirical material and of discovering the structure of the schema simply presupposed thereby and indicating its derivation" (*PSS*, vol. 1, p. 101). This endeavor breaks down into a two-part task. The first part of the task, enunciating the principles of the empirical material, is only vaguely stated. Could Hegel mean here that the pure psychologist is responsible for all the work of the theoretician, namely, stating laws and making empirical generalizations to be tested against empirical data? In this case the "pure" psychologist would hardly differ from the normal empirical psychologist, for we could hardly expect the empirical psychologist to be content with merely gathering data without reworking it into a theory.[11] By the "principles" of the empirical material, however, Hegel does not mean the empirical generalizations covering that material; rather, he has in mind the principles governing the organization and form of such first-level generalizations. The pure psychologist is a metatheorist clarifying the principles (and the concepts, we might add) that govern the construction of particular descriptions and explanations in empirical psychology. Hegel engages in such reflections in his own philosophy of subjective spirit when he attempts to clarify the concepts of imagination, feeling, sensation, or thought and when he attacks associationist psychology in general as being built on faulty assumptions.

The second part of the pure psychologist's task is to discover the construction and the derivation of the schema thereby presup-

11. In Hegel's terminology the empirical investigator, qua empirical, is confined to gathering data—but such an investigator is not a scientist. Theorization is essential to science.

posed. Again Hegel's description is far from clear, particularly because it is not clear whether it is the empirical material that presupposes the schema to be discovered or the enunciation of the principles of the material which presupposes the sought-for schema. I think it is the latter that Hegel intends, that is, that the second part of the pure psychologist's task is to put the set of principles he promulgates in the first part of his task into a broader context and onto a firm philosophical foundation. Thus Hegel says, a bit later in the 1822 manuscript, "In each particular philosophical science, what is logical is presupposed as the purely universal science, and so as the scientific factor in all science" (*PSS*, vol. 1, p. 103). The pure psychologist who discovers a set of principles that will handily deal with all the empirical material at hand is not yet finished, for an explanation of why the principles take the form they do and how they fulfill the conditions of science in general must also be given. The philosophical psychologist must therefore operate on three levels, developing both the empirical theory and the metatheory of empirical psychology and putting them into a broader context. These tasks cannot be performed serially, either; the pure psychologist cannot await the completion of either the empirical theory of psychology or its metatheory before beginning to develop the broader viewpoint. These distinguishable tasks must in fact be in constant reciprocal contact, for the goal is the development of a maximally coherent worldview.

We must ask, however, what would count as indicating the derivation of the model with which one explains empirical material. This task belongs to the third level of reflection isolated above. There seem to be two alternatives: either the model is itself derived from the empirical materials it is eventually used to explain, or it is derived from a priori principles. Hegel insists that "all cognition derives subjectively from perception and observations, and the cognition of appearances is not only of the utmost importance, but is completely indispensable" (*PSS*, vol. 1, p. 97); thus he recognizes the causal role perception plays in knowledge. Yet philosophy— that is, the justification of philosophical truth—is also supposed to be pure and (at least relatively) independent of experience. The three different levels of psychological investigation cannot be independently practiced, for bottom-level observations play a necessary causal role in spurring our *thinking*, whereas our observational and experimental techniques, as well as the categorial structures employed, all have aspects that are extremely empirically insensitive, aspects deeply enough ingrained into our practices to be resistant, though not necessarily impervious, to empirical counterexample.

Such solutions are never really neat, and this one leaves us with a residual problem. The highest level of philosophical reflection is apparently a priori, according to Hegel. The practice of empirical psychology, though, is clearly empirical. How, then, do these entirely different enterprises mesh? All theorizing, and therefore all science, involves the application of concepts that are empirically insensitive, concepts that are, for all intents and purposes, a priori (this much Hegel shares with Kant). The theorizer employs no concepts that do not have an a priori basis, for even those concepts that seem paradigmatically abstracted from sense experience alone contain or implicate a categorial structure that could only have an a priori justification.[12] This is why Hegel accuses the empiricist of operating with metaphysical concepts without appreciating that fact. There can be no clear boundaries drawn between the philosophical and the empirical, for all attempts to describe or theorize about even the simplest empirical phenomena involve philosophical commitments. The conscientious theoretician must therefore also be a philosopher.

THE PHILOSOPHY OF SPIRIT

Let me attempt to summarize Hegel's understanding of the philosophy of mind. As he himself explicitly acknowledges, "the Philosophy of Spirit can be neither empirical nor metaphysical" (*PSS*, vol. 1, p. 103); that is, the philosophy of spirit is not an empirical effort to systematize a certain set of phenomena, nor is it concerned to elaborate an abstract concept of soul which has no contact at all with empirical reality. The philosophy of spirit attempts to uncover the universal and necessary structure inherent in the empirical phenomena of spirit. Because it is concerned with the embodiment of this structure in empirical, individual facts, it must answer to

---

12. The simplest and most straightforward example is Hegel's insistence that the use of the copula, even predication itself, involves metaphysical concepts (see §38).

them by being able to cast light on their nature. But the structures it claims to find embodied in the world must themselves ultimately prove themselves universal and necessary. It is to this degree a pure, a priori science. Whether we accept Hegel's attempt to balance the empirical and the a priori, we can recognize several significant advances in his treatment of the philosophy of mind.

First, he wrenches the attention of philosophers away from the fruitless, age-old questions of rational psychology. He does not try to refute the rationalists' answers; if he says anything one way or the other, he most likely agrees with the rationalists. But he breaks the fascination of these questions all the more radically by simply ignoring them and spending his time and energy in more fruitful pursuits. After Descartes, the apparently central problem of the philosophy of mind was the nature of mental substance and how it differs from and is related to material substance. Hume and Kant realized that there are other, more important questions about mind to be answered, but only with Hegel is there recognition of the fact that Descartes's whole line of thought is founded on a mistake.

Second, because he does not worry about the attributes of the soul, Hegel focuses more on explicating the structure of spirit, that is, the structure of the explanatory principles to which the use of the concept commits us. We shall see that Hegel has a keen sense of the nature and complexity of the concepts necessary to do justice to human activity.

Finally, in his attempt to accommodate the wealth of empirical phenomena as well as the transcendental aspects of our knowledge, Hegel develops a nonreductive approach to mind, which we explore in more detail in Chapter 3. Such an approach is finding increasing sympathy among contemporary philosophers. It offers us a more sophisticated understanding of the relations between the various sciences and promises deeper insight in particular within the sciences of man. Contemporary philosophy of mind can now reclaim Hegel as an ancestor.

3

Nature and Spirit

METAPHYSICS AND THE STRUCTURE OF THE SCIENCES

Hegel's goal in his philosophy of subjective spirit is an empirically sensitive yet basically a priori science of mind. That sounds oxymoronic: How can a discipline be at once a priori and empirically sensitive? Here the elaborate structure of the Hegelian system serves a clear purpose. We have, first of all, the logic—the a priori element in all thought.[1] The system's following two parts, the philosophies of nature and of spirit, bring the a priori structures of logic to bear on the empirical phenomena and thus are empirically sensitive as well as containing an a priori element.

But empirical sensitivity is a matter of degree. What kinds of empirical discoveries would persuade Hegel (or us) to abandon the distinction between nature and spirit altogether? Certainly there are cases in which the distinction is far from clear, just as the distinction between the living and the non-living is unclear. But that there are indeed such distinctions, and that they are highly immune to empirical potshots, seems apparent. Hegel's system offers him a way

1. Philosophy, according to Hegel, is a circle of circles. One of the consequences of this doctrine, which I believe Hegel willingly accepts, is that even logic is not absolutely a priori. The system is a closed curve: the achievement of the final stage of the philosophy of spirit cycles one into the logic. Logic therefore also has roots in the empirical, for it has emerged out of nature itself. Hegel denies any absolute distinction between the a priori and the a posteriori—the a priori is rather an element or aspect of every truth in varying degrees (see §12).

to represent the differing empirical sensitivities of the distinctions and concepts used in the sciences. The more subordinate the concept is, the more sensitive it is to the empirical.[2] Nature and spirit are superordinate concepts and relatively immune to empirical considerations, as is the essential contrast between them. The more subordinate concepts are more empirically sensitive. At least in the *Philosophy of Subjective Spirit*, the placement or explanation of subordinate concepts (e.g., feeling) was more readily altered by Hegel in apparent response to empirical developments, and further research on the development of the *Encyclopedia* will probably show that to be a pattern throughout.

The fundamental conceptual relations are worked out in the *Logic*. Nature and spirit manifest the conceptual structures discussed in the *Logic*, and the general structures of nature and spirit can be determined without much empirical input accordingly. This means that within the realms of nature and spirit we can expect to find structures that embody the distinctions between being, essence, and concept, and that the subordinate structures of these divisions again roughly limn those of the *Logic*. But the further we move from the general features of the realization of the conceptual structures discussed in the *Logic*, the less able are we to describe a priori the more particular features and the more vulnerable to empirical refutation is our attempt to organize the phenomena.[3]

We have not yet distinguished between the philosophy of nature and the philosophy of spirit. The methodological remarks of my first two chapters hold equally for both. What is the difference between nature and spirit? We need some account of the differences and the relations between various stages of the *Encyclopedia*.

2. I call more subordinate those concepts occurring within tertiary, fourth-level, or deeper triads. Every philosophical concept occurs within some triad and most concepts have further triads subordinated to them. Perhaps ideally every concept governs some other concepts, but Hegel is not clear on this point. In a typical listing of the system's determinations (such as the outline of subjective spirit included here), simple indentation shows subordination. Thus the concepts of spirit and nature are superordinate concepts, whereas those of imagination and galvanism are subordinate concepts.

3. One might imagine Kant getting quite bothered trying to locate precisely the synthetic a priori and the empirical elements in, say, physics. But Hegel would not have thought such a project very sensible, for even the lowliest assertion presupposes and contains metaphysical categories. Seeking to draw a boundary between the a priori and the empirical in our knowledge shows a thorough lack of comprehension of the absolute interpenetration of the two.

And though we need to distinguish nature and spirit, we must also distinguish subjective spirit from objective spirit and from absolute spirit. Finally, we must be able to explain the relations between the various levels within the philosophy of subjective spirit.

One noticeable feature of the progression in the *Encyclopedia* is that at the higher levels the distinctions correspond fairly well with the disciplinary boundaries between sciences (at least to the degree they are still recognizable). It has been common in the twentieth century to treat questions about relations between the various sciences in a linguistic mode; I follow suit here, for little is lost by such a treatment, and it brings out with striking clarity the relevance of Hegel's philosophy to present concerns.

The Languages of Nature and Spirit

Let us ask, then, what Hegel takes to be the differences between the language by which we explain and describe nature and the language by which we explain and describe spirit. It is certainly not often easy to separate these two "languages,"[4] but it is clear that Hegel thinks that the concepts structuring these two different forms of discourse are quite different from each other. Furthermore, in his discussions of the differences between nature and spirit, Hegel does not intend to summarize and condense an understanding of their relation which is already common coin. We each possess the beginnings of a fully adequate understanding of the differences and relations between nature and spirit, but the common view is still mired in the rigid and reifying distinctions characteristic of the understanding. Hegel is therefore offering us a revised and improved understanding of nature and spirit, one that avoids the pitfalls plaguing the common understanding. In the linguistic mode,

---

4. Separating a language for describing and explaining the mental from the language for describing and explaining the physical is a convenient mode of speech. The two vocabularies are, of course, not separate languages at all, but parts of unitary natural languages. They are not separable in anything like the way two different natural languages are. With this warning, I adhere to present convention and talk of two (or more) languages. Discussing philosophical issues in a linguistic mode is not as foreign to Hegel as might be thought. It is not uncommon that he makes use of linguistic facts in his own argumentation, but, more important, he expressly affirms that "the forms of thought are, in the first instance, displayed and stored in human *language*" (*SL* p. 3, Miller tr.). Approaching philosophical problems through a focus on language is entirely consistent with Hegel's beliefs.

Hegel is trying to reveal the ideal language pointed at by our present, imperfect, ordinary languages of the understanding.

But in Hegel's view there is no simple distinction between the language by which we describe and explain nature and the language by which we describe and explain spirit. Although he distinguishes nature and spirit, it would be a major mistake to think that that is the end of the matter. Beginning in the seventeenth century, a straightforward dichotomy between the two realms was common, typified in Descartes's distinction between extended and thinking substances. Descartes's distinction amounts to the claim that there are two (and only two) vocabularies necessary for a complete description and explanation of the world—the geometric vocabulary of physics and the mentalistic vocabulary of the soul. For Descartes, all extended things are of a kind, with only accidental differences between them; the animate body is just more complex than a stone, not in any other way different from it. Similarly, in the realm of the nonextended, all things are of a kind, namely, thinking substances and their modifications. Hegel, however, makes no such claims about the homogeneity of nature or spirit. In his system there is no one language of nature, nor any one language of spirit. We find, rather, that the language of nature includes languages for describing and explaining the mechanical, the chemical, the organic, and that none of these can be simply eliminated without loss. Both nature and spirit have various stages, each of which builds on its predecessors. To each of these stages corresponds a special science, and thus we have to consider not only the relation of the Naturwissenschaften to the Geisteswissenschaften but also the relations among the subdisciplines in each of these categories.

These relations have been a subject of much concern in contemporary philosophy of science, so we have several different models for them. The classical reductionist model claims that each of the predicates of a higher science is connected by some bridge law to (a set of) predicates of the reducing science. Any law of the higher science can then be rewritten, perhaps clumsily, but preserving its nomological character, in the vocabulary of the reducing science.[5]

5. See John G. Kemeny and Paul Oppenheim, "On Reduction," in *Readings in the Philosophy of Science*, ed. B. Brody, pp. 307–18; and Ernest Nagel, *The Structure of Science: Problems in the Logic of Scientific Explanation*. See also Jerry A. Fodor, *The Language of Thought*, and Hilary Putnam, *Philosophical Papers*, vol. 2: *Mind, Language and Reality*.

This would be a convenient and pretty picture of the relation among the sciences, for then (supposedly) physics would be the only essential science, statements of any other science being mere abbreviations of much longer and more complex physical laws. But, unfortunately or not, this picture of a unified science is just too simple. There is no good reason to think that there are any such bridge laws between the realms of nature and spirit. To use Fodor's example, there is no good reason to believe that there is a bridge *law* connecting "monetary exchange," a theoretical term in economic theory, to any set of predicates from physics. Monetary exchanges vary widely; they can be exchanges of metal, paper, or wampum, or changes in binary data in a computer. There is simply no reason for believing that monetary exchanges are connected in a *lawlike* fashion with any set, however, disjunctive, of physical predicates.[6]

Once the reductionist model of interscience relations has been rejected, there are two different directions one can go. Those of strong reductionist conviction make the radical move to eliminative materialism, claiming that the reducing science, usually physics, answers every worthwhile question. Even if some slight expressive power is lost, it is argued, the language of higher theories, including psychology, can be simply eliminated without significant loss.

Because it is supposedly the inadequacies of the earlier stages that drive the dialectic onward in the philosophies of nature and spirit, it is clear that Hegel could not accept the eliminability of higher sciences; the whole *Encyclopedia* is an argument for their ineliminability. Eliminative materialism is not independently attractive either. One could at most claim that psychology and other higher sciences are totally eliminable only in principle. That we could never in practice eliminate them is clear. Second, to argue for eliminative materialism one has to maintain that in eliminating the vocabularies of the higher sciences nothing essential is lost. But what exactly counts as essential? Is the usefulness of the vocabulary essential? If so, the game is lost at the outset, for the vocabulary of physics is unusable for describing and explaining psychological or economic or many other kinds of events in any practical manner. The eliminative materialist must write a promissory note on an imperceivable future to claim plausibility for this doctrine.

A less radical and more attractive alternative to classical reduc-

6. See Fodor, *Language of Thought*, pp. 9–26.

tionism is the token-identity version of noneliminative materialism. According to this view, although the predicates of a higher science cannot be either eliminated or redefined in favor of the predicates of the reducing science, it is still the case that any instance of the predicates of a higher science is also an instance of the predicates of the lower science, and that the lower science (again, physics), as more universal, retains priority.[7] Thus, although there is no lawlike relation between monetary exchanges and the predicates of physics, it is nonetheless the case that every monetary exchange is also a physical event (albeit a complex one). Instance by instance, then, there is an identity between the events described and explained by the higher science and those described and explained by physics.

There are several things to be noted about this position. Phrased as it often is as a thesis about objects, it says, for example, that one and the same object can have the mental property of now wanting to go sailing and the physical property of weighing 164 pounds— mental and physical predicates pertain to the same subject of predication. But this account does not yet clarify the relation between the mental and the physical. The token-identity thesis is that my wanting to go sailing is itself *identical* to some (complex) physical property I instantiate. The difference between type and token identity is this: type identity would be correct if every desire to go sailing (or at least all *my* desires to go sailing) were identical to one and the same physical property, whereas token identity requires only that any instance of a desire to go sailing be identical to some instance of some physical property (but not necessarily always the same one).

Here is an analogy. The quarters of the 6th Battalion are the quarters of Harry, Sammy, Ben. . . . But although this is an identity statement, it does not express a type identity, only a token identity, for when Harry is mustered out of the service, the quarters of the 6th Battalion are no longer the quarters of Harry, Sammy, Ben. . . . Surely there is a different identity statement, namely, that the quarters of the 6th Battalion are the quarters of Tommy, Sammy, Ben . . . , which has taken its place. There is no one set of persons to which the 6th Battalion is identical in every case, although in every case it is identical to some set of persons.

This view has seemed quite promising, but it too has difficulties.

7. Ibid.

The doctrine has often been framed in terms of events, with the assertion that, although mental events are not type-identical to physical events, they are token-identical to them. Let us assume for the moment that events are exemplifications of properties by individuals at a time (so-called Kim events); that is, we can identify an event with the ordered triple of an individual, a property, and a time. This is a simplification of our ordinary concept of an event, but it will do nicely for now. Token-identity theorists claim that all mental events are token-identical with physical events. This must mean that every exemplification of a mental property at a time is identical with some exemplification of a physical property at that time. Assuming that the individuals and times involved are the same, the ordered triples constituting the events can be identified only if the properties involved are the same. This seems inevitably to push us back toward type identity, for properties *are* types. It is difficult to say what exactly constitutes identity between properties, but it does seem clear that two properties could not be identical in one instantiation but disparate otherwise. If the properties are not identical, neither can we say that they are coextensive in one instance but not otherwise. We can at most say that they are coinstantiated in this instance but not otherwise. But coinstantiation is not strong enough to please a token-identity partisan.

In discussions of token-identity theories, these points are often obscured by the treatment of the mental and physical events themselves as particulars that are identified, apparently, in virtue of *their* properties. But we must not lose sight of the fact that it is one and the same thing—a person—that has both mental and physical attributes. We need not explicate the unity of the person by identifying the two different kinds of attributes with each other.

An important question remains to be answered: Is there no relation at all between a person's mental and physical properties? Are these so distinct that any set of mental properties can coexist with any set of physical properties? Our immediate reaction is that this cannot be the case; there is some important connection between one's physical and mental properties. It has long been supposed that there are at least causal connections between mental and physical states, but this is not the kind of relation we are looking for here. The causal relation is a dynamic relation; we are looking for some nondynamic, ontological relation between the mental and the physical that captures our belief that my mental attributes depend, in their very being, on my body and its attributes—that mental attributes require a physical substratum.

A new tack on this problem has received a great deal of attention lately, namely, the claim that mental properties *supervene* upon physical properties. The concept of supervenience was first introduced in discussions of the relations between moral properties and natural (or physical) properties. The idea is that what physical properties a person has determine that person's mental (or moral) properties, so that anyone with just those physical properties (and relations, of course) has the same mental (or moral) properties, and a change in mental (or moral) properties means a change in physical properties as well.[8] This claim that mental or moral properties can be *determined* by physical properties is then complemented by a claim that this determination does not yield a *reduction* of the mental or moral properties to the physical.

To avoid getting too technical for our purposes, I offer a metaphor. Philosophers often talk of properties or predicates as ways of "cutting up" or sorting the world. Let us take this metaphor seriously for a moment; suppose that there is no privileged catalogue of the entities in the world. It is possible that there are several different, nonconflicting ways of sorting the world but no direct way of getting from one way of sorting (or even the entities sorted) to another, or of inferring from an item's place in one classification to its place (or even its occurrence) in another. In this sense the two sorting schemes are simply independent and no reduction is possible, although they sort "the same thing." Nonetheless, it could still be the case that one sorting scheme is basic in the sense that a *complete* inventory of the world in the basic scheme determines the world sufficiently well that only one sorting in the other scheme is possible, though not vice versa. This is particularly possible if the second, supervenient scheme is in some way *partial* and simply does not attempt a universal classification. This is the picture that supervenience theorists propose of our world: there is no mapping on an entity-by-entity, or property-by-property basis, even using logical constructs of the entities or properties, between the mental

8. See D. Davidson, "Mental Events," in *Experience and Theory*, ed. L. Foster and J. W. Swanson, p. 88. Davidson uses the notion of supervenience to defend the token-identity thesis, but the two need not go together (see sources cited in note 10).

and the physical, but a complete physical history of the world suffices to fix the psychological history as well (and not vice versa).

My thinking that Cookie Rojas was a great ballplayer, although not identical with any physical state I am in, may supervene upon my physical states—that is, any person in an indistinguishable physical state is also thinking that Cookie Rojas was a great ball-player. This leaves open the possiblity that two persons have content-identical thoughts without being in physically indistinguishable states.

This notion has attracted attention because it seems to offer confirmation of our intuitions about the primacy of the material without the untoward consequences of identity theories. An interesting further development of this new position is that there also seems reason to abandon individualism, the position that the mental properties a person instantiates supervene only upon the physical state of that person's body. The relevant physical state upon which a given mental state supervenes is certain to be very complex, and it may include states of objects outside the person's body. The arguments against individualism are too complex to rehearse here, however.[9]

To recast the supervenience thesis in the linguistic mode, we can say that the statements of a higher language S supervene upon those of a lower language P if fixing all the truths of the lower language also fixes the truths of the higher language. Alternatively, we can also say that S supervenes upon P if two worlds indistinguishable with the resources of P are also indistinguishable with those of S.[10]

Hegel as a Weak Monist

How does this modern speculation about intertheoretic relations bear on Hegel? Does one of these patterns fit the subdisciplines in

9. Tyler Burge, "Individualism and the Mental," *Midwest Studies in Philosophy* 4 (1979):73–121; "Other Bodies," in *Thought and Object*, ed. A. Woodfield; Jay Garfield, "Propositional Attitudes and the Ontology of the Mental," *Cognition and Brain Theory* 6 (1983):319–31.

10. Jaegwon Kim, "Supervenience and Nomological Incommensurables," *American Philosophical Quarterly* 15 (April 1978):149–56; John Haugeland, "Weak Supervenience," *American Philosophical Quarterly* 19 (January 1982):93–104; Garfield, "Propositional Attitudes."

Hegel's system? Most of these models of intertheoretic relations were motivated by the unity-of-science doctrine, a doctrine with which, in its positivistic, particularly physicalistic, guise, Hegel would have had little patience. Hegel shows no interest in any form of reductionism, so the classical pictures of theory reduction and eliminative materialism are both nonstarters for capturing Hegel's view.

One might wonder whether Hegel's idealism is not just materialist reductionism stood on its head, but I find no indication that Hegel thinks he is reducing mechanics to psychology, nor any indication that he intends to eliminate mechanics. He could not eliminate, because he claims that each stage of the dialectic has a certain truth that must be preserved, and I take it that that means it makes some sort of ineliminable contribution to our ultimate understanding of the world. He never proposes that an earlier stage of the philosophies of nature or spirit be simply abandoned in favor of a later stage. Moreover, reductionism is not an open possiblity, because then the stages he discovers in nature and spirit—the whole complex articulation of his system—would collapse into one basic level.

It seems more plausible that Hegel might be a token-identity theorist, for this position would at least preserve the specialness of the individual sciences while also accounting for the overall monism of the system. But this characterization does not work either. Hegel intimates that physical explanations are not applicable to functioning organisms, nor physiological explanations to rational agents.[11] A token-identity theorist must claim that both explanatory forms are applicable; any differences can be only pragmatic or instrumental. Moreover, since identity is an equivalence relation, this would commit Hegel to the identity of spiritual events with natural (physical) events, and there is no indication that he would accept that position.

There are, however, some powerful reasons for thinking that Hegel has something like supervenience in mind as the relation between adjacent special sciences. This interpretation would account for the relative independence of each level of nature and spirit

11. See Crawford Elder, *Appropriating Hegel*, and my review of this book in *The Owl of Minerva* 14 (December 1982):5–8, and 14 (March 1983):4–8

without losing sight of the unity of the world. It would also account for Hegel's ability to order the special sciences serially, for each would then supervene upon its immediate predecessor. It would also account for the systole and diastole of the dialectic, the movement from immediacy through mediation to return to a higher immediacy. At each stage of nature the vocabulary appropriate to that stage picks out certain basic objects that are not further analyzable in that language. Complexes of these objects and complex interactions among them can then be described and explained within the language, but at some point there may occur complexes that possess properties unanalyzable within the old vocabulary. A new vocabulary must be introduced in which these complexes are now treated as basic, simple units. These new, higher simples supervene upon the complexes of the old vocabulary. Most of all, such an interpretation would allow us to grant the autonomy of the spiritual without divorcing it entirely and irreparably from the natural.

Contemporary theories of supervenience are far from physicalistic positivism trumpeting the unity of science, yet they show their dialiectical origin in such positivism by retaining a conviction that physics is the foundation on which all others supervene. Surely, one would think, this is counter to Hegelian idealism. We could, however, invert the supervenience hierarchy and take natural facts to supervene upon spiritual facts, but this is at best unconvincing. First, we would have to sacrifice the stepwise fashion of the hierarchy to make it work, since there are natural events where there are no biological or psychological events. Second, fixing the facts in the highest theory (which would be what exactly? history? philosophy itself?) would be tantamount to fixing all the other facts of the world. And while some of the things Hegel says point in this direction, this view is ultimately irreconcilable with his doctrine of the contingency of nature. As a matter of fact, the retention of matter as the basic set of objects/events upon which all others supervene is thoroughly consistent with Hegel's idealism. Hegel in general has no particular respect for beginning points; the result, the end of a process, is usually what he is interested in.[12]

12. The end of a process need not be a final product. There are processes the end of which is the process itself (for example, the performance of a piece of music).

One might question whether a supervenience of spirit upon nature threatens the *freedom* of spirit, since supervenience is a form of dependence. Here several answers are possible. First, the facts of the spiritual realm are themselves a many-layered complex. The "dependence" on the natural would be very distant—mediated by the biological, the anthropological, the psychological, and so forth—by the time the true freedom of philosophical speculation is achieved. Second, supervenient dependence is definitely not a form of causal dependence, and there is no question of its constituting a form of freedom-depriving compulsion. The freedom of the spiritual is its self-determination, which essentially means that truths about spirit have their ground in the necessary ends of spirit. Given the global nature of the supervenience relation, there is no dependence relation between individual spiritual and material phenomena, only one form of general dependence of the spiritual on the material. The only real problem, then, is at the very beginning: the spiritual depends on nature at least as the object in which it realizes itself. How, then, can it turn around and determine nature's own existence as well? Hegel's answer is that spirit determines nature's own existence because spirit is nature's telos. Since nature is the realm of efficient causation, looking for an efficient cause of nature itself makes no sense. Thus, although supervenient on nature, spirit is still entirely self-determined and therefore free.

We can understand this point better by observing the deep similarities between Hegel and Aristotle. Aristotle's metaphysics is hylomorphic; every object is taken to be a certain form inhering in a matter appropriate to it. A hierarchy of forms is thus generated, the realization of each presupposing the availability of an appropriate matter. How far down this hierarchy reaches and what its bottom looks like has been the subject of much debate, which I can ignore. Aristotle's natural philosophy can be seen as a kind of nonreductive materialism, for matter is, in one sense, basic in his scheme.[13] Yet calling Aristotle's philosophy a materialism is also quite misleading, for it plays down far too much the absolutely central role of form. It is Aristotle's emphasis on the notion of form, what Hegel calls the ideal element, that prompts Hegel to see Aristotle as an important predecessor of idealism.

13. We get something like this in E. Hartmann, *Body, Soul, and Substance.*

Hegel's philosophies of nature and spirit are very much Aristotelian, and it is profitable to think of Hegel's view of nature as similar to Aristotle's hylomorphism; the objects of a lower stage offer the material for the further mediation, the new structures and forms of the higher stages.[14] Even more important, Hegel also adopts a teleological worldview like that we find in Aristotle. That the lower stages of nature are material for the higher stages, are the potentiality of the higher stages, entails that their own actuality is achieved in the higher stage. Nature points toward and exists for the sake of spirit, not because nature is someone's means for realizing an intention to create spirit, but because spirit is the force dwelling within the differentiation of nature. It is the nature of nature, its Concept, to provide the necessary conditions for the realization of spirit and to be itself an essential part of that realization. But make no mistake—spirit, the formal and final cause, retains metaphysical priority.

Hegel's teleologism, his discounting of the philosophical importance of such natural relations as generation or material constitution (see *PN* §249), makes it possible to assert that he believes that something like a supervenience relation holds between individual stages of nature without violating his idealism, his conviction that spirit is the true reality of the world, for his idealism is essentially supported by his teleologism.[15] What we today most commonly see as a thoroughly contingent emergence of supervenient objects and events on top of a complex of subvenient objects and events, Hegel understands to be the embodiment of a goal-directed, self-actualizing process, the self-realization of the Idea, the Absolute.

Let me summarize what I take Hegel's view to be. Nature is to be understood as consisting of various stages or levels. These levels form a hierarchy, one supervening upon another, and the whole ultimately serves the self-realization of the Absolute. For each level

14. G. R. G. Mure has emphasized Hegel's indebtedness to Aristotle very heavily in his works on Hegel. See also N. Hartmann, "Hegel und Aristoteles," *Beiträgen zur Philosophie* (1923).

15. One could say that, according to Hegel, the real mistake materialists make is in thinking that what something consists of is the most important thing to know about it. He would rather have us ask about its role in the realization of the Absolute, without denying that questions of material constitution are also worthwhile. The materialist does not usually pay Hegel similar respect; materialism denies that asking about roles in the realization of the Absolute makes sense.

there is a set of concepts in which the objects of that stage can be described and explained; these concepts are neither eliminable nor reducible. The empirical sciences are consequently also irreducible; each develops and applies the concepts peculiar to a particular level to describe and explain individual phenomena at that level. Inquiry is not, however, exhausted by these empirical disciplines. We can inquire further into the nature of the concepts employed by the empirical disciplines and their interrelations (thus philosophies of nature and spirit), into the nature of concepts in general (logic), and finally into the self-realization of the Absolute (philosophy über-haupt). These philosophical inquiries are all highly nonempirical, of course.

Distinguishing Nature and Spirt

Externality and Self-determination

Given Hegel's stepwise arrangement of empirical disciplines, we must now ask more specifically what motivates the distinction be-tween nature and spirit for Hegel. How can he draw any deeper cleft between the language of organisms and the language of an-thropology than he draws between any two other adjacent disci-plines? The answer is that Hegel perceives certain structural sim-ilarities within the sciences of nature and within the Geisteswissen-schaften, along with some important differences between nature and spirit, the first of which is a contrast between the external and the internal.[16] I have already discussed this distinction briefly. Na-ture is self-external because it and natural objects are not self-determining. This means, first of all, that in explaining some natu-ral phenomenon (the movement of a billiard ball, for instance), one looks outside that phenomenon for an external cause, some other natural phenomenon. Explanations continually lead into the thicket of natural phenomena; natural facts are determined by other, dis-tinct natural facts. In contrast, the Absolute is totally self-determin-ing; there is nowhere else to turn. The stages of nature and spirit leading up to the Absolute are stages of increasing self-determina-tion.

16. *PN* §247ff; *PSS* §381, *Zusatz*; cf. *PSS*, vol. 1, pp. 105ff.

The externality of nature has another, deeper meaning in Hegel's philosophy: "Nature's essential and distinctive characteristic is to be the Idea in the form of otherness." (*PN* §247, *Zusatz*). It is not just the case that understanding any natural phenomenon inevitably leads one to other natural phenomena, but also that understanding such phenomena *as natural* involves seeing them in contrast to the spiritual. Spirit is self-explanatory, self-subsistent, total actuality. In its contrast to spirit, nature is none of these. It must, according to Hegel, be conceived of as pointing to spirit, working toward its own fulfillment in the complete actuality of spirit. Nature as a whole is itself a spiritual phenomenon; the existence and general structure of nature cannot be understood solely on natural principles but must be referred to spirit. In that the very being of nature is realized only through spirit, nature is self-external.

These characteristics constitute the externality of nature in general, but not all the levels of nature are self-external to the same degree. In particular, in the final stage of nature, the animal organism, the first form of externality is *almost* completely overcome, for the organism is a self-maintaining system: "An even more complete triumph over externality is exhibited in the animal organism; in this not only does each member generate the other, is its cause and effect, its means and end, so that it is at the same time itself and its Other, but the whole is so pervaded by its unity that nothing in it appears as independent, every determinateness is at once ideal, the animal remaining in every determinateness the same one universal, so that in the animal body the complete untruth of asunderness is revealed" (*PN* §381, *Zusatz*, Miller tr.). The story of nature is the story of the increasing self-determination present in nature, a story that continues with spirit, for it is not brought to an end with the animal organism. Although the animal has acquired considerable freedom within its environment, it is still bound to its natural conditions. Any further step toward greater self-determination would involve somehow transcending the animal's natural conditions. There is therefore no truly self-sustaining being in the natural world. The closest thing to a self-sustaining being in nature is the animal genus, which persists in and through the demise of its members. But the genus is also self-external in that it has no existence apart from the manifold individuals, which have no consciousness of their species being. The genus is still scattered in mutually external objects. In the realm of spirit, the universal is to come into its own—to achieve an existence that is not merely scattered among different, mutually external individuals. How exactly this occurs we discuss in detail later.

The distinction between nature and spirit, then, is not an absolute cleft; nature itself has successively more spiritual stages. In this sense the break between nature and spirit is arbitrary; there is place for a line here somewhere, but Hegel could have displaced it in either direction without obviously upsetting the fine-grained structure of the whole. Sensation, for instance, occurs as a major topic of consideration in both the *Philosophy of Nature* and the *Philosophy of Subjective Spirit*, and it offers us an interesting case study. In the post-Cartesian tradition, sensation is clearly mental, not physical.[17] Denying minds to animals entailed denying them sensations. In Hegel's system, sensation is clearly a property of complex organisms, but it is also the immediate, simple, first reality of the spiritual. Sensation offers a pivot point, a phenomenon with one foot in both the natural and the spiritual realms. The dualist would like to force a decision one way or the other; sensation is either natural or spiritual, but not both. Hegel rejects this simple disjunction. Sensation emerges as a property of complex organisms and is a form of *assimilation* of the external object. It is correctly considered natural because in sensation the animal organism is still largely determined from the outside, not self-determined. On the other hand, as a form of the assimilation of the external object, sensation is also spiritual insofar as it is an internalization of the external object which allows further, new relations to that external object to develop as forms of self-determination on the part of the organism; that is, in organizing its sensations in ever more complex ways, the organism also acquires new relations to the external object, but now through a process that is self-determined and internal. Thus sensation has two faces—and the point of view from which one looks at it becomes crucial. As a simple property of complex organisms, sensation is decidedly natural; as the nondestructive internalization of the external object, it is the fundament of the spiritual.[18]

17. Descartes himself was not so straightforward.
18. In my discussion here it sounds as if sensation is the turning point between nature and spirit—the last stage of nature and the first of spirit. This is not, however, the case. The *Philosophy of Nature* ends with "the process of the genus" (that is, the life cycle of the organism), and the *Philosophy of Subjective Spirit* begins with "the

There is no clear break between nature and spirit; rather, these are two poles between which there is a complex series of intermediate stages. Hegel draws the line between nature and spirit where he does, not because there is some one clear mark of the spiritual that suddenly appears on the scene, but because at that point a sufficient number of the characteristics of the spiritual have appeared to justify a distinction. From this point on, the spiritual makes itself ever more evident.

The Nature of Spirit

I have so far talked of spirit as if the only feature distinguishing it from nature were degree of self-determination. Hegel does, however, say quite a bit more than this, and we must now turn to his fuller pronouncements about the nature of spirit to see how these further illuminate the status of the individual mind in his theory.

Three principle characteristics emerge in his exposition of the concept of spirit at the beginning of the *Philosophy of Spirit*—the ideality of spirit, its freedom, and its existence as self-manifestation: "We must designate as the distinctive determinateness of the concept of Spirit, *ideality,* that is, the overcoming of the Idea's otherness, the process of returning—and the accomplished return—into itself of the Idea from its Other" (§381, *Zusatz*). Hegel probably derives this use of "ideality" from the Kantian notion of the Ideal of Reason, the unconditioned. Spirit overcomes its other in that that other is the manifestation of spirit, its revelation. By overcoming its other, making its other a moment within itself, spirit ceases to be conditioned by anything external. It is as unconditioned that it is ideal. Since spirit is precisely its self-revelation, nature—as one form of this revelation of spirit—is no longer absolutely opposed to spirit. Nonetheless, nature is not the complete or perfect revelation of spirit, and insofar as spirit's essential nature is this self-revelation, nature is not yet spirit.

Spirit reveals itself in three forms (§383, *Zusatz*). The first and

natural soul" (including discussions of the ways the soul is attuned to large-scale phenomena and situations, such as geographic location, climate, and cosmic influences). I have therefore oversimplified the complex relations between spirit and nature to some extent, but without losing anything essential for our purposes.

lowest form, the form we find in nature, is revelation of spirit only to another, that is, some external observer. Second, the idea "creates for itself an existence conformable to its inwardness and universality" (§384, *Zusatz*), that is, it creates the human being. In the human being, spirit not only reveals itself but, more important, it reveals itself *to itself*. We know ourselves to be the revelation of spirit. Yet, even so, as finite minds we are not yet the perfect revelation of spirit, the revelation in which all otherness is overcome:

> Spirit converts nature into an object confronting it, reflects upon it, takes back the externality of nature into its own inwardness, idealizes nature and thus in the object becomes for itself. But this first being-for-self of spirit is itself still immediate, abstract, not absolute; the self-externality of spirit is not absolutely overcome by it. The awakening spirit does not yet discern here its unity with the spirit concealed and implicit in nature, to which it stands, therefore, in an external relation. (§384, *Zusatz*, Miller tr., adapted)

In the third and last form of spirit's self-revelation, spirit knows nature as its own creation, and nature and finite spirit lose all externality; they are but forms of spirit's self-revelation. We normally distinguish between what is manifested or revealed (the content of the revelation) and how it is revealed (the form). I may manifest an inner insecurity either by withdrawing from responsibility or by seeking out ever new responsibilities with which to prove myself, for example. But the self-revelation of spirit is not subject to this distinction (§383, *Zusatz*); rather, spirit's self-revelation is precisely what is revealed.

So far we have connected two of the three important characteristics of spirit, its ideality and its self-revelation. Spirit is ideal, without an absolute other, because its apparent other—nature—is already a form of the self-manifestation that spirit *is*. Spirit is, further, free. Hegel also calls this "absolute negativity." But freedom is precisely the absence of dependence on an other (§382, *Zusatz*), self-determination. Spirit is only what it makes itself.

Hegel's concept of spirit is difficult and confusing. Even with the above list of major characteristics, one cannot seem to put one's finger on the concept.[19] But because I am concerned only with one particular set of stages of finite spirit, I shall not try to do what I think I cannot do—make all the aspects of Hegel's concept of *Geist* perfectly clear. It is helpful to think of spirit as the ordering activity operative within the universe, an activity that is capable of self-reflection in that it is in some sense capable of metaordering, ordering its own ordering activity. Such a conception of spirit fits the three characteristics I have focused on here. The universal ordering activity is the overcoming of its other, namely, the lack of order. Even a lack of order is not absolutely opposed to such an activity, for it is the presupposition of such activity, and it is far from clear that the notion of an absolute lack of order makes real sense.[20] Order makes itself manifest, it need not reveal something else. And the ordering activity is free, for determination is a form of order, so nothing else can determine it, bind it. Determination is a form of order, so the source of all order can only be self-determined. This account is still very general, but it is enough to give us a sense of the direction of Hegel's thought. In later chapters more detail about the way finite, subjective spirit is an ordering activity is added, piece by piece, supporting this approach to spirit.

We must still specify the notion of spirit a bit further, so that we can finally begin to deal with finite, subjective spirit, the subject of the philosophy of mind. According to Hegel, the point of calling anything finite is to assert a discrepancy between its concept and the reality (§386) and, in particular, to claim that the reality falls short of the concept. In finite mind (spirit is in itself infinite, although it contains finitude) we therefore have spirit that is not fully manifest, nor fully ideal, nor fully free. Finite mind is, as it were, spirit still struggling to gain control of itself, to free itself from nature, which is something it simply finds over against it. Absolute spirit finds itself everywhere; finite spirit "does not yet discern here its unity with the spirit concealed and implicit in nature, to which it

19. But see Solomon, "Hegel's Concept of *Geist*"; and Charles Taylor, *Hegel*. I also find Josiah Royce's *Lectures on Modern Idealism*, which seems to have been forgotten lately, quite helpful.

20. In view of the fact that nature is spirit's other, and that nature itself is not a complete lack of order, I think that we should conclude that the notion of a complete lack of order cannot be made out according to Hegel any more than a concept of pure nothing can.

stands, therefore, in an external relation. . . . Here, consequently, spirit still has in nature a limitation and just by this limitation is finite spirit" (§384, *Zusatz,* my tr.).

But we are concerned in particular with subjective spirit, which is a stage of finite spirit. How does it differ from objective spirit? "As long as spirit stands related to itself as to an Other, it is only *subjective* spirit, originating in Nature and at first itself natural spirit. But the entire activity of subjective spirit is directed to grasping itself as its own self, proving itself to be the ideality of its immediate reality. When it has attained to a being-for-self, then it is no longer merely subjective, but *objective* spirit" (§385, *Zusatz,* Miller tr.). The distinction seems primarily to be that, in subjective spirit, spirit *finds* itself revealed in a *given* material, whereas in objective spirit, spirit is set on constructing its own revelation, making the world over in its own image, as it were, by constructing a society and a civil state. Subjective spirit is still essentially tinged with passivity; it receives a given passively, as if from the outside, which it subsequently recognizes as being a manifestation of the spiritual. Equally important, objective spirit is the realm of intersubjectivity. Subjective spirit is the treatment of the individual "I." Objective spirit treats the "We," a no less essential phase in spirit's self-actualization. This leads to a peculiarity in the Hegelian system: theorization and cognition seem already to be perfected in subjective spirit, whereas practical being must still traverse all of objective and absolute spirit.[21] This imbalance, I believe, can be overcome only if absolute spirit is also the fulfillment of man's cognitive being as well as his practical being.

21. This imbalance is tellingly pointed out in T. Litt, *Hegel: Versuch einer kritischen Erneuerung.*

4

Sensation: Mind's Material

If the question of sensation or perception arises in a discussion of Hegel, the focus of the discussion is likely to be the opening chapters of the *Phenomenology of Spirit* of 1807.[1] Such a focus is, however, a mistake. The examination of sense certainty and perception in the *Phenomenology* bears on the question of the proper categories to be applied *within* experience, but there is no discussion there of the actual nature of sensation or perception as states of organic and spiritual beings within a natural world. To understand what Hegel thinks sensation and perception themselves are we must turn to his Anthropology and Psychology.

Hegel's theory of sensibility tries to do justice to the insights of such predecessors as Aristotle, Hume, and Kant while also providing a framework within which the empirical research of the day can be comprehended systematically. His theory does not answer all the desiderata imposed on philosophical theories of perception by analytic philosophers today, such as detailing a set of necessary and sufficient conditions to distinguish veridical from nonveridical per-

1. D. W. Hamlyn, in his *Sensation and Perception: A History of the Philosophy of Perception*, commits precisely this error and makes the mistakes such an error could be expected to foster; he attributes to Hegel a "minimum of attention to the role of sensation in perception" and the notion that "the only thing which is 'given' is experience as a whole," and claims that "idealism makes it difficult for itself to justify the claim that anything independent of ourselves exists" (pp. 144–45). Others among English-speaking authors who emphasize the *Phenomenology of Spirit* too heavily in this regard include Charles Taylor and R. C. Solomon.

ception, or mere perceptual mistake from hallucination, but it does show a sensitive consideration of problems in the ontology of sense and the differentiation of various levels of perceptual experience.

Hegel's distinction between sensation and the higher mental activities, like Kant's, is phrased in terms of a distinction between active and passive. Although, as he repeatedly claims, spirit is essentially active, Hegel does not believe that there is no passive, receptive element in the individual, subjective spirit. His theory of sensation and intuition is best seen as an attempt to explicate the nature of the receptive element in spirit and its relation to the spontaneous, rational essence. His most important theses are these:

1. Sensation, though clearly mental, is not itself cognitive; the intentionality of sensation is not the intentionality of thought.
2. Sensation is nonetheless basic to cognition and is the starting point of all knowledge and experience.
3. The world of one's direct sensory experience is a phenomenal world in the sense that it is a construction by the mind out of its affections. Given Hegel's metaphysics, however, this does not entail that we are confined to knowledge of a merely phenomenal world.
4. There are different levels of spirit's emergence from the passivity of pure sensation as spirit liberates itself from its dependence on the body and its immediate physical environment.

We begin by discussing the nature of sensation in Hegel's theory. Hegel makes several related attempts to differentiate the sentient from the nonsentient; after looking at these, we discuss in greater detail the nature of the relation between mind and object in sensation.

The Sentient and the Nonsentient

Sensation is a property of animals as well as humans, but we cannot recount the whole of the *Philosophy of Nature* here in order to get the proper background for understanding the emergence of sensation within the animal organism. In what follows I summarize what I take to be the most important points.

The Nature of the Animal Organism

The animal organism is a highly organized chunk of nature, composed of the objects of the lower levels of nature, the physical and the chemical. But it is not simply a conglomeration of such objects (see §350, *Zusatz*). What, then, is the animal itself? The animal is a unity in a way no inorganic conglomeration is. The unifying telos is, in the case of the animal, internal, unlike the inorganic, the telos of which is some external goal. Hegel expresses this important difference, perhaps unfortunately, in terms of the animal being its own universal over against its particular aspects:[2] "An even more complete triumph over externality is exhibited in the animal organism; in this not only does each member generate the other, is its cause and effect, its means and end, so that it is at the same time itself and its Other, but the whole is so pervaded by its unity that nothing appears as independent, every determinateness is at once ideal, the animal remaining in every determinateness the same one universal, so that in the animal body the complete untruth of asunderness is revealed" (§381, *Zusatz*, Miller tr.).

Hegel wants to maintain that the mode of being of the animal organism and even more so of the human involves a rather special relation between universality and particularity. The relation of an inanimate object to its genus is, according to Hegel, external. The individual is merely subsumed under the genus, which just collects a set of otherwise disparate individuals; there is no intrinsic uniting power active in them. There is, for instance, no intrinsic, active essence that all red things have in common.[3] To this extent the inanimate individual and its universal are both abstract. In the animate object, on the contrary, its universal, its concept, is distinctly active within it, and the animate, organic individual actualizes and maintains itself from within.[4] In the animal the externality

2. If one recalls here the Aristotelian doctrine of substantial forms and its applications in biology and psychology, these views do not seem as strange.

3. Not all properties of inanimate things are equally external. The natural kind to which a thing belongs has a closer relation to the thing than do its other characteristics.

4. The self-organization Kant attributes to organisms (*Naturzwecke*) is, along with Aristotle's concept of the organism, an important influence on this aspect of Hegel's theory.

of nature is overcome, for we can only explain and understand the animal's structure and behavior, Hegel thinks, by thinking of its structure and behavior as the expression of a unitary (though complex) concrete universal active within the animal.[5]

Botanical, animal, and human beings are self-organizing. The animal, qua universal, is the principle that orders and gives coherence to its various elements and properties, but in contrast to a desk or a rock it does so itself, from inside. A rock, for instance, is at best only nominally organized; even in complex crystal structures there is no need to refer to functions within a system to explain the organization of the crystal. That a rock has the structure it has and behaves as it does depends solely on the stuff it consists of and its external situation. Artifacts are more highly organized. The properties and behavior of a desk are explained in large part by the function it is intended to serve. It can be made of wood, metal, plastic; we can even slowly replace wood with metal parts and retain the same desk. The desk is free of strict dependence on its material constitution. Nonetheless, its principle of organization or essence is extrinsic, bestowed on it by some person. In an organism the principle of organization is intrinsic—organisms are not designed by someone to fulfill a purpose but are themselves their own purpose. The organism is an active universal because, although a universal in relation to its parts, it must be mentioned in any adequate explanation of them. The organism is its own effect and therefore must be active.

The Sentient Organism

Feeling occurs in the animal, according to Hegel, "as the individuality which in the determinateness[6] is immediately universal to itself, simply remains with and preserves itself: the existing ideality

---

5. Hegel makes the contrast between internal and external do a great deal of work; it separates animal organisms from inanimate nature, but it is also used, as we have seen, to separate spirit from nature. It has been suggested that there is a simple ambiguity in Hegel's usage, there really being two different contrasts—one Aristotelian, which culminates in the internality of the organism, and the second Cartesian, which culminates in the internality of a subjectivity (E. Heintel, "Aristotelismus und Transzendentalismus in 'Begriff' bei Hegel"). I prefer to think that there is one univocal contrast with an articulated structure, but I am not yet sure of that.

6. "Determinateness" is Hegelian for a quality of something.

of being determined" (*PN*, §351, Miller tr.). "Feeling is just this om-
nipresence of the unity of the animal in all its members which immediately communicate every impression to the one whole which,
in the animal, is an incipient being-for-self" (§381, *Zusatz*, Miller
tr.). These are obscure passages, to say the least, but not unusually
so among passages in which Hegel tries to distinguish the sentient
from the nonsentient. The most complete statement Hegel makes
on the subject is in an only recently published unfinished manuscript of a projected, book-length version of the *Philosophy of Subjective Spirit:*

> If neutral water is coloured, for example, and so simply possesses this
> quality, is simply in this condition, it would be sentient if it were not
> only for us or as a matter of possibility that it differed from the
> condition, but it were at the same time to distinguish itself from itself
> as being so determined. Differently expressed: the genus color only
> exists as blue, or as a certain specific color; in that it is blue, it remains
> the *genus* color. But if the color as color, i.e., not as blue but at the same
> time as color, persisted in opposition to itself as blue color—if the
> difference between its universality and its particularity were not sim-
> ply *for us* but existed within itself, it would be sensation of blue. (*PSS*,
> vol. 1, p. 123)

These passages are confusing and obscure, but Hegel is trying to
describe something the evanescence of which has frustrated all
philosophers. He is trying to describe what it is in the nature of
certain beings that makes them sentient, that qualifies them for the
predicate "aware."

A nonsentient being, a stone, for example, can have a color
property, say gray. The distinction between the stone and its grayness is a simple modal distinction (to use the Cartesian terminology). An animal can be colored in precisely the same way. But if the
animal senses something gray, how is it then related to grayness? A
dualist might say that this is again a simple modal distinction between the mind (instead of the body) and one of its properties.
Being gray and sensing gray have two different subjects. In contrast
to this dualistic picture, Hegel wants to keep a unitary subject. The
same thing—the animal—can both be gray and sense gray. The
difference between being gray and sensing gray lies in the relation
the subject bears to the properties of its sense organs.

The nonsentient subject is exhausted in its properties, Hegel seems to be claiming; *it* makes no distinction between itself and its properties, although *we* do. The sentient being, however, retains for itself an identity over against its particular properties, it makes a distinction between itself and its properties. This is all pretty mystifying, but I think some sense can be made of it.

Hegel insists that the sensible quality is now posited within the soul as ideal. Hegel often uses "ideal" to characterize something as being unconditioned by anything external, and we would normally think of sensation as a prime example of determination by the external. "That the soul finds *itself* so determined, that is why the determinateness is at the same time posited as *ideal* in the soul, and is not a quality of it. In that the ideality of this determinateness is not another determinateness, which takes its place and drives out the first, but rather that the soul itself is the ideality of the determinateness and is reflected into itself, the finite, i.e., is infinite, the determinateness is also not a mere state" (*PSS,* vol. 1, p. 122; my tr.) Hegel's notion seems to be that sensations are peculiar because, although they are in one sense properties brought about by external factors (by and large), what they are depends crucially on their occurrence in the context of a complex organic whole. Hegel's point is, I believe, that there is no simple connection between the physical state of a sensory organ and the organism's sensory state. Particular sensations—how the state of the sense organs affects the total sensory state—are dependent on that total sensory state as well. To the extent that each sensation is also dependent on the total state of the organism, the sensation does not upset the self-determination of the organism.

Perhaps an example can help. Thermostats are sensitive to temperature—but they do not *sense* heat or cold. Hegel would say, it seems, something like this: "If the temperature as temperature, that is, not as 78° but at the same time as temperature, persisted in opposition to itself as 78°, it would sense 78°." In some ways our sense organs are meters of our environment, capable of recording its state with sometimes surprising accuracy. We might, then, try to think of our possession of a certain sense as our possession of a metering subsystem that feeds its output into some central processor where it can be calculated into our total behavior function. In such a complex system, we might claim, the temperature as temperature, in the form of the special metering subsystem, persists in opposition to any specific value it may output. But clearly there are many such systems—for example, central heating systems—which do not literally sense heat or cold.

What Hegel would find repugnant in the above example is not the isolation of a particular metering system—this would correspond to a sense organ, and Hegel never doubts the existence of those. Rather, he would object to the form of connection between the metering system and the central processor. The meter is conceived of as fully independent of the central processor, adding its isolable input without regard to the state of any other part of the whole. In other words, the meter is fully modular. This is not an organic unity. The input-output function of the meter would also at least have to have a reciprocal dependence on the total state of the whole system in order for this condition to be met. Only to a system exhibiting strong reciprocity between the particular states of its parts and the total state (for Hegel its universal) could we attribute sensation.

Is Hegel's view of sensation and the mind itself therefore refuted by the contemporary evidence that a number of our psychological abilities are modular?[7] Although he consistently rails against faculty psychology, Hegel does make distinctions among sensation, feeling, intuition, and imagination. Modularity is not all or nothing, and Hegel does not seem to require total nonmodularity in the mind. We therefore cannot say that the apparent modularity presently attributed to a number of our psychological capacities is a refutation of Hegel. But it certainly seems fair to say that the more highly modular are our abilities, the less attractive is a Hegelian theory of mind. In his emphasis on the rationality of spirit and human nature, Hegel may well have gone too far in thinking that all

---

7. See Jerry Fodor, *The Modularity of Mind*, for a general discussion of modularity. Fodor explains his terms as follows: "By saying that confirmation is isotropic, I mean that the facts relevant to the confirmation of a scientific hypothesis may be drawn from anywhere in the field of previously established empirical (or, of course, demonstrative) truths. Crudely: everything that the scientist knows is, in principle, relevant to determining what else he ought to believe. . . . By saying that scientific confirmation is Quinean, I mean that the degree of confirmation assigned to any given hypothesis is sensitive to properties of the entire belief system; as it were, the shape of our whole science bears on the epistemic status of each scientific hypothesis" (pp. 105–7).

our mental abilities have the Quinean, isotropic (that is, multidimensionally holistic) nature reasoning exhibits.

Hegel's confusing but tantalizing remarks about sentience and nonsentience do not help us much in the end. Ultimately we are only told that the sensible organism relates to some of its states in very peculiar ways, ways that are understood by reference to the holistic, organic context in which they occur. At best, Hegel is insisting that there is a limit on the modularity of a sentient system. A sentient being must be more tightly unified or more closely and complexly self-related than a conglomeration of modular metering systems attached to some central processing device. This may be true, but without further specification of the relations involved it is not very helpful.

THE OBJECT OF SENSATION

Hegel's attempt to distinguish the sentient from the nonsentient does not succeed, but neither has anyone else's. There is more to be found, however, when we consider the *object* or *content* of sensation and the nature of the relation between the sensation and its object. Hegel talks rather loosely of the content or object of sensation, and it appears that there are three candidates for the position: (a) the external object involved in the causal process that culminates in the perceiver's having a certain sensation; (b) the proper sensible itself—a color, tone, taste; (c) the animal or human itself.

The first two candidates are familiar, but the third seems unlikely, so let me note some of the textual evidence that shows that this alternative must be taken seriously. Hegel continually insists that in sensation, feeling, and intuition the subject finds *itself*, and that such mental activities are the immediate being-for-self of the organism. As a metaphor, the self-directedness of sensation pervades Hegel's discussion. Furthermore, there are plenty of explicit passages such as the following: "In that the animal senses, it doesn't only sense itself, but itself as determined in a particular way" (§357a, *Zusatz*).

The three objects of sensation—the external object, the proper sensible, and the animal itself—are "objects" of sensation in different senses, and Hegel keeps the senses clearly separate. There are, however, extra complications arising because of Hegel's distinction between inner and outer sense.

Inner and Outer Sense

The distinction between inner and outer sense does not consist in certain sensations being given *as* inner and others *as* outer, for as we shall see, sensations are not given *as* anything at all. Neither does this distinction have anything to do with the Kantian distinction between the forms of inner and outer sense. Rather, in Hegel's system, the distinction is founded on the etiology of the sensation and its content. External sensations are those determined by causal processes originating in some physical object and affecting the sense organs: "One sphere of sentience distinguishes itself principally as the determination of corporeity (of the eye etc., of the parts of the body in general) and becomes sensation in that it is recollected, internalized within the being-for-self of the soul" (§401). Internal sensations, on the other hand, are not the result of the causal influence of a physical object on a sensory organ; they arise instead through the agency of spirit acting on itself, embodying some higher mental state, for example, a thought, in order that it may be sensed: "Another [sphere of sentience] distinguishes itself as the determinatenesses which have originated in and pertain to spirit, and which are embodied in order to be as if they had been found, or sensed" (§401).

Hegel leaves it unclear whether internal sensation is something that uses its own particular organ of sense.[8] The examples he gives lead one to believe that the actual sensing of an internal sensation is accomplished by the organs of external sensation, for he gives the feelings of anger and courage sensed in the breast and blood, the flushing of the face in shame, the trembling and pallor of fear, and the sensation of meditation in the head as examples, and these can be considered to be sensibles proper to touch. They might, however, be considered sensibles proper to proprioception, the status of

---

8. Hegel does say this: "It is not to be denied however, that in accordance with the variety of their content, the inner sensations have at the same time a *particular* organ within which their primary and predominant embodiment takes place" (§401, *Zusatz*), but this does not answer the question of how we sense such things.

which is a bit muddy. Proprioception is not one of the standard five senses, and it is peculiar in that one proprioceives only one's own body, never an external object. Nonetheless, by inner sense Hegel clearly does not mean proprioception, for he does not recognize proprioception as a separate sense, and proprioception does not have the proper etiology. Proprioceptive knowledge of the disposition of our limbs or of gastric distress does not rest on inner sensations in Hegel's sense. The etiology of the sensation is the most important difference between the inner and the outer.

But inner and outer sensation are also distinguished with respect to their content. In the *Zusatz* to §401 Hegel talks more specifically about inner sensations, placing them into two categories. First, "there are those which concern my immediate individuality in some particular relationship or condition." His instances of this category are all emotions. By treating emotions as inner sensations Hegel can account for both their purely occurrent felt quality and the often complex intentional structure they contain, since they are the embodiment of and therefore are involved in higher spiritual activities. The second kind of internal sensations consists of those "which relate to that which, in and for itself, is a *universal*, to right, to the ethical, to religion, to the beautiful and the true." Yet at other places Hegel insists that the object of sensation is always something singular: "Now since what is unmediated is a singularization, everything sensed has the form of *singularity*" (§400, *Zusatz*). Besides the specific list of universals he gives as objects of inner sensation, however, Hegel also claims that *all* the content of the mental sphere—including the objects of thought itself—exists in sensation. How is this conflict to be resolved?

What would count as a sensation of right? It seems to me that we would talk of such a sensation (though we might prefer the phrase "feeling of rightness") in a situation in which we are confronted with a certain state of affairs to which we immediately react, "But that's wrong!" or "That's right!" Hegel's point is that in their mental structure those reactions, insofar as they have a purely felt, noncognitive, affective aspect (that "gut feeling"), are forms of sensation. The pure occurrent felt quality is confined to a particular agent at a particular time in response to a particular situation. It has the "form of singularity." Such sensations presuppose considerable sophisticated mental activity; they need to be learned. The ability to embody sophisticated contents in the simple form of sensation is extremely important. Hegel insists that the ideas of right, of justice, and so on are only truly and completely appropriated by spirit when they are not merely the objects of thought but have become internalized in this way. "Principles, religion etc. must be in the heart, they must be *sensed*, it is not enough that they should be only in the head. . . . One should not have to be reminded however, that what is religious, ethical, true, just, etc. is not *justified* by the form of sensation and of the heart, and that an appeal in this context to the heart or to sensation is either simply meaningless or downright pernicious" (§400).

Hegel explicitly states that the *content* of inner sensation is itself properly handled only in the Psychology, the last stage of subjective spirit. At the early stage of the Anthropology, where he introduces the distinction, the concern is the *embodiment* of inner sensations. Thus the sensation of sin, qua sensation, need not be anything more than a peculiar sensation in the pit of one's stomach or some such. What makes it an inner sensation is its etiology, the fact that it is the embodiment of a higher spiritual act and the capturing of the more complex act in the immediacy of sensation. In making the distinction between inner and outer sensation, Hegel is concerned to account for the fact that our higher mental activities can acquire a purely occurrent affective aspect. The occurrent inner sensation has a content solely in virtue of its causal connection with other states of the organism. One must take this functionalist trend in Hegel's thought seriously.

Mediate and Immediate Objects of Sense

Let us now return to the problem of the object of sensation. The point here is that such things as flashes of light, earthquakes, and one's beloved are mediate objects of sensation; states of the sensory organs are the immediate objects of sensation. The mediate object is the thing that explains why the sense organ is in the sensation state it is in. In the case of external sensation, this is the object at the other end of the causal chain that accounts for that state of the sensory organs are the immediate objects of sensation. The mediate object is sioning object, the concept of right or justice. In this context Hegel places sensation in the middle of a syllogism involving the thing and the organism:[9] "Touch, for example, is the mediation between me and the other, for although it is distinct from both sides of the opposition, it at the same time unites them" (§399, *Zusatz*).

In sensation the animal stands in immediate relation to itself, in particular to the body. The relation of the body to the external object determines the properties of the body or sense organ, and this property of the sense organ *exists as ideal* in the soul, and as such it *is* the sensation.[10] As I have tried to explain Hegel's position, the animal itself is to be more or less identified with the total state of the organism. When the external object acts on the sense organ, the sense organ's change of state is reflected in the change of the total state, although not in any neat way. The state of the sense organ, by contributing in this complex way to the total state of the organism, is a "moment" within it and in this sense exists as ideal in the animal. This moment is the sensation.

To be able to assign a sensation the proper mediate determinate object—indeed *any* mediate object—a complex diagnostic task must be performed, a task beyond the ability of the sensitive soul as such. Such diagnosis requires conceptual abilities that go well beyond sensibility. Thus the soul as such makes no such assignation. An external object as such is present to spirit only at the higher stage discussed in the Phenomenology.

We have now explained the sense in which the external thing is the object of sensation and the sense in which the animal senses itself in sensation. But what of the proper sensible? Where do the sensible qualities such as color, texture, or tone fit in? In a discussion in the *Encyclopedia* that occurs in expanded form in the discussion of Aristotle's theory of sensation in the *Lectures on the History of Philosophy*, Hegel says that when he senses red or hardness his sensation is itself red or hard.[11] And he says, "Heat, warmth, etc.

9. Hegel was familiar with the Aristotelian logic in which terms, not propositions, are the basic elements. He thought of a syllogism as a mediated relation between terms. This is discussed in much detail in Chapter 12.

10. In this Hegel was probably influenced by Spinoza's view that the *ideatum* of the lowest-order ideas of the mind is the body of which the mind is the idea. Spinoza says accordingly that the human mind perceives the modifications of the body, which means that the mind contains the ideas that are in the attribute of thought those modifications the body has in the attribute of extension; see B. Spinoza, *Ethics*, ed. J. Gutmann, pt. II, prop. 22.

11. G. W. F. Hegel, *Vorlesungen über die Geschichte der Philosophie*, Bd. 2, pp. 205–12.

are independent and outside, but they are just as much immediately transformed, made *ideal*, a determinateness of my feelings;
the content in me is the same as it is outside, only the form is
different" (§357a, *Zusatz*). Hegel is drawing here on the Aristotelian
account of sensation, according to which "the actuality of the sensible object and that of the sense are one and the same, though
differently definable" (*De Anima*, 425b26ff)[12]. As Aquinas says in
his commentary on this passage, "Color has two modes of being: a
material mode in the object, a spiritual mode in sensation."[13]

Wherever we run into a claim of shared content in different form
in Hegel it is helpful to think of the content as being determined by a
functional role in a larger system. There are, then, several ways two
things can have the same content but different form. They can have
the same content either by playing relevantly similar roles in two
different systems or by serving the same function (perhaps more or
less adequately) within a common system. Their forms differ insofar as the means by which the common role or function fulfilled
differs. Neither of these senses of "same content/different form"
seems to apply to the proper sensibles in their objective and subjective existences. Sensations of red play a role in my acquisition of
beliefs, in my directing my action, and so on, but the redness of
things themselves cannot be said to play *that* role, though sensations of red can play the role they do only in virtue of their connections to red things.

If having a content is playing a functional role, then many philosophers would object in principle to the idea that the proper
sensibles are contents. The sensation of red, it is claimed, cannot be
defined or explained in terms of its causal powers, for something
could be functionally equivalent to a sensation of red—that is, give
rise to the same beliefs, desires, behavior—and not be a sensation
of red. There are two ways to try to make this claim out: either the
organism (or machine) has *some* sensation that is functionally equivalent to a sensation of red but is not a sensation of red, or, alter-

---

12. In the first edition of the *Encyclopedia* we find the following remark: "*Aristotle*
also recognized the determination of sensation, in that while he recognized the
sentient subject and the sensed object into which it is divided by consciousness as
only the *possibility of what sensing is*, he said of sensation that the *entelechy* of the
sentiment being and what is sensed are one and the same" (*PSS*, vol. 3, p. 121).

13. K. Foster and S. Humphries, trans., *Aristotle's "De Anima" in the Version of
William of Moerbeke and the Commentary of St. Thomas Aquinas*, p. 362.

natively, the thing has some state—but not a sensation at all—that is functionally equivalent to a sensation of red.

The first formulation raises, in effect, the problem of the inverted spectrum. I know of no discussion of this problem in Hegel, but I think his Aristotelian theory of sensation would have led him to deny the meaningful possibility of someone's phenomenal spectrum being the inverse of other people's. After all, it is the same thing—red—that exists in the object and in the mind. But since Hegel describes the sensation as ideal and as having a content, we still might be able to preserve everything he says about sensations while admitting the possibility of an inverted spectrum. In that case the content of the sensation, Hegel would maintain, is unaffected, for the sensation typically caused by red things would be a sensation of red, given that functional equivalence is maintained (where functional equivalence includes preservation of the typical connections to emotional states, aesthetic properties, etc.) Otherwise, Hegel would claim, we would be trapped in a subjective idealism.

I am less sure of Hegel's response to the notion of a complete, but sensationless, imitation human. Such a notion is surely not a live option for him. If such an imitation is supposed to do *everything* we do but sense, that is, imagine, understand, and reason, Hegel would declare it an impossibility, for sensation is a necessary condition of these higher activities. Hegel would also deny the possibility of a complete behavioral imitation devoid of internal reasoning. But how are we to take the impossibility of sensationless imitation? Does it mean that any rational agent ipso facto senses (so that if we succeed in building a rational agent, it will have sensations), or that to build an imitation of us one must not only make it reason but also make it sense? Surely Hegel would reject the latter alternative—it destroys the unity of spirit, chopping it into separable, autonomous units.

Hegel seems well on the way to denying the possibility of absent qualia and thus sustaining the notion that sensations are specified by content, by functional role. We need, then, to worry a bit more about what role that is exactly, so that, for example, heat as an inner and an outer state shares one content with different forms. The point seems to be that, while nature and spirit constitute significantly different systems on their own, our sensation states do map some of the natural properties of things, preserving their most important relations, and are the sensations they are because of these ties to their typical causes. The content is primarily determined by the abstract relations within the sensory range and the causal links to the object, although, as we have seen, it must be open to other influences as well.

SENSATION AS NONCOGNITIVE

There is a more radical thesis about sensation lurking here which it is now time to flush out: that sensation is, although mental, noncognitive. The individual qua individual is, for Hegel, unknowable—another easily recognizable Aristotelian principle. Sensation is entirely singular and devoid of universality and can therefore be cognitive, conceptual, at best only potentially.

One criterion of cognitivity—a necessary but not sufficient condition—is that cognitive activities be subject to standards of correctness. But when considering sensation as a pure affection of the subject, it makes no sense to ask whether the sensing was done correctly or whether it is true. Hegel adopts the Kantian view that knowledge requires the organization of experience under certain objective constraints. Although a state may be called a sensation only when it participates in a complex, organically structured unity in a certain way, calling it a sensation is still treating it as a simple, without consideration of the specific role it may play in the cognitive life of the organism. Occupying a place in a cognitive system, sensations are no longer considered merely the passive affections of the animal and are no longer merely sensations; they have become what Hegel calls feelings.[14]

Since concepts are that which organize our experience, the unorganized material of experience must itself be nonconceptual. In a sense Hegel believes that there is a given element in our experience—he uses the metaphor that these elements are *found* by the soul within itself rather than *given* to it—but it is not an epistemological given, and terms of epistemological appraisal are not appli-

---

14. Hegel uses "feeling" (*Gefühl*) for both the sense of touch and a later stage of subjective spirit beyond sensation; see Chapter 5.

cable.[15] It is true that all experience has its root in the sensations found within the individual organism and taken up by spirit. But the sense in which spirit is rooted in sensation must be properly understood. Sensation is the genetic, causal root of the spiritual, but no sensory episode plays a foundational epistemological role.

That Hegel's approach to the individual's epistemological situation is so Kantian is also seen in the following passages:

> The *subjectivity* of sensation must be sought not indeterminately in man's positing something *within himself* through sensing, for he also does this in thinking, but more precisely in his positing something not in his free, spiritual, universal subjectivity, but in his natural, immediate, singular subjectivity. This *natural* subjectivity is not yet a self-determining one, pursuing its own laws, activating itself in a necessary manner, but a subjectivity determined from without, bound to *this* space and *this* time, dependent upon contingent circumstances. (§400, *Zusatz*)

> Mere sensation . . . has to do only with the singular and contingent, the immediately given and present, and this content appears to the sentient soul as its own concrete actuality. In that I raise myself to the standpoint of consciousness, in contrast, I relate to a world external to me, to an objective totality, to an internally connected circle of manifold and complex objects standing over against me. (§402, *Zusatz*; my tr.)

Furthermore, one must take seriously the idea that Hegel believes sensation to be the immediate material of mental activity. Over against this stands the form-giving activity of spirit. Sensation can at best only be considered such as is ripe for the agency of spirit; it is potentially, but not actually, cognitive. How spirit's activity on this raw material of sensation ultimately produces true knowledge is the story of the remainder of the philosophy of subjective spirit. This process begins with the next stage, feeling. But, although absolute knowledge has its roots in man's sensory encounter with the world,

---

15. D. W. Hamlyn's criticism that only the whole of experience can be thought of as given according to Hegel simply does not hold up against the texts beyond the early *Phenomenology of Spirit*. The whole of experience is something that spirit constructs—it is a result of the activity of spirit. See Hamlyn, *Sensation and Perception*.

Hegel claims that this beginning is ultimately overcome, that true thought, free of any sensory admixture, is ultimately achieved.

Hegel's theory does not escape some of the problems that also ensnare his predecessors. We can capture several of these problems in our net by pointing out the slide that tempted so many philosophers: a sensation of pain is *of* pain because it *is* a pain; the pain has its proper existence in the mind. A sensation of blue is similarly treated; it can be *of* blue because it is an actual case of blue in the mind. But patches of color usually have an outline and shape. If there is an actual case of blue in the mind, we then ask, is there also an actual case of shape, say, triangularity? Here, of course, the philosopher balks. The mind is traditionally treated as nonextended, shapes are certainly modes of extension, and therefore there can be no shapes in the mind.

Are problems also generated for Hegel's system by this line of reasoning? There is one immediate difference to be noticed. In contrast to his predecessors, Hegel believes that shape is a proper sensible, a proper sensible of touch: "Three dimensional *shape* also falls to the lot of feeling, for feeling alone is concerned with general mechanical determinateness" (§401, *Zusatz*). We can thus state the problem in a very straightforward way. Hegel claims that, when he sees something red, his sensation is itself red. Would he also agree that when he touches something triangular, his sensation is triangular? This question is made still more complex by the fact that in the system it is not until we reach the more sophisticated level of intuition that space and time are explicitly introduced and constructed. Hegel has not really thought out the way spatiality enters into our perceptual experience. Some remarks in the *Encyclopedia* imply that our visual field is two-dimensional and that we infer the third dimension. But then it would seem that we have separate access to at least two-dimensional shapes through a sense other than touch. Can it be possible for sensations to have dimensions like this and yet not be spatial? A similar kind of problem is caused by the universal objects of inner sensation. If in sensing red my sensation is itself red, in sensing right or wrong is my sensation itself right or wrong?

Our earlier analysis of the content of sensations, however, shows that Hegel need not be smothered by these problems. If a sensation has a certain content in virtue of occupying a position in a (mental) quality-space isomorphic in the essential respects to the quality-space applicable to the object by which it is typically caused, then some mental analogue of space suffices for us to be able to sense shapes. Inner sensations are still a problem, but if we remember that Hegel is after the "gut feeling" in such sensations, and that justice and right are the mediate objects of the sensation and not the proper sensibles, the problem evaporates.

Perhaps the major source of disquiet in Hegel's treatment of sensation is the fact that he seemingly denies that sensations are cognitive while still attributing them content. The notion of a contentful state seems already to invoke cognitive notions. We have seen in what sense sensations have a content: preserving within the mind a quality-space equally applicable to the outer objects causally responsible for the sensations. The sense in which higher cognitive states have a content is different, though not unrelated. The intentionality of sense is not the full intentionality of the higher cognitive processes.

5

Feeling

In sensation mind is passive, receptive, unorganized, aimed at the individual, dispersed in a manifold. Its content is merely found within itself, not freely created by it. Feeling is the first step toward the free, creative, thinking mind, but it is only the first step, the introduction of the barest unity into the manifold of sensation. We have several more levels to move through before we reach normal perception.

The distinction between sensation and feeling is never given an extremely clear formulation and is not to be found in Hegel's work before the third edition of the *Encyclopedia*. I believe that this distinction was one that Hegel was led to in his later years in order to preserve the pure immediacy, singularity, and lack of universality of sensations themselves. In the earlier version of the *Philosophy of Subjective Spirit* Hegel talks of sensation more loosely, allowing the concept to stray from its defining relation to singularity. I argue here that the distinction between a sensation and a feeling is simply that a feeling is a sensation that has a place in a very low-level, basic, organized system of sensations.[1]

The fuzziness of his early concept of sensation led Hegel to see that he needed an intermediate stage at which sensations could

1. This might seem to conflict with the position I have taken on the nature of sensation's content, for attributing content to a sensation presupposes its participation in a system sufficiently organized to map a quality-space. In feeling, however, the relevant system must be of much greater scope than simply a mapped quality-space; it is the total system of all the animal's sensations.

acquire some of the characteristics of the universal. This could be accomplished if they were to occupy a place in a system and thereby acquire a functional role within that system, because then the particular sensation loses importance in contrast to the role it plays— and roles are universals and can be taken by many different role players. Feeling, however, is still not explicitly cognitive, and the sensations are not organized yet through the conceptual categories that we meet in the Phenomenology:

> The sensing of the *universal* seems to involve a contradiction, for as we know, sensation as such has as its content only that which is single. What we call the *feeling* soul does not involve this contradiction however, for it is neither confined to the *immediate sensuousness* of *sensation* and dependent upon the *immediate sensuousness* of what is present, nor does it relate itself to the *wholly universal being* which can be grasped only through the mediation of pure *thought*. It has, on the contrary, a content which has not yet developed into the separation of the universal and the singular, the subjective and the objective. . . . This content still relates itself to the feeling soul as accidents do to substance; the soul still appears as the subject and central point of all determinations of content, as the power which dominates the world of feeling in an immediate manner. (§402, *Zusatz*)

THE ROLE OF FEELING

Feeling is still clearly an animal function; it is not confined to humans. As the mention of sense and feeling in the *Philosophy of Nature* (§356ff.) makes clear, the functions of these powers of the animal soul are directed toward enabling the animal organism to maintain itself within, but also over against, its environment.

The medievals noticed that on the basis of mere sensation the animal cannot be expected to succeed in its efforts to preserve itself, and that we cannot explain animal behavior solely by reference to the pure data of sense. As Aquinas says, "The sheep runs away when it sees a wolf, not because of its color or shape, but as a natural enemy" (*Summa Theologica*, q. 78, art. 4). There must be some synthetic activity of the animal beyond even that of the common sense to account for the animal's behavior. Yet the medievals could not go so far as to attribute intellect to animals. They solved the puzzle by postulating an *estimative power*, which apprehended nonsensible properties of things. To explain similar unthinking behavior patterns in man, Aquinas postulates the same power, but calls it instead the *cogitative power*. This was also called *particular reason*, "for it compares individual intentions [objects of mind], just as the intellectual reason compares universal intentions." Gardeil says of this *ratio particularis* that, "in general, its function consists in being a sort of mediating faculty between sense on the one hand, which grasps the material singular, and intellect on the other hand, which is the faculty of the abstracted essence. Thus, it serves to prepare the immediate phantasms for the consideration of the intellect."[2] This *vis aestimativa* is grouped by Aquinas with common sense, imagination, fantasy, and memory as an internal sense.

The feeling soul plays a role in Hegel's theory of mind similar to that played by the estimative power in Aquinas's theory. The feeling soul is a nonintellectual, immediate synthesis of the sensory material. Unlike Aquinas, Hegel takes imagination and memory to be powers of the intellect and treats them in the Psychology. Yet, although he deals with these powers or activities of the mind explicitly as operations of the intellect, it is clear that Hegel uses the capacities of the feeling soul to account for some things we might normally attribute to imagination or memory. In Feeling, Hegel considers those powers of the soul which, to use Aquinas's phrase, are "a preamble to the intellect."

Hegel's concept of feeling is one of the earliest modern attempts we can find to work out a theory of our preconscious mental activity. But there is a constant danger in reading Hegel's texts and thinking about his examples, for there is no purely preconscious human behavior that has not been transformed by our consciousness and our thought. Hegel devotes much attention to pathological and abnormal phenomena in the Anthropology, where feeling is discussed. This is certainly not because feeling is itself something pathological or abnormal, but because it is in such cases that the otherwise buried preconscious activities produce a noticeable ef-

2. H. P. Gardeil, *Introduction to the Philosophy of St. Thomas Aquinas*, vol. 3: *Psychology*, pp. 75–76.

fect. Inferring the existence and nature of unconscious psychological activities from the data of pathology is today a standard practice.
But when we read his discussion of a pathological phenomenon
with which he wants to illustrate some aspect of feeling and in turn
to explain the phenomenon with that concept, we must be careful
not to think that the person involved is operating solely at the level
of feeling. Perhaps there are some morons who, Hegel would say,
have not progressed beyond the animal stage of feeling, but normally humans are well beyond that stage, and the phenomena
peculiar to feeling make their appearance only in abnormal circumstances—in cases where, due to a breakdown in these lower, preconscious functions of mind, the higher, truer being of the spiritual
is not achieved. It is sometimes hard to know which aspects of the
case belong to feeling.

> For observation the concrete nature of spirit carries with it the peculiar
> difficulty that the particular stages and determinations of the develop-
> ment of its concept do not remain behind as particular existences over
> against its deeper forms. . . . The determinations and stages of spirit,
> in contrast, remain essentially as only moments, states, or determina-
> tions at the higher stages of development. It thereby happens that the
> higher shows itself empirically present in a lower, more abstract deter-
> mination. (§380, my tr.)

> Although it [the feeling soul] is therefore entirely formal, it is of
> particular interest insofar as it has being *as form,* and so appears as a
> *state* (§380) into which the development of the soul may relapse after
> having advanced to the determination of consciousness and under-
> standing. (§404)

Feeling and the Self

The notion of the self enters Hegel's discussions of feeling in two
different ways. First, he claims that the notion of a self is intimately
bound up with the notion of the feeling soul: "Sensation involves
sensitivity, and there is reason for maintaining therefore, that while
sensation puts more emphasis upon the passive aspect of feeling,

upon *finding,* i.e., upon the immediacy of feeling's determinate-ness, feeling refers more to the self-hood involved here" (§402).

That the concept of the self is emphasized in feeling as opposed to sensation is quite clear, given my interpretation of feeling. Sensations considered as such exhibit no organization; organization first appears in feeling. But until some at least rudimentary organization appears among the sensations, there is no sense in talking of a self. Sensations, furthermore, do not simply fall into organized patterns; they have to be organized into them. Spirit, in this case as soul, is the organizer.

Feeling is therefore the other side, the active side, of sensation and is as much animal as human, for the animal soul must also bring the sensations into a unitary self to be said to have sensation at all. Nonetheless, there are considerable differences between the nature of the connectedness an animal can give its sensations and that given by humans to their sensations, both because humans can do more than feel and because, due to their higher capacities that need to be embodied in feeling, they have feelings of which animals are not capable. Feeling is the preconscious organization of sensation, a "blind but indispensible function of the soul," which is the presupposition, but not the actuality, of having a concept of the subjective and the objective, and a presupposition of having the concept of self.

In the later stages of the dialectic in the Phenomenology and Intuition there are categorial requirements on the way sensation is organized, but this is not the case here. There are, however, some pragmatic requirements on the organization—namely, that it by and large suffice to enable the animal to manuever successfully in its environment. But this does not require the animal to organize its sensations through *concepts.* Only certain success-promoting *patterns* of response to the environment are called for. In feeling, the soul does not construct a spatio temporally extended, law-governed, physical world of experience over against itself on the basis of the material provided by sensation—such a construction would involve making use of those categories, universal rules of construction, which characterize the higher stages of consciousness and intuition.

Although we can, from the third-person perspective, already

start applying the notion of a self to the feeling soul, without the feeling soul's having any such concept itself, Hegel does attribute a minimal, nonobjective awareness of self to the feeling soul, which he calls self-feeling [*Selbstgefühl*]:[3]

> As individuality, the feeling totality is essentially an internal division of itself and an awakening to the *Urtheil* [the judgment, the basic division] within itself in accordance with which it has particular feelings and as a subject stands in relation to these its determinations. The subject as such posits these within itself as its feelings. It is sunken into the particularity of these sensations, and at the same time it unites with itself therein as a subjective unity through the ideality of the particular. In this way it is self-feeling—and it is at the same time only in the particular feeling. (§407, my tr.)

Self-feeling is a problematic concept, for how can a being have a concept of self without having the concept of the non-self, and in particular the concept of an external world, which we know the feeling soul does not have? But this question itself is misleading in that it presupposes that in self-feeling we are concerned with a *concept* of self. Such, I want to argue, is not the case.

The only contrast available to the feeling soul on the basis of which it could have something that deserves to be called a feeling of self is that between its own contents and itself, the possessor of those contents. The feeling soul cannot assign some contents to itself and some to something else, for that would be equivalent to positing an external world, so self-feeling is not a matter of classifying feelings into two different kinds, feelings of self and feelings of not-self. But the contrast between itself and its contents is not a contrast that exhibits itself in the sensations or feelings themselves. Since all feelings are its own, in every feeling the soul is feeling itself, is self-feeling.

The soul is not a totally passive receptor, however; as we have seen, its own state is a significant factor in its sensibility, and quite naturally the forms of organization present in the feeling soul are significant determinants of the higher-level organization of its sen-

---

3. Petry translates this, incorrectly I think, as "self-awareness." The connotations of this translation are too cognitive, for in self-feeling we are certainly not aware of a self as a self.

sible states. Self-feeling is present in every feeling, because the organization of the whole, already present in the feeling soul, is a determinant of each feeling: "We have before us here feeling subjectivity; it realizes itself, is active, emerges from simple unity as liveliness. This activity belongs to the determination of liveliness; it awakens the opposition in itself, but it sublates and preserves it thereby, giving itself self-feeling, giving itself determinate being" (*PSS*, vol. 2, p. 325; my tr.).[4] The soul feels itself in every feeling insofar as the content of the particular feeling, determined as it is in part by the total organization in which it participates, implies that total organization, the self.

Hegel applies the notion of self-feeling to the explanation of mental illness. Mental illness, he says, is the pathological dominance of this lower level of spirit. Hegel's reasoning is something like this. The sane subject is the one who has a solid understanding of its world and its place in it; it lives in a well-ordered world. Any subject has certainly progressed far enough that it possesses the categorial structure necessary to having a concept of self, but in derangement it puts its self-feeling in its place. This means that, rather than constructing an objective world in accordance with the categories of the understanding, it takes the immediate unity found in its feelings to be objective itself, removing its thinking from the constraints of the objective world.

> As healthy and self-possessed the subject has the present consciousness of the ordered totality of its individual world and it subsumes into that system each particular content of sensation, representation, desire, inclination that occurs and it classifies them in the proper place.

> Caught in a particular determinateness, however, it does not assign such a content the proper place and rank that belongs to it in the individual world system that is a subject. In this way the subject finds itself in contradiction to the totality systematized in its consciousness and to the particular determinateness that neither flows with nor is classified or ranked within that totality—derangement. (§408, my tr.)

4. This passage is given in Petry's text as a *Zusatz* to §407, but it is not one of the *Zusätze* supplied in the original posthumous edition by Boumann. No other edition of the *Encyclopedia* gives a *Zusatz* for §407. This passage comes from Griesheim's notes. Parallel passages in other manuscripts authenticate it. See Petry's apparatus, *PSS*, vol. 2, p. 325.

Yet, if derangement were a matter of inconsistency in one's beliefs, there would seem to be no difference between error and insanity:

> I can, of course, be mistaken about myself as well as about the external world. People of no understanding have empty, subjective representations, unfulfillable wishes that they nonetheless hope to realize in the future. They restrict themselves to totally singular goals and interests, hold fast to one-sided principles, come into conflict with actuality. But neither this narrowmindedness nor this error are yet deranged as long as the benighted still know that their subjective representation does not yet exist objectively. Error and folly become derangement only when someone takes his merely subjective representation to be objectively present and holds to it in the face of the objective reality that contradicts it. (§408, *Zusatz*, my tr.)

There is no clear line between stubborn error and derangement, and we cannot, in the very nature of things, confront anyone with the independent, objective truth. Self-feeling has the upper hand when it is untempered by the complex principles of the understanding and tries to maintain its simple organization in the face of a world incoherent with it. "Consequently, when someone speaks in a deranged manner, one should always begin by reminding him of his overall situation, his concrete actuality. If, when he is brought to consider and to be aware of this objective context, he still fails to relinquish his false presentation, there can be no doubt that he is in a state of derangement" (§408, *Zusatz*).

THE SOUL'S RELATION TO REALITY

The most puzzling aspect of the soul as Hegel describes it in the Anthropology is its ontological status and its relation to the rest of reality. Early in the Anthropology, "soul" is treated almost like a mass term—soul does not come in packaged units but is the "ideality" of nature in general. In the progress of the Anthropology the soul is supposed to crystallize, as it were, into separate individualities. Yet even in the relatively late stages of feeling and habit this individualization is not absolute; the boundaries between otherwise distinct persons can still be violated, for example, by two different persons sharing the same sensation. "The soul is truly immaterial, even in its concreteness, and proof that it is capable of this *substantial identity* with another is to be found in the somnambulent [hypnotized] individual's sensing within itself the tastes and smells present within the individual to whom it is thus related. . . . In this substantial identity, consciousness has only one subjectivity" (§406). Similarly, Hegel talks of the feeling soul having an immediate access to the whole world, so that one can have direct feelings (one is tempted to say "intuitions," but not as Hegel uses that term) of spatially distant objects and events without, apparently, any objective, causal chain mediating between the event and the feeling: "With regard, firstly, to what is spatially distant from us, insofar as we are conscious and awake, we can only know something of it on condition that we sublate the distance in a *mediate* manner. The *envisioning* soul is not bound by this condition however. Space is of *external nature*, not of the *soul*, and in that it is apprehended by the soul this externality ceases to be spatial, for it is no longer external either to itself or us once the ideality of the soul has transformed it" (§406, *Zusatz*).

Hegel wants a peculiar double status for the soul. He wants it to be individuated by persons and their bodies for some purposes, so that, for example, it makes sense to speak of states of the soul (sensations, feelings, etc.) as having an owner, being *someone's* states. For other purposes, for example, explaining the phenomena of national character or clairvoyance and hypnotism, he wants soul to be something shareable across persons, the "ideality" of a much larger piece of the world than just a single body.[5]

Hegel cannot have it both ways. When he treats the soul as a supraindividual reality, he seems to have to treat its states, in

5. Hegel not only deals with derangement in his discussion of feeling but also discusses hypnosis, clairvoyance, and other psychic phenomena. At the turn of the nineteenth century, before the rise of modern psychology, before modern biology, a theory with no room for such phenomena was in trouble. "Confirmation of the factual aspect could appear to be the primary need. For those from whom it might be required it would be superfluous however, since they simplify their consideration of the matter by dismissing accounts of it as delusion and imposture, infinitely numerous though they are, and accredited by the education, character, etc. of the witnesses. They are so set in their apriori understanding, that it is not only immune to all evidence, but they have even denied what they have seen with their own eyes. . . . Comprehension of it is impossible insofar as one presupposes personalities independent of one another and of the content as an objective world, and assumes spatial and material extrinsicality to be generally absolute" (§406).

particular sensations and feelings, as quite independent entities in their own right; the boundaries of the soul are wide because souls are simply conglomerations of sensations. Thus two people can share the same sensation; sensations are Humean, the soul is a bundle of such states, and, since the grouping principle is not spatial, the same sensation can be in two different bundles. But a bundle theory of the soul comports ill with the alleged singularity and unity of the soul and clearly violates the progression of the Anthropology from soul as a general existent standing over against nature as a whole to something singularized in individual souls and individual sensations.

Hegel tries to combine the generality and the individuality of the soul by describing it as a monad, an individual that nonetheless contains a complete world. Leibnizian monads are active and generate the whole world in representation from within themselves. Similarly, the soul is (though admittedly only potentially) the locus of the whole world, a "featureless mine" out of which the entire world can be generated or brought to light.

> The filling of the soul has yet another aspect however, for apart from this material [sensation], as an actual individuality we are also *implicitly a world* of concrete content with an infinite periphery, and have within us a numberless multitude of relations and connections, which even if it does not enter into our sensation and presentation is always within us, and still belongs to the concrete content of the human soul regardless of the extent to which these relations are able to change constantly even without our knowing of it. On account of its infinite wealth of content, the human soul may be said to be the soul of a world, the *individually* determined *world-soul*. Since the human soul is a *singularity*, determined in all its aspects and therefore *limited*, it also relates itself to a universe determined in accordance with its *individual* standpoint. That by which the soul is confronted is by no means a being external to it, for the totality of relationships within which the individual human soul finds itself is rather the actual life and subjectivity of this universe. (§402, *Zusatz*)

In another place Hegel says, "The *concrete* being of an individual involves the entirety of its basic interests, of the essential and particular empirical relationships in which he stands to other people and the world at large" (§406).

This comparison of the soul to a monad limps badly, for a monad is a complete world in representation only. But the notion of representation does not have clear application in the realm of soul, for the soul is supposed to be pre-representational. The fact that Hegel attributes content to feelings inevitably forces us toward interpreting them as representational states. Yet the categorial (and syntactic) structures necessary for being truly representational are lacking. There is a weaker sense of representation according to which anything registering a feature of the world in some law-governed fashion can be said to represent that feature—this is the sense in which sensations represent the properties of physical objects. But feelings are supposed to be more complex than sensations, without achieving the status of representations in the full sense.

What Hegel could be getting at is puzzling, but the interpretation I have been developing casts some interesting light. Hegel seems to be denying that the state of one's body is the sole important factor in determining the state of the soul. We earlier described sensations as being, in the first place, the being-for-mind of states of the sensory organs. But here, in feeling, where such states begin to acquire a meaning in virtue of their participation in an organized system, we find that the scope of the factors relevant to that organization goes far beyond the immediate state of the sensory organs. The soul, as a totality, includes as part of its "filling" everything relevant to it.

One way to uncover what Hegel might be driving at here is to return to our suggestion that the spiritual supervenes upon the material. The point has been made several times by those investigating the supervenience relation that mental facts, if supervenient upon the physical, must supervene upon very large sets of physical facts; not even an exhaustive set of physical facts about one person's body would suffice to determine that person's mental states.[6] Hegel may be making a similar point here. What he calls the

6. See Burge, "Individualism and the Mental"; idem., "Other Bodies"; Garfield, "Propositional Attitudes and the Ontology of the Mental." But notice that the arguments given in this literature all explicitly concern intentional, representational mental states. It remains an open question whether the individuation of sensations or feelings is individualistic.

concrete being of a soul involves virtually the entire world and in such a way that it need not enter into sensation or representation. The soul is to be thought of as the ideality of this broad-ranging "world" of facts, and I think we can take this to mean that the soul supervenes upon this whole "world." In the interpretation of someone's feelings, which involves the specification of their role in the unconscious organizational pattern of the soul, it is this world that forms the appropriate background for the interpretation. In hypnosis and clairvoyance, sensations and feelings occur which Hegel believes can only be appropriately interpreted as being the immediate appearance to the mind of some event or object to which there can be no normal, causally mediated perceptual access. Should a woman have a sudden image of her husband dying and experience a feeling of loss, when at that moment her husband is in fact dying in an army hospital on a distant continent, Hegel might be perfectly willing to countenance the possibility of some fairly mundane explanation of the image and feeling—that it was occasioned perhaps by a piece of spoiled mustard taken at dinner. But he would object to an insistence that this must be all there is to the occurrence, for such an insistence humbles the soul to a mere upshot of the corporeal. One's bodily states are causally coherent, but the states of one's soul are not subject to that same requirement, for, as nonspatial and immaterial, they lack the proper ontological presuppositions for causal interaction. The net of events relevant to the interpretation of a spiritual event is wider than the immediate causal substratum.

Another way to put this is that what counts as a coherent explanatory account of our feelings is not logically required to coincide with the causal account of our sensory states. Our feelings are explained by an interpretation against the background of our "concrete being," the entirety of our basic interests and so forth. In our example, we are not logically required to insist that what the woman felt was a bit of spoiled mustard, and to do so is to misunderstand the relative priorities of spirt and matter. In the long run, it may well be more enlightening to regard the occurrence as a case of immediate spiritual contact between loved ones. The spoiled mustard would, as it were, sink to an enabling condition.

Hegel seems to be assuming that we are implicitly representing the entire supervenience base, and this is a mistake. The supervenience base determines the character of our representation, no doubt, but we cannot infer that we are therefore constantly, though only implicitly, representing the entire base in such a way as to be able to call up distant portions of it directly on occasion. Hegel appears to be taking the relation between nature and spirit, which I have classified as a supervenience relation, to be the relation of *expression*. Just as the Leibnizian monad expresses the world from a certain point of view, the Hegelian soul expresses the world from a point of view. My feelings are the expression of my entire concrete actuality, my world. And indeed, the correct description of numerous feelings depends on my broader situation—on, for example, the difference between pride and false pride or anger and righteous indignation. But it seems illegitimate to move from the fact that my mental states, at whatever level of description, have a broad supervenience base that extends far beyond my own body to the idea that spatial determinations have no true reality for souls or persons, that souls are expressions of the whole world from a point of view. "Expression" itself also has a weak and a strong sense. In the weak sense, expression is just reliable indication; in the strong sense it involves full representation. Feelings can express the world at most in the weak sense—yet Hegel decries their unreliability. A written text constitutes an expressive being, and what it expresses—its meaning—supervenes on the physical text. But it does not (apart from questionable cases of self-reference) express the written text it supervenes on. The expression and supervenience relations rarely, if ever, coincide.

As complex as the metaphysical issues are in Hegel's account of hypnosis, clairvoyance, and the feeling soul, the epistemological issues are treated straightforwardly. Knowledge strictu sensu involves rule-governed construction of the fact or object known within the mind. But so-called immediate knowledge can access its internal world without recourse to the stepwise construction of consciousness. The soul can be the "soul of a world" without external limit because the constraints of space and time, which are exact, determinate, and give the rule to the understanding, are not operative here. This immediate access to the whole of the world is unreliable and not objective, and it is cognitive at all only when the content dredged up is subjected to categorial construction to some minimal degree. "Visionary knowledge," as Hegel sometimes calls

it, is really a misnomer—it would be better described as a "visionary cognitive state" because it is not knowledge at all.

THE LIBERATION OF THE SOUL

The material and the spiritual are not divorced from one another—although they are certainly not strictly identical, they are
unified. But the merely formal organization of spiritual material
which constitutes the form of feeling must express itself in the
body, for otherwise the bodily states of the individual would diverge increasingly from the self-determination of spirit. If spirit is
not divorced from body, it must gain control of the body, make the
body its means of expression. This organization of the body, if it is
to embody the spiritual unity of the determinations of the soul,
must be an organization of the body over and above that merely
organic organization already present. This form of organization is
habit. Notice that habit is purely formal; virtually any content can be
embodied in habit. "The form of habit, like any other, is certainly
open to complete contingency of content. . . . At the same time
however, habit is what is most essential to the existence of all
spirituality within the individual subject. It enables the subject to be
a concrete immediacy, an ideality of soul, so that the religious or
moral etc. content belongs to him as this self, this soul, and is in him
neither merely implicitly as an endowment, nor as a transient sensation or presentation, nor as an abstract inwardness cut off from
action and actuality, but as a part of his being" (§410).
    Hegel says several times that grasping the determination of habit
is very difficult, and he seems to have considered the emphasis he
places on habit and the role he gives it to be a fairly novel and
important contribution to our knowledge of the mental. We can
question the novelty of such an emphasis in the light of the importance of custom in Hume and his followers, but not its importance.
The essential determination of habit, Hegel says, is that it is our
liberation from sensation and feeling. It is this we must now seek to
understand.
    The life of feeling and sensation is that of a soul totally sunken in
its sensations and feelings—it has no "distance" from them, but it is
overwhelmed by them and indeed is at best a merely formal point of

unity within them. When the soul acquires habits, however, sensation and feeling lose their commanding grip on the soul; they no longer dominate it. "It is *free* of these determinations insofar as it is neither interested in nor occupied with them" (§410). This aspect of habit is called inurement when considered as a theoretical attitude; in its subjective practical aspect it is indifference to satisfaction, and as objectively practical the soul is liberated from the particularities of its existence by acquiring skill. "In habit the soul makes an abstract universal being of itself and reduces what is particular in feelings and consciousness to a mere determination of its being" (§410).

Up to this stage the soul has been a self only formally, which means not in complete actuality. At its simplest level, soul is a panoply of singular determinations; these are then connected with one another and even come to wear their connectedness on their sleeves, although only abstractly, in self-feeling. But when in habit the soul makes itself an abstract universal, it must free itself from the immersion into its particular feelings and sensations which characterizes even the level of self-feeling. It does so in taking the patterns of unification in feeling and making them *natural*, immediacies presupposed by and within which spirit realizes itself. Habit makes the feeling organization of the determinations of soul into a second nature. Thus this whole level of organization is now related to the further progress of spirit as sensation and feeling are to organic being. In habit the particular sensation or feeling is unimportant, as the particular pieces of matter are unimportant to the body. And the soul, in having habits, relates itself not to a singular determination of itself but to a universal and persistent determination of itself. Since the ego is the universal itself (according to Hegel), it relates itself to itself more adequately in habit.[7] "Nevertheless, the universal to which the soul relates itself in habit differs from the self-determining concrete universal present in pure thinking, in that it is only the abstract universality brought forth through reflection from the repetition of numerous singularities" (§410, *Zusatz*).

Because in habit its immediate determinatenesses are reduced to unimportance, the soul, as their abstract universality, is now left

7. Hegel's conception of the ego or self is discussed more thoroughly in Chapter 6.

free of them. By no longer being exhausted in its particular states, by acquiring interesting higher-order and longer-term properties, the soul gains independence, a character of its own, an identity. Thus through habit soul also gains dominance over its corporeality and comes to control its body, which is now "something unresistingly pervaded by the soul, something subjected to the liberating power of the soul's ideality. It is therefore through this separation of the soul from its corporeity and the sublation of this separation, that this *inwardness* of soul and *externality* of corporeity emerge as a mediated unity" (§411, *Zusatz*). In this, the soul as actual, the body is the sign and the expression of the soul. In acquiring habits the soul has learned to withstand certain pains, to forgo or ignore certain pleasures, to go beyond the immediate material of sensation. By acquiring set patterns of simple behaviors, it is ready to make the leap into larger and larger compounded patterns that mark a significant increase in complexity and sophistication. The patterns of habitual action form the presupposition for the rule-governed forms of behavior of later stages. The behaviorists were not totally off the mark; they just mistook one of the lowest levels of mental organization for the totality of mind.

Actual soul is both the conclusion of the Anthropology and the germ of the Phenomenology, for the self now sets itself as an abstract universality over against its particular determinations, and "soul which posits its being over against itself, having sublated and determined it as its own, has lost the significance of being soul" (§412). This abstract universality is the I, the ego.

6

Phenomenology:
The I Emerges

The Phenomenology of Spirit poses a major problem for Hegel scholarship. Hegel composed a book entitled the *Phenomenology of Spirit* in 1806 while at Jena.[1] This volume was to provide an introduction to Hegel's system, showing the reader how natural consciousness (and therefore the reader's own as well) achieves the standpoint of absolute knowledge, the standpoint of the system.

Ten years later the Phenomenology of Spirit appears embedded within the *Encyclopedia* system, surrounded by the Anthropology and the Psychology. Indeed, it is clear that very soon after the earlier book had been published Hegel began treating the Phenomenology as preliminary to the Psychology, rather than prefatory to the Logic. By 1812 the Anthropology had made its appearance as the predecessor to the Phenomenology.[2]

The two Phenomenologies do not correspond exactly in content either. In the early Phenomenology the major divisions include Consciousness, Self-consciousness, Reason, and Spirit. The version

---

1. This volume's original title, changed in proof, was *Science of the Experience of Consciousness.*

2. There is an extensive debate over the relation of the Phenomenology to the Logic and the rest of the system; see Hans Friedrich Fulda, *Das Problem einer Einleitung in Hegels Wissenschaft der Logik;* and Otto Pöggeler, *Hegels Idee einer Phänomenologie des Geistes,* for some of the principal contributions to that debate. Unfortunately, much of this debate has taken little account of the evolution in Hegel's thought during his Nürnberg period. At present, however, there is simply no reliable edition of the Nürnberg materials. Until a reliable edition appears, Hegel scholarship must acknowledge a serious handicap.

we find in the *Encyclopedia* is much briefer. Spirit is no longer included (many of the topics discussed there show up in the philosophies of objective and absolute spirit), and Reason is highly truncated as well, shrinking to a mere transition paragraph to the Psychology.

The early Phenomenology seems to start where the later, *Encyclopedia* version does, but it continues on, including most of the themes and topics of the rest of the system.[3] Yet we cannot say that in writing the early Phenomenology Hegel simply forgot to stop and added on the rest of the system, for there is good evidence that he did not see the book that way. Furthermore, inspection of Hegel's collateral work in 1805–6 indicates that what is presented in the early Phenomenology does not coincide with his explicit attempts at the time to elaborate his system.

It seems reasonable to suppose that Hegel did indeed continue beyond what started as the "Science of the Experience of Consciousness" to write something larger and slightly different, but not that he simply annexed a chunk of his system to his original manuscript; the Phenomenology is far too organically unified to be such an amalgam. I believe, rather, although I lack the space to argue it here, that the core of the Phenomenology in both versions is the analysis of the concept of an independent object of experience. The Phenomenology is about the subject-object relation; it is an analysis of what must be the case if that relation is to be *truthful*.

Hegel's analysis is essentially complete by the end of the sections on Self-consciousness. The early Phenomenology then goes on to interpret an astonishingly wide range of phenomena in terms of the basic structures identified in the early chapters. In the *Encyclopedia* the conceptual structures outlined in the Phenomenology are not abandoned, but neither are they the explicit model for the interpretation of all higher phenomena. The early Phenomenology is intended to show that the structures constitutive of consciousness (the subject-object relation) are revealingly applicable to all forms of human life—that a form of life (or social institution, etc.)

---

3. Even their beginnings are not perfectly congruent, for Hegel admits in the *Encyclopedia* version that it was a mistake to include specifically spatiotemporal concepts like "here" and "now" in the argumentation of the chapter on sense certainty (see §418).

is also a form of consciousness and vice versa. It is to demonstrate that neither abstract discussions of the foundations of our knowledge, such as Descartes's, nor psychological explanations, such as Hume's, adequately portray the concrete, social reality of the subject-object relation. Thus scientific observation, morality, and religion are all treated as manifestations of knowledge, as forms of consciousness, which means interpreting them in terms of the subject-object structure. In the *Encyclopedia,* on the other hand, each phenomenon is examined on its own terms, not primarily as a form of consciousness. There is no commitment to putting the subject-object relation at the center of every case. In the *Encyclopedia,* therefore, the Phenomenology is confined to the examination of the forms of consciousness as such.

According to Hegel, Kant's philosophy is nothing more than a phenomenology, since it is concerned with the analysis of the subject-object relation (§415). Kant gives us a theory of consciousness, according to Hegel, a theory of how an object can appear to a subject—but Kant does not successfully push through to understanding the basis of the whole subject-object relation, to showing us the truth of that relation, for he never goes beyond the appearance relation.

Because Hegel's phenomenology (primarily in the version of 1807) has already attracted so much commentary and critical attention, I do not rehearse its dialectic in this chapter. Because our topic is the philosophy of mind per se, I focus instead on Hegel's conception of the subject of consciousness, the I, or, as he sometimes calls it, the abstract ego.[4]

CONSCIOUSNESS AND THE I

There is considerable transcendental confusion surrounding Hegel's concept of the I. To minimize the dangers, I treat this topic, like the topics of my opening chapters, in a linguistic mode. All the

4. As Petry remarks in the introduction to his edition of the *Encyclopedia Phenomenology,* there has never been a systematic comparison of the two Phenomenologies. (Actually, there may be more Phenomenologies, since the *Encyclopedia* went through three editions, and there are versions left from the Nürnberg period.) This is a study begging to be written.

essential points can be made for my purpose without treading heavily on swampy, transcendental ground. Accordingly, I try to answer two questions in this chapter:[5] (a) What does the word "I" mean, according to Hegel; in Fregean terms, what are its sense and its reference? (b) What kind of creature can use the word "I"; that is, what is presupposed about the utterer in any significant use of the word?

Does "I" Refer?

Because sense supposedly determines reference, it might seem best to start by asking what the sense of "I" is for Hegel.[6] But there is a prior issue: a common interpretation of Hegel claims that "I" does not refer at all, that reference to individuals, or at least singular demonstrative reference, is impossible.[7] This claim is based on passages like the following:

> [When I say "I"] I do indeed *mean* a single 'I', but I can no more say what I *mean* in the case of 'I' than I can in the case of 'Now' and 'Here'. When I say 'this Here', 'this Now', or a 'single item', I am saying all Thises, Heres, Nows, all single items. Similarly, when I say 'I', this singular 'I', I say in general all 'I's'; everyone is what I say, everyone is 'I', this singular 'I'. (*PhG*, p. 83; *PhS*, p. 62. Quotation marks added by Miller)

A parallel passage from the much later Berlin *Encyclopedia* shows that Hegel retained this view throughout his career.

> Since language is the product of thought, nothing can be said in it which is not universal. What I only *mean* [*meine*] is *mine* [*mein*], belongs

---

5. Although Hegel does treat the word "I," his principal interest is in the concept expressed by the word and what it stands for. His discussions shift without much warning between the explicitly metalinguistic and the straightforwardly metaphysical. I follow suit and shift rather casually between the formal and the material modes.

6. I employ the Fregean terminology of sense and reference in this work without worrying about faithfulness to Frege's own use and without attributing any such distinctions to Hegel. This terminology allows us to raise some important questions about Hegel's understanding of the I.

7. Hamlyn, *Sensation and Perception*, pp. 140–46; Ivan Soll, *An Introduction to Hegel's Metaphysics*, pp. 91–110; Gilbert Plumer, "Hegel on Singular Demonstrative Reference," *Southwestern Journal of Philosophy* (1980); M. J. Inwood, *Hegel*, pp. 311–17.

only to me as this particular individual; but if language expresses only what is universal, I cannot say what I only *mean*. And what is *unsayable,* feeling, sensation, is not the most excellent, the most true, but rather the least significant, the least true. If I say: "the *individual,*" "*this* individual," "here," "now," then these are all universalities; *anything* and *everything* is an individual, a this, and, if it is sensuous, it is here and now. Similarly when I say "I," I *mean* myself *as this* self which excludes all others; but what I say, "I," is just everyone; I, which excludes all others from itself. (§20, my tr.)

From our supposed inability to refer to individual objects it is thought that Hegel infers their metaphysical unreality as well as the impossibility of any knowledge of them.[8] But in these passages Hegel does not deny that we can refer to individual objects. His argument is directed against a different doctrine: the belief that indexical reference affords us a direct, preconceptual access to individuals.[9] He attacks the position that "our approach to the object must also be *immediate* or *receptive;* we must alter nothing in the object as it presents itself. In *app*rehending it, we must refrain from trying to *comp*rehend it" (*PhG*, p. 79; *PhS*, p. 58).

Besides direct referential access, the empiricist Hegel is attacking also attributes to indexicals an epistemological role—that of providing direct, preconceptual epistemological access to objects. Hegel attacks this position by arguing that even indexical reference is conceptually mediated and therefore cannot afford us preconceptual epistemological access.[10]

8. G. E. M. Anscombe has lately defended the position that "I" is not a referring expression. Hegel's supposed rejection of indexical reference cannot be assimilated to Anscombe's position, however. Anscombe wants to treat "I" as similar in use to the "it" in "It's raining," claiming that "I" has only a *use,* and neither a Fregean sense nor a reference. Hegel, in contrast, seems to say that "I" is a universal, implying that it is a general term applying to all conscious beings—really a predicate in its depth grammar, not a singular referring expression at all. Again, Anscombe thinks that "I" is quite peculiar, different from other indexicals, whereas Hegel lumps them all together. See G. E. M. Anscombe, "The First Person," in *Mind and Language,* ed. S. Guttenplan, pp. 45–66.

9. The position Hegel is attacking seems to have been most closely approximated by Bertrand Russell. I have discussed Hegel's position on indexical reference, names, and knowledge in more detail in "Hegel on Reference and Knowledge," *Journal of the History of Philosophy* 26 (1988): 297–307.

10. Plumer misinterprets Hegel's position here because he thinks that sense certainty's "basic aspiration is the relation of [singular demonstrative] reference"; "Singular Demonstrative Reference," p. 73. But this is not right. Sense certainty's basic aspiration is immediate, direct knowledge.

Denying our ability to refer to individuals is unnecessary to Hegel's goals; the arguments he presents actually assume that we can successfully refer to individuals. He returns again and again to the point that utterances containing "now" change truth-value over time, that utterances containing "here" change truth-value depending on the place of utterance, and that utterances containing "I" change truth-value depending on the utterer. These changes in truth-value depend on the reference of the indexicals. " 'Here' is, e.g., the tree. If I turn round, this truth has vanished and is converted into its opposite: 'No tree is here, but a house instead' " (*PhG*, p. 82; *PhS*, p. 60).

Hegel's position on indexical reference is an attempt to assimilate indexical reference to descriptive reference. Reference via a description is clearly mediated by the concepts (the universals) involved in the description. Contrasting to descriptive reference is reference via a proper name, which Hegel admits is immediate, for proper names have no meaning:

> Even the expression *this* contains no distinction; each and every something is exactly as much a *this* as it is an other. One *means* to express something completely determinate by "this"; but it is overlooked that language, as the work of the understanding, says only what is universal, except for the *name* of an individual object; the individual name, however, is something meaningless [*Sinnloses*] in the sense that it does not express a universal and appears as something simply posited, arbitrary, for the same reason that proper names [*Einzelnamen*] can be arbitrarily assumed, given, or even changed. (*WdL*, vol. 1, pp. 104–5, my tr.; *SL*, p. 117)

But if indexicals and descriptions both refer in a conceptually mediated manner, they nevertheless refer. Furthermore, indexicals, unlike names, have a meaning. This returns us to our original question, What does the word "I" mean?

The Sense of "I"

Hegel himself never precisely explains the meaning of "I." What, then, should we be looking for? The previous discussion of Hegel's treatment of indexical reference gives us a hint. Hegel classes "I" together with "here," "now," and "this." It has not been uncommon to take the word "this" as the basic indexical word, treating the others as somehow derivative. And several things Hegel says indicate that he also thinks of indexicals in this way: "if we take the 'This' in the twofold shape of its being, as 'Now' and 'Here' . . . " (*PhS*, p. 60; see also the passages from *PhS*, p. 62, and *WdL*, vol. 1, pp. 104–5, quoted above).[11]

Hegel seems aware that "this," unlike the other indexicals, admits of completion by sortal predicates: "this man," "this ball," "this color." Indeed, given that indexical reference is always conceptually mediated, there *must* be some sortal completion at least implicit in any use of "this." The obvious derivations of "now" and "here" from "this" seem, then, to treat them as already having a sortal built in—"this time" and "this place." Such an approach seems consistent with what Hegel says about "here" and "now" and suggests what we need to look for in the case of "I": some appropriate completion or specification of "this _____ ."

But what counts as an appropriate specification? Even if we could assume that persons are the appropriate referents of "I," we still could not infer that "person" is the correct completion for "this _____ ," because coextensionality does not guarantee sameness of sense. Furthermore, many of the things Hegel says about "I" seem to preclude its having the sense of "this person." We must therefore look more closely at what he actually says about the I.

The passage quoted earlier from *Encyclopedia* §20 is a useful starting point; in its continuation Hegel sounds most of the themes that dominate his discussions of the I:

> Kant made use of the awkward expression that I *accompany* all my representations, also sensations, desires, actions, etc. The I is the universal in and for itself, and commonality is also a form of universality, though an external one. All other men [*Menschen*] have it in common with me to be an I, just as it is common to all *my* sensations,

11. In the *Phenomenology* of 1807, Hegel's treatment of "I" and "this" sometimes seems to imply that they are coordinate—neither subordinated to the other, both arising, as it were, together. There is much to be said for this interpretation, and I cannot rule it out, but the preponderance of the passages seems to treat "this" as prior. I doubt that Hegel had a clearly thought out position on whether "I" and "this" were coordinated or subordinated.

representations, etc., to be *mine.* The *I,* however, abstractly as such, is
pure relation to itself, in which all representation [*Vorstellen*], sensation, every state and every particularity of nature, talent, experience,
etc., is abstracted from. The I is insofar the existence of wholly *abstract*
universality, the abstractly free. That is why the I is *thinking* as a
subject, and in that I am simultaneously in all my sensations, representations, states, etc., thought is everywhere present and runs through
all these determinations as a category. (§20, my tr.)

The I is thus claimed to be (a) a wholly abstract universality, (b) pure
relation to itself, (c) abstracted from all its particular states, and (d)
thinking as a subject. And we are also given at least a partial
specification of the things to which "I" can be correctly applied—to
all humans. This passage, when correctly interpreted, is a key to
Hegel's concept of the word "I." The important clue is what Hegel
says about the I as such, for the "as such" locution is essentially an
operator restricting what can be correctly said about its argument to
things that are specially connected to the sense of the argument
expression. During the time Winston Churchill was the prime minister of England, it was true that the prime minister of England was
a leisure-time bricklayer; but it is certainly false that the prime
minister of England, as such, was a leisure-time bricklayer. The
prime minister, as such, is a member of the cabinet, advisor to the
throne, and resident of No. 10 Downing Street; but the prime
minister, as such, is neither male nor female, short nor tall, Labour
nor Conservative. To be more general, not everything true of *A* as
such can be reckoned as *part* of the sense of "*A*"; but everything true
of *A* as such must have some special connection with the sense of
"*A.*" What is true of *A* as such is true of it because it can be correctly
referred to by "*A.*" Of course, we must remember that even if it is
false that *A* as such is *F,* it does not follow that *A* is not *F.* It is false
that the president of the United States, as such, is a former screen
actor, but it is nonetheless true that the president is in fact a former
screen actor.

Hegel asserts that "the I, however, abstractly as such, is pure
relation to itself, in which all representation, sensation, every state
and every particularity of nature, talent, experience, etc., is abstracted from." Let me put aside for the moment the idea that the I
is pure self-relation. The I as such is abstracted from all of its

particular states; that is, there is no particular state that an I, qua I, must have. But this apparently leaves the I totally indeterminate.

Hegel does not, however, think of the I as indeterminate. For one thing, that would not distinguish "I" from "this."[12] It is important that the I is abstracted from a specific group of states, namely, as we see from the list he gives, primarily mental states (in a suitably broad sense). But there is another important fact about the list from which the I as such is abstracted: *thinking* is missing from the list. Few philosophers distinguish mental representation and thought. Yet for Hegel there is a clear difference; representation is a sensuous, imagistic type of mental processing, whereas pure thinking is formal and nonsensuous (i.e., its phenomenology is not constitutive of it). Indeed, it is quite significant that thinking is omitted from the list of things from which the I is abstracted; only a few lines later, thinking is asserted to *be* the I. These considerations give us a preliminary understanding of the sense of "I," namely, "this thinking subject."[13]

This is not an entirely happy choice on Hegel's part, for there are problems with thinking that "I" has as its sense "this thinking subject." First, "this thinking subject" could refer to someone besides the utterer. "This thinking subject" could have the peculiarly first-person sense essential to "I" only if there were some special form of demonstration that necessarily indicates its user. But "this" used with that special form of demonstration would already be equivalent to "I," and the sortal would not be necessary. We would not need to specify what kind of thing—namely, a thinking thing— the "this" picked out. "I" would be as *conceptually* indeterminate as "this."

---

12. I have not tried to specify the sense of "this." A number of things Hegel says about "this" indicate that a "this as such" could only be a bare particular, something picked out as an individual shorn of all its properties. There are no bare particulars, however. See Aquila's interesting discussion in "Predication and Hegel's Metaphysics." If "I" and "this" are coordinate terms, then a "this as such" would be a pure or bare object contrasted with the pure or bare subject of the I.

13. This view obviously ties in with Kant's use of the first-person pronoun to express the transcendental unity of apperception. Hegel's interpretation of "I" is deeply influenced by Kant's reflections in the transcendental deduction (see *WdL*, vol. 2, p. 219ff.; *SL*, p. 583ff.). For an illuminating treatment of the thinking self in Kant, see Patricia Kitcher, "Kant's Real Self," in *Self and Nature in Kant's Philosophy*, ed. Allan Wood, pp. 113–47.

One might try to give the demonstrative a smaller scope and take "I" to have the sense "the subject of this thought," but this has difficulties as well. This move seems to assume some form of inner demonstration, which is just as suspect as a form of demonstration that applies only to oneself. It also presupposes that we can individuate thoughts before individuating their subjects. As a way around this latter problem, we might suggest that there is a special access to my own thoughts, so that I need not individuate them by first individuating myself, but in that case again the simple "this" expressing such access would be sufficient. Adding that a *thought* is the kind of thing demonstrated is otiose.

In general, equating the sense of "I" with some form of the demonstrative use of "this" seems to necessitate postulating some special form of demonstrative contact that guarantees first-personness. This strikes me as implausible and ad hoc. And if I must employ a special access available only to me in thinking of myself, how can others understand my thoughts or assertions about myself? There is no adequate way to capture the essential first-personness of "I" using the essentially third-person resources of "this." Such considerations make it more plausible that "I" and "this" are coordinate, or even that "I" is the primary indexical.[14]

Nonetheless, according to the most natural interpretation of the texts, "I" has a two-part sense for Hegel: first, it designates a thinker, indeed, an individual thinker; second, it is the expression of that thinker's pure self-relation, which itself is partly constitutive of being a thinker. This pure self-relation is poorly expressed by an objective mode indexical like "this." (The nature of the pure self-relation intimated by the use of "I" is explored in the last section of this chapter.)

14. When Hegel calls something a "this," his intent is usually to emphasize the object's individuality. Hegel's concern with the metaphysical questions surrounding the relation between the individual and the universal dominates such discussions. He never explicitly discusses the specifically linguistic nature of the uses of "this" (or "I," for that matter) as a demonstrative or anaphorical term, or the conditions of its successful use. It is thus not surprising that Hegel fails to consider explicitly all the technical difficulties in the use of "this" or "I." Nor is it surprising that the natural proposal for the meaning of "I" stemming from the texts is subject to shortcomings. Hegel is so interested in emphasizing the involvement of universals in indexical reference that he pays only cursory attention to the specific differences between the indexicals and between indexicals and definite descriptions.

The Reference of "I"

Taking "this thinking subject" as our understanding of the sense of "I," we can now ask what the normal reference of a use of "I" is. Traditionally, one of four alternative referents for "I" has been defended: a body, a Cartesian-style soul, a concrete person (an animate organism strictly identical with neither body nor soul), or some different thing such as a transcendental ego.

We can take it for granted that Hegel, a self-styled idealist, would not take one's body to be the normal reference of one's use of "I." In the same vein, however, we might think that a good idealist ought to deny body or matter any essential role in the constitution of the thinking subject to which the "I" refers. This would disqualify the concrete person as the referent of "I," leaving only the substantial Cartesian soul or the abstract transcendental ego as appropriate candidates.

Hegel clearly rejects the whole notion of a Cartesian soul. The "soul" of rational psychology, Hegel complains, is a confused notion—an attempt to think of the human spirit on the model of a natural, material thing. Rational psychology attempts to distinguish the soul from natural things by simply denying certain natural predicates to it. But, Hegel in effect maintains, the predicates that capture the nature of spirit have an entirely different logical grammar and cannot be simply compounded from sense experience. Because the very notion of a Cartesian soul is confused, Cartesian souls can hardly be the referents of "I."[15]

Is the balance of reasons then thrown in favor of the "I" standardly referring to a transcendental ego, some relatively abstract entity, neither body nor soul nor concrete person, which lies behind the phenomena of the self? Kant was reluctant to identify the I that thinks with the empirical self and sometimes even with the noumenal self (*Critique of Pure Reason*, B423a). Given the importance of the Kantian conception of the transcendental ego for post-Kantian German idealism, it would seem plausible that Hegel followed suit and posited some transcendental entity as the referent of "I." But, despite these appearances, Hegel does not take this path. None of the motivations that pushed Kant to distinguish the empirical self

15. Recall the discussion of Hegel's critique of rational psychology in Chapter 1.

and the thinking subject have any significant hold on Hegel. Kant has three different motivations for regarding the I that thinks as nonempirical: his convictions about the nature and possibility of ethics, his belief that thinking things are in principle unknowable, and his belief that phenomenal properties are ultimately unreal.[16] Hegel thoroughly rejects Kant's incompatibilism and the distinction between the moral and phenomenal self; morality must be a this-worldly affair or it is useless, according to Hegel. Because Hegel rejects the phenomenal-noumenal split, he can hardly maintain the irreality of phenomenal properties, or that natural properties are somehow fake (although they are false in the sense that they do not reveal the complete truth of things). Finally, rather than believing that the thinking subject must be unknowable in principle, Hegel believes the opposite. Only insofar as something exhibits the structure of thought is it knowable, and only thought is absolutely knowable.

We are forced, it seems, to reconsider the notion that a concrete person is always the referent of "I." There is, however, an objection to this—the fact that Hegel claims that the I as such is abstract. Because of the abstractness of the I, it seems capable of maintaining its identity across conditions in which the identity of a concrete person would not be maintained. For instance, I can imagine being the Emperor Claudius, and it seems plausible to claim that I might have been Claudius. In one sense it is clear that I, Willem de Vries, a man of the twentieth century, cannot have been Claudius; I have a certain objective reality that cannot be altered so radically without the destruction of the person I am. Nevertheless, we are able to imagine ourselves to be quite different beings from what we objectively are, and Hegel recognizes the importance of this ability to divorce ourselves from our objective reality and to project ourselves into a different, call it subjective, reality.[17] But the abstractness of

16. See Kitcher, "Kant's Real Self," p. 122.

17. Zeno Vendler, in his article "A Note to the Paralogisms," attempts to exploit our ability to abstract ourselves from our objective situation to argue for a distinction between the transcendental I and the concrete person, but his argument assumes that our ability to imagine being something else means that it is really possible to be that thing. Then, assuming the necessity of all identities, it must be the case that either I am not identical to Willem deVries or "I" is not a rigid designator. But both "Willem deVries" and "I" seem to function as rigid designators. "The answer is that

the I does not mean that the concrete person is not the I, any more than the abstractness of "this" means that it cannot pick out a concrete object. Our earlier distinction between names and demonstratives shows that this objection is fallacious, for it assumes that "I" is a name, not a demonstrative.

Kant *ought* to have endorsed the Aristotelian dictum that it is the same thing that thinks that runs,[18] but it is clear that Hegel *does* endorse it. Thinking (at least in its subjective variety) is a human activity. To be sure, it is a very special kind of activity, but no activity can occur without being realized in some particular, natural embodiment. To consider a human an I is to abstract from that particular embodiment of thinking. That the I can be abstracted from its embodiment no more implies their separability than the abstractability of shape from color or equilaterality from equiangularity implies their separability.

THE THINKING SUBJECT

Universality and Self-relation

Let me summarize the position we have reached. Hegel takes the sense of "I" to be (roughly) "this thinking subject." The referent of "I," as we see in more detail below, is an individual human [*Mensch*] in a complex situation. Our apparent ability to wrest the I from its

---

the 'I', the subject of such a transference, has no content and no essence; it is a mere frame in which any picture fits; it is the bare form of consciousness" (Vendler, p. 117). This leaves it difficult to understand just what the transcendental I is, but we can already see that Hegel rejects several of the crucial assumptions in Vendler's Kant-inspired argument. First, Hegel rejects the assumption that the impossible cannot be imagined. The ability to divorce ourselves in imagination from our empirical reality does not show that the self is something different from its empirical reality. Second, Vendler also seems to be arguing that because the sense of "I" is abstract, its referent must be an abstraction, because it designates rigidly. If the "I" designates rigidly, though, it does so via an abstract description, and the designatum need not be abstract. There is nothing here to force Hegel away from "I" referring to a concrete person. See Zeno Vendler, "A Note to the Paralogisms," in *Contemporary Aspects of Philosophy*, ed. G. Ryle, pp. 111–21.

18. It has been argued that there is no good reason for Kant to divorce the empirical self and the thinking self, and that the thinking self must indeed be the empirical self; see, for example, P. F. Strawson, *The Bounds of Sense*, pp. 162ff; or Kitcher, "Kant's Real Self."

concrete actuality is due to the fact that the coherence of counterfactual suppositions about x is controlled by the sense of the expression used to refer to x. Because the sense of "I" is highly abstract, there are few counterfactual suppositions that are absolutely incoherent for something referred to solely as "I." But the fact remains that I am a man, according to Hegel, not a Cartesian ego.

The discussion of the sense of "I" began with a passage in which Hegel characterizes the I as (a) wholly abstract universality, (b) pure relation to itself, (c) abstracted from all its particular states, and (d) thinking as a subject. So far, only the third and fourth characteristics have been considered. To present a rounded account of Hegel's understanding of the "I," something must be said about its universality and self-relation. This also necessitates an explication of Hegel's conception of thinking, for a thinking subject is universality and pure relation to itself in virtue of being a *thinking* subject.

There are two aspects to the claim that the I is self-relation—material and formal. The sense in which an I is materially self-related is the most directly understandable, for it concerns our relations to our own internal states. More important, the formal self-relation is made possible by the material self-relation. We therefore begin by looking at Hegel's conception of the way each thinker is materially self-related. This really only requires a review of the previous development of subjective spirit with an eye to the emergence of a self, for the material self-relation of the thinking subject *is* the self-relation of the organism. As a preface to this discussion, let me remind the reader that the overall structure and intent of Hegel's mature system is decidedly more Aristotelian in style than it is Cartesian. Beginning with his logic cum metaphysics, Hegel traces the overall, fundamental structures of reality. The structures formally specified in the Logic are then applied to the analysis of particular phenomena in ascending orders of complexity, each building on the previous order, from mechanics through biology. The philosophy of spirit picks up this progression, but one should not think that the dividing line between nature and spirit is clearcut; we have a great deal in common with animals. The Anthropology is the transition point between the animal and the human; it describes those structures essential to the emergence of the I.

The crucial stages of the emergence, as far as we are concerned, start with sensation. A sensation has a peculiar two-sideness:

viewed naturalistically, it is a state of the body centered around a sense organ, but from the point of view of spirit (from within, as it were) it is an absolutely simple, given reality, without structure, without connection. The Anthropology describes a set of structures in which the particular sensations involved become increasingly less important as the functional organization of the structures becomes increasingly complex.

Sensations are, from one point of view, bodily states. The higher-level organizations into which the sensations are brought, however, are not per se bodily; rather, they are functionally specified and explained, and as such, they are only abstractly specified, the particular sensations involved being contingent to them. These structures of sensations exist as habits. "That the soul thus makes itself into an abstract universal being and reduces what is particular in feeling (and in consciousness) to a determination of it that merely *is*—this is *habit*. . . . It [the soul] is free of [these determinations] in so far as it is neither interested in nor occupied by them; in that it exists in these forms as its possession it is at the same time open to the further activity and occupation of sensation as well as of the consciousness of spirit in general" (§410, my tr.). In an organism that has developed large-scale habitual patterns of behavior, individual sensations are important only insofar as they figure in these patterns. The soul is an abstract universal being insofar as it is best described and explained in terms of these abstractly specified, dynamic structures of sensations. The soul is the totality of them. But it is not in virtue of habit alone that man is capable of having an I: "This abstract being-for-self of the soul in its corporeality is not yet I, not yet the existence of the universal which is for the universal" (§409, my tr.). Achieving a self, an I, requires a further recursion. Freed from the particularities of sensation by reducing the role of sensation to that of mere contingent occasion for the soul's (abstractly specified) activity, the soul now reduces the role of those patterns of activity to occasions for higher-order structures. With this move the I—the subject of consciousness—emerges: "This being-for-self of free universality is the higher awakening of the soul to the I, to the abstract universality insofar as it is *for* the abstract universality, which is thus *thinking* and *subject* for itself and indeed subject of its judgment [*Urtheil*], in which it excludes from itself the natural totality of its determinations as [i.e., in the form of] an object, a world *external to itself,* and so relates itself to it that it is immediately in that world reflected into itself—Consciousness" (§412, my tr.).

Habit, as Hegel describes it, can be thought of as the organization of sensory experience; the I emerges, not in that organization, but as the possibility of a further unitary organization of the various modes of first-order organization of sensory experience. A habit is an abstract universality in that it is the same across times and places, ready to manifest itself whenever it is elicited. It is in imposing a further, higher-order structure on our habitually structured sensory experience that the I and consciousness emerge. The I, then, apparently depends on the existence of a second-order functional organization.

If this is the nature of the I, we should be able to use it to illuminate the difference between animals and humans. Animals certainly have habits, but, if Hegel is right, these habits simply coexist within the animal, as it were. They are not subject to any higher organizing principle. Should two (or more) habits come into conflict, say, because the eliciting stimuli for two mutually exclusive behavioral patterns are present, the conflict is only resolved de facto, depending on which habit is more firmly entrenched. With humans, in contrast, there is a higher level of organization. Conflicts between habitual patterns are (often) resolved in a principled and not merely de facto manner. The human is self-regulating in a way the animal is not.

The picture obtained from the above discussion might be misleading, for some may be unable to resist the temptation to think of man's initial reflective turn as essentially *conscious,* in which man is aware of the behavioral patterns or mental structures reflected on *as* either behavioral patterns or mental structures. This, however, would be a major mistake, a serious jumping of the gun. When Hegel insists that the natural determinations of the soul (the sensations, feelings, and first-order habits) are excluded from the soul in the form of an external world, in the form of objects, he should be taken at his word. The objects to which consciousness relates throughout the Phenomenology are, strictly speaking, internal constructions of consciousness out of the manifold of sensation. This is why Hegel can insist that "the Kantian philosophy is most accurately assessed as having grasped spirit as consciousness; and as containing throughout not the philosophy of spirit, but only the determinations of its phenomenology" (§415, my tr.). The first-order patterns of mental activity on which consciousness directs itself do not appear to it as patterns of mental activity, but as constituting independent objects.

We can now see the sense in which the I, the subject of consciousness, stands in a material relation to itself. The objects it takes to be independent of itself, and in relation to which it defines itself, are in reality determinations of itself, for they are the complex structures of sensory data we have (subconsciously) prepared for further conceptualization.[19]

The I is a higher-order organizing principle. Strictly speaking, it relates itself directly only to other organizing principles, and thus only to things of its own basic ontological type. If we grant that organizing principles are always universals in some suitable sense (whether abstract or concrete universals), then the I, itself a universal, relates directly only to other universals, which are, furthermore, contained within it. This is the formal sense in which the I is a pure self-related universal. It is, to use the Aristotelian vocabulary, the form of forms. It is also important to note that this formal self-

---

19. Because of the essential self-relatedness of the I, it is tempting to attribute to Hegel the belief that all propositional attitudes are de se, a la David Lewis or Roderick Chisholm. The belief that all reference is directly to one's self and only indirectly, by means of individuating descriptions, to other things does not sit comfortably with other Hegelian doctrines. First, whereas Hegel sometimes seems to treat "I" and the other indexicals as coordinate, he never seems tempted to make "I" primary. Second, the idea that we are, in thought, directly related to and directly aware only of ourselves flies in the face of the phenomenology (in the non-Hegelian sense) of thought; deep thought is precisely when we *forget* ourselves, *lose* ourselves, as Hegel remarks in several places. Third, insisting that we act as our own intermediary between our thought and the world still leaves us with an intermediary and thus threatens to revive the problem of a thing-in-itself inaccessible to us.

There are, however, other elements of Hegel's philosophy that indicate such an interpretation—his comparisons of the feeling soul to a monad, for instance. At a deeper level, Hegel's confinement to an Aristotelian logic of terms, which underlies his conviction that judgments and syllogisms are ways the internal structure of a concept (universal) unfolds itself, also encourages the view that thought and belief ought to be understood as self-attribution of a universal, whether in the still implicit form of a concept, the dirempted form of a judgment, or the fully unfolded form of a syllogism.

Hegel did not have a clearly articulated theory of the propositional attitudes; it was not a clear issue for the age. I presently believe that Hegel's position is indeterminate with respect to this question, although I hope to return to it in future work.

relation supervenes upon the material self-relation. Anything with the material self-relation exhibited by a normal human being would ipso facto also exhibit the formal self-relation of the I (though not necessarily vice versa).

Thinking as a Subject

The major characteristic of the I—thinking as a subject—needs to be further explicated. Thought is seen by Hegel as the universal ordering activity manifested as much in the order of objective reality as in our subjective mental activity. Pure thinking is the structure or organizing activity necessary to any (metaphysically) possible world; it is the system traced in Hegel's Logic.

M. J. Inwood interprets Hegel's claim that the I is thinking as a subject to mean that Hegel identifies the pure I with the self-determining system of pure thoughts.[20] There are several startling consequences of such an identification. First, there is no distinction between individual thinkers.[21] Inwood suggests that different particular egos might be identified with different chunks of the total system of pure thoughts—namely, with that part of the system an ego commands. But this seems already to presuppose the identification of egos in some other way, for there is no way intrinsic to the system of pure thoughts to differentiate egos. Second, identifying the I with the system of pure thoughts would make it impossible to distinguish any particular thinker from that system, from the Absolute. A Kojevean vision of a megalomaniacal Hegel, who having understood his own system has become the very intellect of God, would be right after all. Another untoward consequence of such a position is that it seems to make it impossible to draw the distinction between occurrent thinkings, attributable to persons at specific times, and the pure thoughts themselves. The system of pure thoughts is always present—the pure thoughts are not datable. But then how can I or my occurrent thoughts, which surely are datable, be identical to (even part of) the system of pure thoughts? I argue

20. Inwood, *Hegel*, pp. 34–42.
21. This consequence can be softened somewhat by taking the position that there is only no distinction between individual egos qua pure thinkers. But if thinkers are truly to be identified with pure thoughts, there can be no distinction among them, for pure thought is one.

below that Hegel believes that at the highest level of mental activity—pure thinking—we *are* the activity that thought is (see also Chapter 11). But it is a mistake to take this to be a strict identity between me and the system of pure thoughts; one batter does not a ballgame make.

The untoward consequences of a strict identification of the pure I with the system of thoughts can be avoided without losing the essential and intimate relation between the two by employing one of Hegel's favorite devices, the distinction between form and content. The pure I and the system of pure thoughts must have, according to Hegel, the same content, but in significantly different forms. This distinction, as employed by Hegel, is not a simple juxtaposition of two independent, separable elements in a complex whole. Although one content can appear in different forms, it is sensitive to the form in which it appears. A mismatch between form and content does violence to both. Without the appropriate form, the content cannot appear as it really is; an inadequate form distorts, or at least conceals, part of the content.

The most familiar example of the use of this distinction within Hegel's system is his description of the relations among the triad of the final stage (Absolute Spirit) of the philosophy of spirit: Art, Religion, and Philosophy. Hegel claims that these three share a common content—the self-knowledge of spirit as Absolute Spirit. But he also claims that they differ in the form this content is given. In Art, spirit's self-knowledge is clothed in an externally perceptible form; in Religion, it takes an imaginative, imagistic form. Only in Philosophy does spirit's self-knowledge attain the fully adequate, explicit form best suited to it.

The system of pure thoughts is a network of interrelated pure concepts. But his is how Hegel conceives of the I as well. Hegel adopts the Kantian idea that the categories (pure concepts) *constitute* the I in their operation. The subject and the object are simultaneously constituted by the activity of thought. But unlike Kant, Hegel sees no reason to confine pure concepts to subjective minds alone. Pure concepts are also constitutive of objectivity; anything supposedly lying "behind" the objects of our thought must be nonobjective, illusory. Thus Hegel's I is an active, self-constituting system of pure thoughts.

The same may be said of the Idea, the total reality of the world.

The important difference between the I and the Idea is that the I is an *existent* self-constituting system of pure concepts (*WdL*, vol. 2, p. 220; *SL*, p. 583). To say that something exists or is existent is to say that it is involved in relations of mutual dependence with an indeterminate number of other things of similar status. "Existence is the immediate unity of self-reflection and reflection in another. It is therefore the indeterminate collection of existents as things reflected into themselves which are just as much appearances in another or relative, and which constitute a *world* of mutual dependence and an infinite connection of grounds and groundeds" (§123, my tr.). Existence is the form, for instance, of spatiotemporal particulars. The world-whole, or the pure Idea, cannot be said to participate in relations of mutual dependence—there is, after all, nothing else it can depend on. The I, however, does participate in such relations, for each person is an I necessarily related to other I's and to nonthinking beings as well. Thus, although the content of the Idea and the I are the same, their forms are significantly different.

Since existence is a matter of entering into dependency relations with other things, there is an inherent tension in the notion of the system of pure thoughts existing. The system is supposed to be absolutely self-determining. How can it adopt a form so antithetic to its nature?

> This last shape of Spirit—the Spirit which at the same time gives its complete and true content the form of the Self and thereby realizes its Concept as remaining in its Concept in this realization—this is absolute knowing. . . . Truth is the *content*, which in religion is still not identical with its certainty. But this identity is now a fact, in that the content has received the shape of the Self. As a result, that which is the very essence, viz. the Concept, has become the element of existence, or has become the *form of objectivity* for consciousness. (*PhG*, p. 556; *PhS*, pp. 485–86)

The system of pure thoughts—the absolute Idea—cannot itself adopt the form of existence, for the system requires a form fully adequate to its content. Its content is the categorial structure governing the constitution of the world. Considered as a pure content, independent of considerations of form, this is the Concept—an abstract structure (explored in the Logic) realized by the world-whole. The only form fully adequate to this content is the world-whole itself. But that abstract structure is also realized *within* the world; there are, as it were, partial, microcosmic realizations of the structure of the macrocosm. An existent individual who possesses sufficient internal complexity with the appropriate categorial structure partially realizes the Concept in a self-reflective mode. The content of each I is the same, but the individual I's, as distinct existences in the natural world, are themselves thereby distinguished.

It is, indeed, part of the very structure of the world that its own structure be internally duplicated in this way, and in this sense the world comes to its own fullest realization in our thought about ourselves as realizing the Concept.

All human activity is imbued with thought; thought is a moment in everything we do. Just as thought is involved in all the structures of the objective world, it permeates all the structures of subjectivity. In this sense we are always thinking, according to Hegel. But surely there are some episodes of mental activity which are pure thoughts in a more straightforward sense—for instance, what someone does in reading and understanding Hegel's *Logik*. Thought is the structure of our mental activity. In pure thinking that structure is also the object of our thinking. Thus thinking as a subject and thinking as an object coincide in pure thought, the self-conscious realization of the Concept.

We began with a question: According to Hegel, what am I? I am a complex organism whose internal states exhibit a self-reflective, multileveled structure enabling me to consciously recreate the structure exhibited in the world as a whole. I am a thinking thing and therefore necessarily also an embodied, sensate thing. Strictly speaking, I am neither a merely material nor an immaterial thing. What is important about me is not what I am made of, but what I do—namely, think. And in thought, at least, I participate in the Absolute.

7

Intuition

THE ROLE OF INTUITION IN THE PSYCHOLOGY

Intuition is the first division of theoretical spirit, and although Hegel could have called it "rational sensibility" or even "perception," its placement after the Phenomenology emphasizes the difference between intuition and sensation or feeling.

The connection between sensation, feeling, and intuition is that they are all mental states with significant sensory content directed on individuals. In Kant's botanization of the genus representation (*Critique of Pure Reason*, A320/B376–7), an intuition is classed as an objective perception that "relates immediately to the object and is single." This is strikingly echoed in the *Zusatz* to §445, where the first stage of theoretical spirit is described as "material knowledge relating to an immediately *single* object,—or *intuition*." In specifying that intuition is a form of *material* knowledge Hegel is excluding cognitive states that relate to a single object, but that do so formally, as for instance a definite description might. A representation with the content "the tallest man in the room" might well relate to a single individual and yet not be a piece of material knowledge. For, if there were such an individual but no sensory contact between him and the representation, the representation could not be immediately applied to the individual. Not all singular representations are intuitions, therefore—only those that represent an individual directly through their sensory content.

As in Kant, the objects to which intuition relates are highly structured. The object of intuition is a spatiotemporally extended object, possessing causal properties and sometimes intentions, desires, and reason. It is only at this relatively late stage that Hegel finds a place for the rich perceptual experience of the world with which we are all so familiar.[1] This is important, for the fact that our ordinary perceptual consciousness of the world is dealt with under intuition means that it is *not* under consideration in the Phenomenology. This reinforces our earlier claim that Hegel's Phenomenology is not the proper place to look for his theory of perception.

Sensation provides the material for intuition. "The content that is raised into intuitions is its [spirit's] sensations, just as its intuitions are changed into representations and immediately its representations into thoughts, etc" (§440, my tr.). But sensation, as we saw earlier, is thoroughly nonconceptual, so there seems to be no room for the concept of "rational sensation." And indeed, Hegel writes very little of sensation in the section on intuition. Hegel rather recapitulates the notion of feeling as forming the first stage of intuition. But the notion has broadened in scope here a bit, for Hegel remarks that "feeling has already occurred earlier (§339ff.) as a mode of the soul's existence. In that case the essential determination of the *finding* or the immediacy is natural being or corporeity. Here however, it is merely *abstract*, immediacy in general" (§446). Notice that his reference here is, perhaps surprisingly, not to the section on feeling in the Anthropology but to the *Philosophy of Nature*. Feeling is a determination of the animal and therefore properly treated in the *Philosophy of Nature* as well. In saying that here, in intuition, feeling has become merely abstract, Hegel is opening the realm of feeling and sensation to things that are not simply the mental counterparts of externally determined bodily states. Thus he fulfills his earlier statement (§401, *Zusatz*) that internal sensations are, properly speaking, to be discussed in the Psychology. The important point is that such feelings have not been mediated by the

---

1. Sellars has argued for years that a Kantian perceptual judgment has the form "This cube is pink," where the subject phrase "this cube" models the intuitive component of the perceptual judgment and therefore the structure of the intuition itself. In Hegel's *Logik* the singular judgment takes precisely this form. If Hegel takes his logic and his statements about the singularity of the object of intuition seriously, he would have to find Sellars's model suggestive and very agreeable. See W. Sellars, *Science and Metaphysics*.

objective, rule-governed constructive processes that constitute in-tuitions.[2]

Intuition is for Hegel, like Kant, the constitution of that form of our cognitive experience in which we relate immediately to the singular as singular. Material relation to the singular as singular, however, can be guaranteed only by a sensory connection. Con-cepts never relate to the singular as singular. In intuition the con-tent retains the form of the found or the given (the immediate), but its givenness is merely the way it appears, for the content is a determination of spirit itself, and in its relation to it spirit relates itself only to itself; that is, the object of intuition seems to be given to us directly, without intermediary process or medium, but in fact the rich structure that the object of intuition is presented as having is itself the work of the constructive processes of spirit itself. Hegel does not believe that this structure is only a subjective artifact of our mental processes—the objective structure of the world and the subjective, cognitive structures of rational beings are ultimately congruent—but that the object as presented in intuition has been constructed in accordance with the categorial structures of con-sciousness, although that activity is not present to the intuiting consciousness itself.

In the Psychology there is a steady progression in the explicitness of the activity of spirit. "Psychology is therefore concerned with the faculties or general modes of the activity of *spirit as such*—intuiting, representing, recollecting, etc., desiring, etc." (§440, my tr.). In intuition the activity of spirit, its constructive contribution, is not

---

2. It is not altogether clear, however, that in his discussion here Hegel respects his own distinction between sensation and feeling. In particular, my interpretation of the distinction seems to be belied by his remark that "cultivated, true sensation is the sensation of a cultivated spirit that has acquired the consciousness of determinate differences, essential relationships, true determinations, etc., and in which it is this rectified matter that enters its feeling, that is, contains this form" (§447, my tr.). This sentence is rather obscure, but I take it to imply, not that sensation comes as loaded with essential relations, but that in their very entry into feeling, as a result of the immediate synthesis of sensation to create feeling, they already obtain this form, since the unconscious synthesis is now informed by reason. This sentence, so interpreted, does not threaten my interpretation of the distinction between sensa-tion and feeling. There are passages in the Additions where these terms seem to be used loosely, but this is not surprising, for in writing the Additions Boumann had a variety of different sets of notes, both from Hegel's hand and from his students', some of which were relatively early, before Hegel had solidified this distinction.

yet evident in the experience, however present it may be to the mind reflecting on the nature of intuition. Theoretical spirit is "the activity by which the seemingly *alien* object [of the stage of Consciousness] receives, instead of the shape of something given, isolated and contingent, the form of something inwardized, subjective, universal, necessary, and rational" (§443, *Zusatz*, Miller tr.).

> It is therefore a mistake when theoretical spirit is sometimes distinguished from practical spirit by characterizing the former as passive and the latter as active. This distinction does, indeed, appear to be correct. Theoretical spirit seems only to accept what is already there, whereas practical spirit has to produce something that is not yet externally to hand. In truth, however, as we already indicated in the *Zusatz* to §442, theoretical spirit is not a merely passive acceptance of an other, of a given object, but reveals itself as active by raising the inherently rational content of the object out of the form of externality and singleness into the form of reason. (§444, *Zusatz*, adapted from Miller tr.)

Theoretical spirit begins with a *found immediacy* (its apprehension of the object of consciousness). In this seemingly immediate apprehension of the object of consciousness spirit indeed knows the external object—but it does not yet apprehend its own self and the extent to which the object of consciousness is its own, its self (because constituted by it). The concepts with which subjective spirit understands its own activity are the subject of the Psychology. The Psychology is a crucial level of Hegel's system, for its thoroughgoing self-reflectivity is the defining characteristic of spirit.

Attention, Space, and Time

Full-fledged intuition is not, of course, present at the lowest level of intuition; as we have seen, the lowest level is simply feeling recapitulated and abstracted. The level above that, called "attention" by Hegel, has (as is common with the second step of a triad) two "moments" within it. The fact that spirit finds itself in intuition implies an internal split, a distinction between that which finds and that which is found. In intuition spirit is self-related, which requires that there be two distinguishable (though not necessarily separable) moments. Naturally, these two moments are thoroughly correlative: the moment of spiritual activity is attention; what is found is a spatiotemporal world.

It is important to note here that attention is apparently conceived of as the mental activity through which experience receives its spatiotemporal form.[3] But this notion seems implausible, for attention (*Aufmerksamkeit*) is a fairly strong word, implying a high degree of conscious mental activity and willful self-control. The constitutive function of the perceiving spirit is not a conscious function of spirit, yet in the Addition to §448 Hegel seems to say that it is. This view would seem to make the constitution of the spatiotemporal world of our experience something we do by paying attention either to our feelings or sensations or to the objects of experience, and this seems patently false.

To understand Hegel's concept of attention we must remember that it occupies a place within the dialectic of intuition parallel to that occupied by self-feeling and by the whole level of consciousness insofar as it is in consciousness that the distinction between the subjective and the objective is made explicit. I take it to be the case that self-feeling, consciousness, and attention are all different levels of one and the same generic form of mental activity, with attention being a more highly developed and articulated level of this activity or function of mind. Each of these levels has as a primary feature a subject-object split in which the object is projected away from the subject or externalized.

Two observations have to be made in respect of the significance of this externality however; firstly, since what is spiritual or rational constitutes the objects' own nature, what is sensed assumes the form of a self-externality in that it becomes an object external to the internality of spirit. Secondly, we have to note that since this transformation of what is sensed proceeds from spirit as such, what is sensed is endowed with a spiritual, that is to say with an abstract externality, and so acquires the same universality as that which can pertain imme-

3. The implication is clear: the objects of consciousness in the Phenomenology do not have a spatiotemporal form. This continues the remark in the Phenomenology (§418) that "here" and "now" are determinations that do not really apply to the object of sense certainty but are properly reserved for intuition. This is made even clearer in the Addition to §418.

diately to what is external, a universality which is still entirely formal
and devoid of content. (§448, *Zusatz*)

These are the two respects in which intuition differs from its earlier
counterparts. First, Hegel says, intuition experiences its objects as
self-external. This means that in intuition we experience objects
as imperfectly manifesting a determinate essence, an essence independent of that singular object and only *fully* realized by us,
through our conceptual grasp of it. Insofar as the object of intuition
is determined by this essence—without which, of course, it would
not be what it is—the object is self-external. Second, the externalization of the sensuous content is performed in intuition by spirit as
such, and this dictates the form in which that content is externalized. The point here is that the external form imposed on something by spirit itself is essentially appropriate—it is the externality
the thing itself has. So when spirit imposes an external form on the
sensuous content presented to it, it imposes the same form of
externality as singular, sensuous things themselves have—space
and time.

But this leads us to ask a more probing question: Are we to
understand that sensations are themselves in a spatiotemporal ordering, even though spirit, although perhaps temporal, is certainly
not spatial? We have already seen a quandary similar to this in our
discussion of sensation, a problem that we decided was a weak spot
in the Hegelian theory. Here however, the situation is different, for
whether Hegel realizes it or not, he has room for a sophisticated
answer to the present problem.

The answer is, as it should be, a decided yes and no. Yes, the
ordering of sensation is spatiotemporal, but no, this does not en-
gender special problems once we realize what Hegel intends by a
spatiotemporal ordering. If we turn to the relevant discussion in the
Philosophy of Nature (§254–59), we find Hegel discussing the idea
that space is a mere form of intuition. To this notion he replies,
eliminate the element of subjective idealism in this statement and it
is right—for "space is a mere form, that is, an abstraction" (§254).
Or, as he says in §448, space is "the form of indifferent juxtaposition
and quiescent subsistence." Time, also a mere form, is the "form of
restlessness, of the immanently negative, of successiveness, of arising and disappearing."

I suggest that we take Hegel seriously here and think of time and space as purely formal ordering relations indifferent to what they order other than that (since they are the forms of self-externality) it be self-external. It might well be the case then that there are two different sorts of items exhibiting these sorts of relations among themselves, the objects that really are "out there" and the sensations that arise in the subjective mind. The idea is that space and time, as formal orderings of items, can apply to different kinds of items as long as the internal structures of the domains are isomorphic. There is in the mind a formal isomorph of the perceived spatial relation between two objects of intuition, and this is sufficient for the spatiality of the intuition, since space is, by its nature, formal.[4]

This idea of counterpart dimensions to account for the spatiotemporality of our experience is not clearly among the arsenal of the eighteenth- and nineteenth-century philosophers. Sellars, in his discussion of Kant, for instance, can only claim that, had Kant made a few of the distinctions Sellars has made, he would have been led to some such idea. Yet the case that something like this was in the back of Hegel's mind seems stronger, for he also makes it clear that "if we have said that what is sensed derives the form of what is spatial and temporal from the intuiting spirit however, this statement must not be taken to mean that space and time are *only subjective* forms. . . . The truth is that the things in *themselves* are spatial and temporal, this dual form of extrinsicality not being one-sidedly imparted to them by our intuition, but in origin already communicated to them by the implicit, infinite spirit, by the eternally creative Idea" (§448, *Zusatz*). Space and time are both internal to the subjective spirit and real forms of nature.

Why are space and time the forms of intuition? Could there be other forms of intuition? Kant, it seems, has to acknowledge the

---

4. I am obviously drawing on some of the suggestions that Sellars has put forward in his interpretation in *Science and Metaphysics* of Kant's views on space and time, but there are some significant differences here. On my reading of Sellars, the sigma- and tau-characteristics of impressions would be properties the impressions have because of their causal history. For Hegel this causal influence is nugatory; they would rather be characteristics assigned to sensations by the mind because the mind here, as spirit, implicitly cognizes their nature as self-external and takes them as having the appropriate form—gives them this form, in effect. Of course, spirit only gives to them what they already are in their nature, but the spontaneity of mind in the constitution of the spatiotemporal order seems to me heavily emphasized in Hegel.

possibility of other forms of intuition and can offer no reason why space and time happen to be the forms of our intuition. For Hegel, though, such a question does not really arise. Space and time are the determinate forms of self-externality in general (see the arguments in *PN* §254ff.); this is why they are not merely subjective forms but are present in nature itself. They are forms of our intuition simply because they are the forms in which self-external individual objects are realized. If those objects could adopt a different form, the form of our intuition of them would change accordingly. Hegel's derivation of space and time from self-externality is overly aprioristic, but his belief that the forms of our intuition depend on the structure of the world, and not vice versa, represents a healthy realism on his part.

Hegel exploits the fact that attention is more determinate and focused than mere consciousness, for the object of attention is more than a relative other, it has become totally determined, located in the determinate metric of space and time, given an independent existence all its own, and thus, since it *is not* really independent, made self-external. "Intelligence thus determines the content of sensation as something that is external to itself, projects it into time and space, which are the forms in which it is intuitive" (§448, Miller tr.). But finite things *are* self-external and spatiotemporal, according to Hegel, and intuition thus gets at their very heart.

It seemed, above, that Hegel might be insisting that we are conscious in intuition of bestowing spatiotemporal form on objects. But I do not think that he is in fact committed to such an implausible doctrine. Even though in attention spirit is actively directing itself on certain aspects of the world rather than others, this need not be a conscious effort, nor need a person be aware of doing so. That would indeed be a higher level of self-consciousness than is present in intuition.

Much of Hegel's talk of attention treats it as the ability to focus on one thing, which involves both the negation of one's self-assertiveness and the ability to give oneself to the matter at hand. Whereas in feeling the distinction between subject and object is indeterminate, "intelligence necessarily goes on to develop this difference however, to distinguish the object from the subject in a *determinate* manner" (§448, *Zusatz*). The focusing of attention emphasizes the subject's activity in cognition and determines the object more fully for the mind, thus sharpening the split between mind and object while also fostering a deeper appropriation of the object in its fullness by the mind and thus overcoming the split between subject and object.

INTUITION PROPER

In feeling proper the item found is "found" as a member of an indeterminate connectedness; in consciousness it is found as external and independent of the ego, and the ontological structure of the object itself comes under investigation. In intuition the item found is found as an item (or as belonging to an item) in an external, spatiotemporal world. The structure of the connectedness among the found sensations is now completely specified. And it is only in intuition that adequate sophistication is reached to account for the experience of a spatiotemporal world as spatiotemporal. On Hegelian principles, animals cannot be attributed the experience of a spatiotemporally ordered world.[5]

The third step in the triad of intuition is the rather bland assertion that intuition proper is the "concrete unity" of the moments already discussed. We may take the time to differentiate intuition proper from some of its other neighbors, as Boumann's *Zusatz* does.

One of the more interesting remarks in the Addition to §449 is the contrast drawn between intuition and the sensuous consciousness of the Phenomenology. As stated, though, it seems to set intuition off, not just from sensuous consciousness, but from all those attitudes summed up under the heading "Consciousness." Such consciousness, he says, "in unmediated and wholly abstract certainty of itself, relates itself to the immediate singularity of the object, which falls apart into a multitude of aspects. Intuition, on the contrary, is a consciousness which is filled with the certainty of reason, its general object having the determination of being something rational, and so of constituting not a single being torn apart

---

5. Hegel takes spatiotemporal relations to be not merely qualitative but also metric, and we cannot attribute to animals knowledge of a metric: "Space is, in general, pure *quantity*. . . . Consequently, nature begins with quantity and not quality" (*PN* §254).

into various aspects, but a totality, a connected profusion of determinations." (§449, *Zusatz*). "True intuition," he goes on to say, "apprehends the genuine substance of the object."

It is clear here that somehow intuition gets a hold on the essences or concepts of things in a way that is impossible for phenomenological consciousness; can we explain how this can be the case without calling on the vague and unhelpful point that intuition is informed with reason and therefore grasps things as they are? We have seen that the big advance in the nature of the object constructed by intuition over consciousness is that it is explicitly spatiotemporal, and this provides us with the key, for the objects constructed by intuition trace a path through space and time. It would seem from most of Hegel's pronouncements about the abstract nature of space and time, their low level of reality, for instance, that the spatiotemporality of an object has very little to do with its essence. But such is not quite the case. It is true that in intuition the grasping of the object is still merely immediate and is not yet true cognition, for "it has not yet achieved the immanent development of the substance of the object, but rather limits itself to apprehending the unexplicated substance still surrounded by the concomitants of the external and contingent" (§449; *Zusatz*, my tr.). But what intuition must have a grasp of is the *recipe* for constructing a spatiotemporally extended object—an object with a backside, an inside, a past, and a future— on the basis of the sensations that have none of these qualities. This recipe is the first step toward possessing the essence, the concept of the thing, for this recipe is the important recombination into a "living" totality of what consciousness has separated and analyzed. The object is no more the simple conglomeration of its causes and effects, its past and its future, its parts and the whole, than bread is the simple conglomeration of flour, yeast, water, sugar, eggs, heat, and pressure.

Because Hegel insists that all content can occur in feeling, and therefore in intuition, he can also use his account of intuition to approximate the more everyday sense of the term (which it has in German as well as English). Thus he talks of a historian's intuition, and of course of the artist's intuition. These remarks, however, dilute the pure epistemic force of his position and have probably led many of his readers astray, but an immediate grasping of the essence of the object is what any kind of intuition is about. In intuition one conceives the object correctly, but it is mere correct belief, for one's justification is not made evident for or by intuition.

When, on reflection, the subject realizes that strictly speaking its object is not really external, but internal and determined by the subject, the move is made into representation, that set of mental activities surrounding memory and imagination. This is the topic for chapters 8–10, but it is fitting to note here that in representation the intuitive activity of the mind provides the material for further, more complex activities. Intuition is extremely complex on Hegel's account, yet it is but the first stage of a series of successively more complex, compounded levels of mental activity.

8

Representation and Recollection

THE ROLE OF REPRESENTATION

A division of the abilities of the mind into perceptive and thinking capacities is old and common; one of Hegel's more noticeable innovations is a tripartite division of the mental faculties into the intuitive, the representative, and the thinking. The middle element here, representation (*Vorstellung*),[1] presents us with particular difficulties. Some of the phenomena Hegel treats under the rubric of "representation" are clearly sensory—such things as delusions, dreams, and hallucinations—yet others are such as we would today unanimously attribute to thought, namely, the phenomenon of language. I begin here by distinguishing representation from intuition. In the second section we turn to recollection, the lowest level

1. *Vorstellung* also presents related difficulties for the translator. For Kant it is the generic term covering mental acts and is usually translated as "representation." In Hegel's usage *Vorstellung* is no longer the genus of all mental acts, for it does not include thought. Petry translates it as "presentation," whereas Wallace and Miller continue to use "representation." I have adopted "representation" partly to prevent confusion with the more general notion of something's being presented to spirit and to mobilize the play on "re-presentation," which captures some of the spirit, although not the exact semantic content, of Hegel's plays on *Vor-stellung*, and partly because Hegel's criticisms of *Vorstellung* are criticisms of what is today called the representational theory of mind. "Representation" is a fortuitous choice as well in that representations are treated by Hegel as re-presentations, or presentations in a new mode, of intuitions.

of representation. We return to the distinction between representation and thought in Chapter 11.

When Hegel separates representation from the phenomena of intuition, he claims that in representation the fact that the mental state or act is subjective becomes explicit:

> However, that the object has the character of being mine is only implicitly present in intuition and is first posited in representation. In intuition the objectivity [*Gegenständlichkeit*] of the content predominates. Only when I reflect that it is I who has the intuition—only then do I step into the standpoint of representation. (§449, *Zusatz*, my tr.)

> Accordingly, spirit posits intuition as its own, penetrates it, makes it into something inward—recollects itself in it, becomes present to itself in it and thereby free. Through this inwardization intelligence raises itself to the stage of representation. Representing spirit has intuition, which is sublated in it and neither has vanished nor is something only past. (§450, *Zusatz*, my tr.)

It might appear that any representation wears its subjectivity on its sleeve, yet such things as hallucinations do not obviously present themselves as any more subjective than any other perceptual states, although Hegel calls them representations. Of course all our mental states, perceptual states as well, are subjective, but what qualifies these mental states to be particularly well suited to be called representations?

At the level of representation, the subjectivity of the content of the mental state, which was only implicit in intuition, is made explicit. Hegel does not think, however, that it must be explicit to the subject having the representation that it is subjective—otherwise hallucinations and delusions could not be considered representations. It must rather be made explicit to an objective point of view. But an objective point of view also realizes that even in intuition the content is subjective, although it agrees with the objective reality. To this extent, intuitions and representations are not exclusive, for intuitions form a special subset of representations.

We still need to distinguish the sense in which the subjectivity of the content of a mental event becomes explicit in a representation. We can understand this by asking what would count as the correct explanation of the presence to mind of that content. If we reflect for a moment on what we have already seen of Hegel's theory, it is apparent that what the manifold of sensation is presented *as* is not an occurrent, simple property of a certain complex of sensations; rather, what a complex of sensations is presented as is a matter both of the internal structure the activity of spirit has endowed that complex of sensations with and of the relations that that complex, again through the activity of spirit, has with other sensate complexes. Thus a mental state that seems to fit in with the course of intuition in us—and is therefore presented as an intuition—may, on later reflection, be discovered to have been a mental state that does not cohere with the order of intuition and is thus a mere representation. In theoretical spirit we adopt an objective standpoint even on that which is subjective. Thus representations are not self-presenting in the sense that, when had, they reveal of necessity all their essential qualities, including whether they are mere representations or representations that also qualify as intuitions in virtue of correct connection with extra-mental objects.

This last remark should also make it clear that there is no absolute demarcation in internal ("felt") qualities between intuitions and mere representations, at least not at the lowest levels of representation, for indeed, in intuition itself we have a representation. One is tempted to say that the difference between intuition and representation is the attitude the mind takes toward its own state, but this way of talking nourishes the misleading picture of a spectator in a theater watching images on a screen and reacting to them. We must rather tell a more complex story and give up the attempt to simplify so radically. The mental life of an individual forms a whole, and even this whole is not a totally isolated atom but interacts in various ways with the subject's environment. Each mental act or state is an item in the course of the world that is open to explanation, and the distinction between some of them as intuitions and some of them as mere representations lies more in the kind of explanatory considerations that must be advanced to explain them than in any properties intrinsic to the states themselves. Thus mental states are classed as mere representations both when they fall short of intuition and when they are at a higher level. Let me explain this.

The first constraint we must recognize is that accounting for a mental state or act is not just a matter of explaining its origin in strict causal terms; one must also show how the act fits in with the subject's other mental states and the state of the environment. Thus it is important to give, not only a causal chain leading from the object to sensations forming the material of the mental state, but also an account of the principles according to which these sensations are unified with all others to form a coherent whole. This is a large part of what we are saying when we describe a mental state in terms of its content. The full explanation of the genesis of a mental state includes as a crucial factor its fit with other mental states— even though this is a matter of interpretation.[2] We must remember that the coherence of any sensation with any other need not be evident to the subject itself; nonetheless, that there is such a coherence is presupposed by our assigning the sensation to the same subject.

There are three important factors to be taken into account in the explanation of a sensuous mental state: the environment, the perceptual apparatus, and the internal spiritual apparatus responsible for the constructive activity. In normal intuition, the activity of the subjective spirit and the operation of the sensory apparatus are standard and therefore not important in explaining that particular state. When a subject is alert, in standard conditions, with perceptual organs operating properly, no reference to the state of the subject other than its orientation in the environment and perhaps perceptual set is necessary to explain why the subject has the experience it has. The subject's own state and activities, since quite normal, form part of the background conditions of the perceptual experience, and the burden of explaining why that particular experience is had is carried by facts about the physical environment of the subject.

In cases of mere representation, the explanatory burden is shifted for whatever reason to facts about the subject itself, whether about the perceptual apparatus or the spiritual apparatus. The subject's own activities are now important in explaining why this experience was had at that time. There is still a causal story to be told about the generation of the sensate material, but now the form that that material is given by spirit is not a normal *re*construction of the cause

2. These considerations of coherence and the process of interpretation are holistic, teleological, and normative, of course; see Chapter 1.

of the sensations. The standard relations between the causal and semantic characteristics of the mental states do not hold. It is this difference that means that the experience is not an intuition, but this difference need not be evident in the experience itself. Such a situation can occur in two ways: (a) there can be some disturbance in the normal operation of the sensory organs; (b) it is possible that there is some breakdown in the activity of construction. This second alternative can occur for two different reasons: (i) the causal input, the material of sensation, does not fully determine the object constructed, and due to lack of or faulty contextual information the wrong object is constructed or the object is constructed with some wrong properties; (ii) the mind itself "processes" the material incorrectly and constructs something that corresponds to nothing in the environment. These possibilities allow for illusion, hallucination, and even madness, and in such cases it is clear that the state of the subject is crucial in the explanation of the experience. In cases of such a breakdown in the otherwise normal course of intuition we are forced to be more aware of the subject's own role in intuition, and of the fact that the subject possesses a *subjective representation* of the extra-mental world. In this way some representations are best understood as falling short of intuition.

There are, however, other ways the contribution of spirit to its own experience can come to the fore. Spirit is free—it determines itself and is not totally dependent on the external world for its content. Insofar as spirit determines its own experience, it is evident that spirit itself bears the explanatory burden in explaining why it has this experience now.[3] The most intuitive example of such self-determination by spirit is a case of imagination, where, for instance, I let my fancy wander amid images of flowered fields and

---

3. It would be a mistake to think that spirit's self-determination is to be understood here as spirit's *willing* a certain state into existence, for a volition itself is something to which spirit determines itself. At this level, spirit's freedom is the freedom of organic self-determination, of the independence of the complex from the environment. The force of saying that spirit determines itself in a certain way is not the imputation of a volition or some such mental state but rather a sign that we are at an explanatory dead end. Since spirit is free, its actions are not externally caused, and saying that spirit has freely determined itself in a certain manner lets us know that the explanation stops with spirit itself. The explanation of a free act of spirit is in terms of spirit's ends, which it has determined for itself and which are ultimately implicit in its essence.

beautiful skies, thus escaping the drear of a winter's day. This need not be an intentional action, something I set out to do, but it is something I do. Alternatively, I could sit down and work on designing a house or solving a problem. We can give reasons for why I am thinking what I am thinking, but these are again internal to me and refer to my thoughts, desires, goals, character, perhaps my physical condition.

This notion of a spirit freely determining its own mental content seems to raise some problems. Do we, by this formulation, commit Hegel to the thesis that a spirit can create sensations, the basic material of mind, freely? Since sensations are, as we have already seen, states of sensory organs having immediate being for mind, this interpretation would involve mind's ability to influence the body directly. Hegel would object to putting the question this way, for it suggests a real separation of mind and body, but the point does confront him with a real difficulty. If there are sensations that do not arise by the standard causal patterns, Hegel must account for such processes—but to my knowledge he does not do so.

Need we suppose that the mind can simply create sensations ex nihilo for use in imagination? Hegel might say that there is a continual though changing fund of sensation, that in creating representations spirit constructs the sensations in novel ways, making use of the material at hand. In talking about a certain case of visions that someone had and recognized to be mere visions, Hegel remarks, "Internally we have before us a representation, and this presence is a moment of corporeity, and through illness this presence can be so augmented that it assumes the form of seeing" (quoted from the Kehler ms. in *PSS*, vol. 2, p. 271, my tr.). But to suppose that the eidetic image of a flower arrangement which an eidetic imager may have while, say, skiing in the mountains is merely a novel reconstruction of the sensations caused in standard ways by the environment seems to stretch plausibility. An eidetic image is too close to the original. Hegel's rather bland explanation that something was brought about by spirit or dredged up from within spirit's "nightlike abyss" (§453) is simply insufficient.

If this is the nature of the self-determination of spirit in imagination, how exactly does it differ from an illusion or hallucination, spirit's merely *incorrect* construction of the material of sensation? Again, internally there need be no difference, except insofar as in spirit's free self-determination the constructs are presented to mind as bearing the stamp of self-creation. This difference, however, can only be cashed in in terms of the relations the construct bears to other mental states or acts. For instance, suppose someone to be having a pink elephant experience, although there are no such elephants around. Whether we say that the person is hallucinating or merely imagining vividly depends to a great extent on the further behavior and reports of the person. If she describes the elephants in detail, matches their color to a printer's sample, and yet does not expect others to see or respond to the elephants, does not cower in front of them, and so on, we may well marvel at her imaginative capabilities but we shall not assert that she is hallucinating or under an illusion. To be hallucinating she must think that there are elephants out there, and we tell this by, for example, her running to escape being trampled. Whether a representation is an imagining or an incorrect intuition depends on the connection it is given to other representations.[4]

RECOLLECTION

Hegel's treatment of Representation is divided triadically, under the headings Recollection (*Erinnerung*), Imagination (*Einbildungskraft*), and Memory (*Gedächtnis*). These headings are a bit misleading; there are perhaps no better words for labeling what he is talking about, but if one takes these in their ordinary meaning certain confusions are bound to arise. In each case Hegel isolates particular mental abilities, and although each retains some relation to the normal sense of the word, it is stripped bare of most of the connotations it normally carries. Furthermore, the finer points go absolutely untouched, as is necessary in an encyclopedic treatment. Hegel warns us also against treating each of these three as different and separate faculties constituting the mind. The three are understood by Hegel to be hierarchically ordered in increasing complexity, each one presupposing and involving its predecessor: "The precise nature of a truly philosophical comprehension consists however in the

4. Some of the material dealing with derangement quoted in Chapter 5 reinforces this interpretation.

grasping of the rational connection present between these forms, in recognizing the sequence of the organic development of intelligence within them" (§451, *Zusatz*).

Recollection, the first of the three main stages of representation, is itself divided triadically. This creates some technical difficulties for us, for Hegel uses the important term "recollection" within each of these three stages without acknowledging explicitly that the meaning has shifted slightly because the term is now applied to a simpler, now to a more complex, ability. To avoid merely verbal confusions at the small expense of some stylistic awkwardness, I simply subscript the terms to make it clear in each case which level I am dealing with.

Recollection$_1$ is described as follows: "As initially recollecting intuition, intelligence posits the content of feeling in its inwardness, in its own space and its own time. It is thus (1) *image* freed from its initial immediacy and abstract singularity against others and taken up into the universality of the I in general. The image no longer has the complete determinateness that intuition has and is arbitrary or contingent; it is in general isolated from the external place, time, and immediate context in which intuition stood" (§452, my tr.). In recollection$_1$ the sensate material present to mind (the content of intuition) is no longer presented as an object external to the mind in space and time. The sensate material is still given an internal structure sufficient to make it a representation of an object, but the particular sensate clump is no longer united with all the others by those strict categorial principles that impose spatiotemporal structure on the field of intuition. Thus the image is no longer presented as in objective space and time, but as an object in no particular space at no particular time. The object imaged has thus been removed or abstracted from its spatiotemporal context. If I consider the objects in my visual field not as physical objects independent of me but as visual images, even though I may be correctly intuiting a typewriter and desk, I have moved up to the recollection$_1$ of these objects, for the objects are no longer located for me in objective space.

This abstraction of the image (whether visual, aural, gustatory, etc.) from its immediate spatiotemporal context is the first important step presupposed by all higher activities of spirit, for all these, especially thought itself, involve the ability to go beyond the immediate situation into the actual past in memory, into nonactual possibilities in the imaginative construction of possible pasts, presents, and futures, and beyond the sensible altogether in the contemplation of the universal per se. The first and elementary step toward these more sophisticated intellectual achievements is this simple abstraction of the present material from its complete context.

Although the content of feeling is no longer completely subjected to those rules or categories that impose complete spatiotemporal determinateness on it, it is certainly not left devoid of such structure, and the entire categorial arsenal developed in the *Encyclopedia Phenomenology* is presupposed here. Without these categories, the subject-object split would remain meaningless to the subject, who would be unable to perform the act of recollection, unable to contrast his states with extra-mental objects at all. In recollection$_1$, "what is represented, however, gains this permanence only at the cost of the clarity and freshness of the immediate, fully determinate singularity of what is intuited. Intuition palls and dims in becoming an image" (§452, *Zusatz*, my tr.). This passage brings to mind Hume's distinction between an impression and an idea. Hume distinguishes the two solely on the basis of their force and vivacity, which seems to be similar to Hegel's distinction between the relative freshness and clarity of intuition and recollection$_1$. But Hume's differentiation between impression and idea is merely phenomenological; he has no other way to explain why an idea is less vivid than an impression other than that ideas derive from impressions, for which conclusion a major argument is that the impressions are more vivid. But since Hume draws several other distinctions on the basis of force and vivacity, it is not clear just what the distinction between impression and idea, which is supposed to be an important distinction in kind, really amounts to.

Hegel, on the other hand, can give a theoretical explanation of the phenomenological difference between intuition and representation. Vivid and strong presence to mind is not merely a matter of the original strength of sensation, according to Hegel, but also of the weight in the constructive process it is given.[5] But if we are to

5. We must remember that the categorial scheme developed in the *Encyclopedia Phenomenology* does not give us rules for the construction of particular objects in general. The construction of particular objects always demands special knowledge; it is, moreover, imbued with thought and is something that we unconsciously and sometimes consciously learn to do. To a trained taster certain flavors in a complex dish or drink may be quite strong and vivid, while to the untrained palate they are lost in the multitude of other flavors.

construct an object abstracted from its spatiotemporal, causal environment, certain of its properties and certain of the sensations it causes to arise within us must be given short shrift in the construction. To give them their full due would involve constructing their impact on the environment, and this would slowly extend itself thoughout the spatiotemporal world. To the extent that these properties of the object (ultimately all of them to varying degrees) are not given their full weight in the construction, the object is presented as less clear, less vivid, less fresh. One might consider as an analogy the phenomenological difference between the sound a familiar voice makes in the various environments in which we normally hear it and the radical change it undergoes in an anechoic chamber, where it is deprived of its normal richness through interaction with the environment.

Recollection$_1$ is a fairly straightforward concept. Recollection$_2$ is a little more problematic, for it is the unconscious preservation of the image isolated in recollection$_1$. Each representation we have is preserved in the "night-like abyss" of intelligence. We encountered a claim like this about the feeling soul earlier, but I said little about it then, so let me say a bit more now. First of all, there is no clear rule for individuating representations or feelings. Is the representation of a typewriter a different representation from the representation of a blue typewriter or the representation of a battered, old typewriter with thirteen keys and the ribbon missing? All our intuitions can be treated as representations, so we must take Hegel to mean that our complete intuitive experience of the world, as well as any inner intuitions we are able to develop at higher stages, is preserved in recollection$_2$. In a stretch of intuitive experience we are able to focus on any of its aspects and turn it into an image, and as potential images the whole panoply is preserved within recollection$_2$.

Second, the mode of preservation in recollection$_2$ is not correctly conceived as an anatomization and pigeonholing operation within the mind: "It is the inability to grasp the universal, which is concrete in itself while yet remaining simple, that occasioned [the notion that] particular representations are preserved in particular fibers and locations; different things are supposed also to need singularized spatial existence" (§453, my tr.). Hegel insists on the "need to grasp the Concept in its concreteness, to grasp it, as it were, as the seed which contains *affirmatively* and as a *virtual* possibility, all the determinatenesses which first come into existence in the development of the tree" (§453). It is clear that thinking of the images as preserved in pigeonholes or as stored in Locke's mental closet promotes a thorough misconception of mind, for then the images would remain independent actualities that are merely rearranged by the mind. But the images no longer *exist*, they are not discrete individuals discoverable within the mind but potentialities capable of being actualized by the mind. Locke's image of a progressively better stocked closet is exactly wrong.

Hegel heavily emphasizes the unity and simplicity of spirit exhibited by the fact that all these images are retained, but not individually and discretely. But an even more important lesson perhaps is the generative power of spirit. Hegel uses the metaphor of a seed: "the germ which contains affirmatively and as a virtual possibility, all the determinatenesses which first come into existence in the development of the tree" (§453). The infinite generative power of our minds has been a central fact in contemporary reflections on the nature of mind—but contemporary theorists have been generally concerned to show how such infinitary capabilities can rest on finite resources. Any attempt to sketch how the infinitary can be generated by the finite is noticeably absent from Hegel's works, however, for he is convinced that the finite really presupposes the infinite. The finite, he believes, might be reached by an "analysis" of the infinite (as a point, perhaps, is an analytic part of a line), but the (true) infinite cannot be generated by synthesizing finite pieces (as a line cannot be built by stringing points together).

Hegel's talk of an "abyss" also constitutes a denial that there is any privileged set of simple ideas or images into which perceptions can be decomposed and from which memory or other images can be recomposed. We preserve the whole of our experience and recall parts of it. Hegel's approach to the mind is antithetical to the contemporary cognitive scientist's analytic approach. Unfortunately, Hegel gives us no concrete suggestions about how to secure infinitary generative capacities without a set of elementary parts and combinatory operations.

It is intriguing to speculate about how Hegel would have considered an analogy drawn between the preservation of an image in this "abyss" of the mind and the preservation of a part of a picture in a hologram. There is no one-to-one correspondence between the parts of an image generated from a hologram and the parts of the hologram itself; from any part of a hologram a complete, though less detailed, image is generable. Another model of "distributed representation" is offered by a new and fascinating branch of cognitive science—connectionism. Connectionist machines can perform apparently difficult and sophisticated tasks in real time by manipulating highly interconnected networks of very simple processors. Unlike standard algorithm-crunching von Neumann machines, there are no separable memory addresses for different pieces of information, either program or data. Whatever representations are attributed to the machine cannot be localized; they are distributed across the machine. It is possible that Hegel would have found even these analogies too materialistic in their treatment of mind, but perhaps such a treatment is still fitting at this low level of representation.

These potential images hidden within the intellect would be an empty fiction unless they could be actualized, but they can be actualized only in an intuition: "To have determinate being such an abstractly preserved image needs an intuition with determinate being. Recollection properly so called is the relation of the image to an intuition, in particular as the subsumption of the immediate singular intuition under what is universal in form, under the representation that has the same content" (§454, my tr.). In recollection proper (recollection$_3$) spirit gains control over the images within it, for they are no longer present as either isolated intuitions or mere potentialities of images. In recollection$_3$ the relation between these two aspects is brought to the fore, and this somehow gives spirit this control. The paragraph is rather murky, but what Hegel is getting at is that in recollection$_1$ there has to be an actual intuition present to the mind, and the potentialities discussed under the heading of recollection$_2$ can only find their actuality in those intuitions. Spirit can, however, produce this product on its own, rather than waiting for it to be elicited by the environment: "In recollection therefore, intelligence is within itself in the determinate sensation and its intuition, and recognizes them as already its own, while at the same time it now knows its image, which in the first instance is merely internal, to be also confirmed in the immediacy of the intuition" (§454). This phrasing is a little misleading, for recognition and knowing are sophisticated cognitive acts, well beyond the

powers of this level of spiritual activity. I shall return to the interpretation of this sense of recognition below. "The image, which in
the abyss of intelligence was its property, is now, with the determination of externality, also in its [intelligence's] possession. It is
thereby at the same time posited as distinguishable from the intuition and separable from the simple night in which it is at first
immersed. Intelligence is therefore the power of being able to express what it possesses, and no longer to require external intuition
in order to have this possession existing within itself" (§454, my tr.).

Two questions are raised in §454: (a) in what sense are these
images general, and (b) what is the nature of the recognition we
gain in recollection₃? The "abstractly preserved image" is the ability
to generate the image, but insofar as this ability is itself something
general, it is a general representation. But why is it that this descen-
dant from a completely determinate intuition can be something
general? There are two ways to understand this new generality,
neither of which excludes the other. One of these involves a general
point about the nature of abilities; the other involves the specific
nature of images as Hegel conceives them.

First, there is something inherently general about abilities. Each
actual action is fully determinate; it is an individual. But I do not
think that we can make sense of having an ability that can logically
be realized in one and only one fully determinate way. I might have
the ability to commit suicide at 10:53 P.M. on March 23, 1989. Is this
an ability that has only one possible realization? True, it is necessary
that it can have only one actual realization, but there are still any
number of fully determinate possible actions that would realize this
ability. I could commit suicide with a knife, a gun, with sleeping
pills, at home, in my car, sorrowfully, or gleefully. We could add all
such conditions onto our specification of the ability, but there are
always others left unspecified. If we attempt to avoid these considerations by picking some fully determinate possible action, naming
it "Harry," and then saying that I have an ability to Harry, there are
several replies to be made. First, the context "an ability to _____"
takes a verbal-action description, not a name or singular term.
Second, if we understand this ability as "the ability to perform
Harry," there is an epistemological problem about assigning such
an ability without assigning the more general ability to perform
other Harry-like actions; our evidence could never be that complete.

Can we think of conditions under which "He has the ability to perform Harry" is justifiably assertable but "He has the ability to perform other Harry-like actions" is not? It seems to me that this makes sense only in a world so thoroughly determined that Harry is the only possibility given the whole state of the world. But if the events of this world are so thoroughly determined, it seems that the notion of an ability becomes trivialized, for things would only have "abilities" to do exactly those things they do. The abilities to construct images are standing abilities of spirit of which one realization does not exclude other earlier or later realizations (unlike the realization of an ability to commit suicide). Even though the image generated may be quite determinate, the same image can be generated again, and the generation of one particular image can also be a realization of several different abilities. In each case the realization is particular but the ability realized is general.

Second, an image, as we have seen, is an abstraction from the objective spatiotemporal order; but once we have abstracted from the spatiotemporal order and can no longer refer to it to individuate cases, the image can present any number of different objects. Locke, for instance, also saw this property of abstractions. As we shall see when we consider the imagination, the more we abstract not only from the object's spatiotemporal context but also from its own spatiotemporal features, the more suitable it becomes as a representation of a wide range of objects and properties. A recollection$_3$ of a triangle is general in being an ability to generate other perspectival views of the triangle, given the intuition of the triangle as stimulus. The image generated is general in the sense that only its internal properties are still fairly determinate, its spatiotemporal position and perhaps other individuating relational properties being abstracted from.

In recollection$_3$ we "subsume" an intuition under the abstract representation, and this constitutes a sort of low-grade *recognition* of the object. This is not full recognition, for no concepts are applied to the thing in this recognitive process. I have talked as if the one-time occurrence of an intuition is enough to preserve its image indelibly in the mind, and although this is theoretically true, from the practical standpoint it is too simple, as Hegel recognizes quite well. The strength with which a content is preserved is proportional to its repetitions within experience. "If I am to *preserve* something by recollecting it therefore, I must have the intuition of it *repeated*. In the first instance of course, the image is revived not so much by me as by the immediate intuition corresponding to it. By means of being thus frequently elicited, however, it acquires within me such a liveliness and presence, that I no longer need the external intuition in order to recollect it" (§454, *Zusatz*). When this ability to call up an image on one's own has been developed, a new and higher stage of spirit, that of the reproductive imagination, has been reached.

We can give another sense to the way a "general" representation—this ability to construct an image—subsumes an intuition, and to the way we recognize the intuition as one we have already had. It must be clear that we do not hold one intuition up against an image and compare the two, deciding that they are the same or that one is a specification of the other. Generally speaking, one thing is subsumed under a second when the first is an *instance* of the second, and this approach can be extended fairly straightforwardly to the case at hand: an actualization of an ability is an instance of it, and a specific intuition is an instance of spirit's ability to construct such an image. This still leaves unanalyzed the manner in which spirit can recognize the content of an intuition as one it has encountered before.

That which is recognized as previously encountered, as our own, is what is familiar. It is easy to fall into the trap of thinking that recognizing something involves assigning it a linguistic or conceptual tag. The recognition we speak of here is definitely prelinguistic, of a sort we might also be able to assign to animals, for instance. Seeing something as familiar does not involve comparing it to any other representation or sticking a tag on it mentally, but, phenomenologically speaking, it is presuming to know how things stand, having certain definite expectations about what would happen if. . . . This form of knowing or recognition is founded on the immediate knowledge of ease in the performance of an ability. All explicit knowing *that* is founded on a set of epistemic skills, knowing *hows*.

If I am exercising a certain skill, I do not need to look at my actions to know what I am doing or what the result of my actions ought to be. Development of a skill brings along with it immediate, noninferential knowledge that the skill is being performed during the performance. This does not mean that in the performance of the skill we are necessarily reflectively aware of the performance, but that when we do have such reflective awareness it is noninferential. Such awareness of ease in construction is immediate and noninferential, but it is not infallible, and it is based on our ability to habituate ourselves to the ordinary course of events. Through this process of familiarization and habituation, spirit gains control over its representations. There is no suggestion here that this is a will-ful learning process; at this stage we are confronted with a brute ability of spirit, one spirit can learn to control consciously, but one that does not depend on such conscious control. After repeated hearings, for instance, one can simply sing a song, without ever having made an effort to learn it. And there are different degrees to which the song can be mastered. Some people might require a good deal of prompting, that is, the repetition of part of the appropriate intuition, to be able to keep going with the song. Others eventually find no prompting at all necessary—they now know the song. Knowing a song is a knowing how, it is a skill, and the kind of knowledge of objects we possess in our recollective activities is a similar kind of knowing how. It is a kind of technical knowledge always limited by the immediate situation in its applicability and usefulness; it is not yet theoretical knowledge, which escapes the limitations of particular situations, transcending the dependence on particular sensate material that still characterizes recollection.

9

Imagination: Universality
and Signification

In Petry's edition of the *Encyclopedia*, it appears from the table of contents that Imagination is subdivided into (a) Reproductive Imagination, (b) Associative Imagination, and (c) Phantasy, which is then itself subdivided into (i) Symbol, (ii) Sign, and (iii) Language. But this division seems to be Boumann's, not Hegel's, for if attention is paid to the architectonic mentioned in the main paragraphs, it is clear that Reproductive Imagination and Associative Imagination are one and the same, and that the three divisions of Imagination are (a) Associative or Reproductive Imagination, (b) Symbolic Imagination, and (c) Sign-making Imagination. I treat them in this order.

ASSOCIATIVE OR REPRODUCTIVE IMAGINATION

Spirit, in the exercise of the ability to set images before itself which are no longer occasioned by the immediate intuition, is the reproductive imagination. As a result of spirit's having gained unconscious control over what is presented to it (which means that reference to the present intuition as stimulus is no longer necessary in the explanation of the occurrence of the mental act), the process of abstraction, analysis, and generalization which was already in evidence in recollection has become more thorough, more advanced. For now, "it is however only within the subject, in which it is preserved, that the image has the individuality in which the determinations of its content are linked together, for its immediate, i.e., its initially merely spatial and temporal concretion, its being a unit within intuition, is dissolved" (§455). In recollection, the contents of the images were still complete spatiotemporal objects as met with in intuition, although abstracted from their spatiotemporal context. But when the skills of construction have reached the sophistication involved in imaginative reproduction, the distinct determinations met with and united in the experience of a spatiotemporal object become dissociable from each other, no longer hanging altogether in natural clumps. The connection between determinations is no longer given by the general rules of construction or the particular knowledge of spirit; in forging the connection, spirit no longer follows the rules constitutive of objectivity but unites the determinations in accordance with some subjective general representation. "The reproduced content, as belonging to the self-identical unity of intelligence and produced from intelligence's universal mine shaft, has a general representation for the associative relation of images, of the representations which, in accordance with other circumstances, are more abstract or more concrete" (§455, my tr.).

The picture of mind operating in reproductive imagination which emerges from these remarks seems to be the following. In recollection, mind achieves the ability to generate images of each particular determinateness an object may possess, but intuition is still a controlling factor. In the reproductive imagination, these abilities are freely exercised, but they are not informed with a rational order either; they are governed by arbitrary associations. In more intuitive language, having only encountered red fire trucks and green lanterns, with the power of imagination I can separate and recombine these into images of green fire trucks and red lanterns. Images of particular determinations are produced, not individually without any connection, but as realizations of a more general representation, which, however, can be quite abstract, a mere association.

What we want to know is the nature of this general representation. We have already noted that images have a certain generality; we must now see that imaginative representations have a higher level of generality: "Images are already more general than intuitions; however, they still have a sensuously concrete content whose relation to other such contents I am. In that I now direct my attention to this relation I obtain general representations—representations in the proper sense of the word. For that through which the individual images relate to each other is precisely what is common to them" (§456, *Zusatz*, my tr.). Hegel goes on immediately to explain this common element: "What is common is either a certain particular aspect of the object raised to the form of universality, such as the red color of the rose for instance, or the concrete universal, the genus; in the case of the rose for instance, the plant" (§456, *Zusatz*).

We can now understand more exactly what has been accomplished in the earlier stage of recollection and here in reproductive imagination. The abstract general representation within the mind in recollection was still the representation of a particular individual object, and its generality was that of subsuming beneath it the multiplicity of intuitions in space and time to which it could give rise. Strictly speaking, it is only now, at the level of the associative imagination, that we have achieved a truly general representation, namely, the first representation of such things as redness and humanity.

It is important to note that Hegel distinguishes two different forms of universality, although they are not distinct for subjective spirit at this level: there are particular abstract properties and there are concrete universals. What is the difference, and why is it so important? Hegel himself identifies the concrete universal with the genus, and other texts make it clear that Hegel thinks of the genus of a thing as giving its essence, its concept, its ideal type, the peculiar unity among the otherwise contingent determinations which makes the thing what it is. In associative imagination both kinds of universal become indifferently available to spirit, but the associative imagination draws no distinctions between them. It is only at the stage of thought that this distinction can be made by spirit, for only at that point has spirit so systematized its own products that it can isolate the crucial nodal points within the system.

It is here within the treatment of the associative imagination that Hegel discusses briefly what he takes to be the shortcomings in the previous treatments of this subject, specifically, the notion of laws of association of ideas and of abstraction. His first attack on the laws of the association of ideas is merely terminological, for he points out that "it is not *ideas* that are associated," which is true in his system, since his definition of "idea" is quite different from any given by anyone working in the empirical tradition he is attacking. But this hardly strikes a death blow. His other criticism, however, cuts deeper. He claims that the "modes of relation" commonly considered under this heading are not *laws*, "the precise reason for this being that the same matter is subject to so *many* laws, that what occurs tends to be quite the opposite of a law in that it is capricious and contingent,—it being matter of chance whether the linking factor is an image or a category of the understanding such as equivalence and disparity, ground and consequence, etc." (§455). Associationists of the time often multiplied their "laws" beyond all plausibility (although Hume certainly did not), and when care was taken to keep the number small, they were stated vaguely enough to be quite unscientific in any case.

There is also a deeper criticism lurking here, which we can restate as follows. In physics the fundamental laws are relatively few, and they apply universally. There can be great complexity in their application, thus rendering the actual calculation and prediction of specific events practically impossible, but this is not a difficulty with the theory; it creates no problem in employing the theory to *explain* events, for they are all explained in parallel fashion. The so-called laws of psychological association, however, are in a very different situation. There are even greater difficulties with prediction—but this might at first be thought to be merely practical. What is more important is that these laws are not treated as universally applicable; in constructing a post hoc explanation, we do not mobilize the full set of laws but choose one that will give the proper result, and accordingly the other laws must not hold. In one case we invoke the law of associating resembling representations, in another case we invoke contiguity, and in a third, causation. There is, or at least seems to be on the Humean account, nothing to decide which laws get invoked until after the fact; the laws are to that extent merely ad hoc. And this points up a nonpractical difficulty in using these laws to construct predictions about what a person will think: even having specified the antecedent conditions, we cannot decide which law will be the one obeyed. Unless we have a higher-order law to give us some method of deciding this, we are in principle barred from predicting. Thus, I believe, it is not merely the multiplicity of purported associative laws which is the focal point of Hegel's criticism—Hume avowed only three and Hartley only the law of contiguity—but their *nonsystematic* multiplicity that bears the brunt of the objection. The "laws" of association simply do not share the characteristics of law-likeness with other laws.

Is this a fair objection to Hume and the other associationists? There are things the associationist can do to hold this objection off, such as insist that the laws of association are measures of the probability of a certain kind of idea following another and must be given various weights relative to the background conditions. Thus, in any particular case, prediction is not possible, since the laws are only probabilistic, but all the laws apply, just with different strengths, and all have universality and necessity. But this is not a very happy move, and I am not aware of anyone making it or a similar move at the time. Hume and the other associationists took themselves to be developing a system of laws for the operation of mind in the same way that Newton gave laws for the operation of natural systems. Hegel has seized on some of the significant differences in the formal nature of the two kinds of laws to demonstrate the inadequacy of the associationist program to its own ideal. The ideal of a predictive psychology modeled on physics never attracted Hegel in any case, of course.

Hegel is not yet finished with the associationists, however; he takes a further look at the concept of abstraction. He does not deny the legitimacy of the concept, but he does find fault with the associationists' attempts to analyze it. He claims that associationists think of the abstraction of a general representation as a kind of superimposition of similar images. This has been a common post-Lockean attempt to explain Locke's rather unfortunate pronouncement that the idea of a triangle "must be neither oblique nor rectangular, neither equilateral, equicrural, nor scalenon, but *all and none* of these at once" (*An Essay Concerning Human Understanding*, bk. IV, pt. 7, sect. ix, my emphasis). Hegel does not attack this rather confused notion of an abstract idea (which was not Locke's reflective position) straightforwardly, however; rather, he points out that with this in mind one still needs to explain how just these images get combined: "In order that this superposing may not be entirely accidental and conceptless, an attractive force or something of the kind had to be assumed between the similar images" (§455, my tr.). This remark of Hegel's immediately brings to mind one of Hume's: after discussing the principles of association that govern the mental world, Hume notes that "here is a kind of *attraction*, which in the mental world will be found to have as extraordinary effects as in the natural, and to shew itself in as many and as various forms. Its effects are every where conspicuous; but as to its causes, they are mostly unknown" (*A Treatise of Human Nature*, bk. I, pt. 1, sect. iv). But, says Hegel, it is silly to treat the bond between different images as some sort of attractive force; the bond is spirit itself.

Hegel's point is that representations have the powers they have—they are the representations they are—because of their role in a complex system. The associationists cling here to the idea that our representations are thoroughly natural and that their interactions are also as natural as the causal relations among physical particles. But the holism of representations defeats the conception, for their interactions are not atomistically determined. The system is primary, not any particular property of the representations. The "attractive force" between representations is not an empirically demonstrable entity on empiricist principles; there is no perception of it, and if there were, that perception would be just another impression. Images are not united by some intrinisic attractive force; the postulation of a natural attractive force between subjective entities constitutes a pseudo-solution to understanding their order and connection. An attempt to construct a mechanical model of the mind and of the nature of an idea or concept must fail, for it fundamentally misconstrues the nature of spiritual activity, which is not mechanical but holistic and teleological. And once spirit is recognized as this force, and the images are understood to be determined by the totality in which they participate, the road to the proper understanding of what is spiritual has been opened.

Yet to talk of a free act of spirit is not to say that the ordering of images is chaotic or indeterminate, for "intelligence itself is not only general form; rather, its inwardness is in itself determinate, concrete subjectivity with its own content or worth [*Gehalt*] which stems from some interest, implicit concept, or idea" (§456, my tr.). But how are we to understand such an internal determination? What is the mechanism of determination here? If we say that we have a form of agent causation, not mechanical causation—understanding the activity of spirit in the terms that seem to spring most quickly to mind given Hegel's own idiom—we have then set up a picture that presupposes an agent, a mind within the mind itself, the "little man" theory of mind. Clearly this is not something we want to attribute to Hegel. But agent causation is not the only alternative to mechanical causation. Another model of determination is that of an element's being determined by its place in a whole. Hegel's point is that the order of particular images and representations can often be legitimately and usefully explained by reference to the whole train in which they occur, which is itself accounted for by reference to some higher-level mental entity, such as an abiding interest or an attempt to solve a problem, which involves even further holistic reference to the mental life of the subject.

On the basis of this functional determination of mental acts, we can then reintroduce a notion of agent causation in the mental sphere, as is clearly necessary at a later stage, since we can cause thought to occur by trying to think of something, setting oneself to consider a problem, and so on.

This possibility of the holistic explanation of series of mental acts shows up another fault in naive associationism: if the associationist principles are adopted as the sole explanatory principles of mental activity, rational, goal directed thought is unintelligible—or, rather, is unintelligible *as* rational thought. On the basis of the associationist laws alone we cannot distinguish flights of fancy from well-controlled problem-solving patterns of thought. The recognition that series of thoughts come as intelligible units or wholes is the first step toward separating "the play of a thoughtless representing" (§455) from rationally informed thought itself.

Symbolic Imagination

Insofar as individual images acquire a place within a train of thought, they begin to point beyond themselves and thus begin to acquire meaning. This is the next level, the symbolic imagination, which together with sign-making imagination Hegel often calls fantasy. We must not presume that because Hegel talks here of meanings he has moved into quasi-linguistic mental activity, nor is the abstract rational content that unifies the subjective representa-

tions a "hovering presence" or a ghost. It exists *in* the representations and needs them in order to have actual existence: "Thus,
while informing [this fund of representations] with its own content,
[intelligence] is in itself determinately recollected in it—fantasy,
symbolizing, allegorizing, or poetical imagination" (§456, my tr.).
Thus a particular image of a particular rose becomes a symbol for all
roses, and it is called to mind at times in order to be the particular
embodiment of or vehicle for, for instance, a representation of
beauty. Which particular rose-image is present to mind when one is
thinking about flowers or roses or beauty is entirely unimportant,
and the explanation of the occurrence of the image does not account
for it in all its particularity, but only in its general formal features.
There are of course certain conditions the image must meet to be
eligible as a symbol for a certain general representation, namely, it
must be an image of something that shares the appropriate property: "This [fantasy] chooses, to express its general representations,
no other sensuous stuff than that whose independent meaning
corresponds to the determinate content of the universal to be imaged. So, for example, the strength of Jupiter is presented through
the eagle, since the eagle is held to be strong" (§457, *Zusatz*, my tr.).
But fantasy can operate with complex sets of symbols, and "it is
rather by a coherence of details that allegory expresses what is
subjective" (§457, *Zusatz*). This level of mental activity underlies the
possibility of art, but the discussion of the particular modes of
symbolization belongs properly to the philosophy of art and is not
discussed here at all. We can note, however, that the art of poetry,
as explicitly linguistic, is a strange hybrid between the symbolic and
the signific. It would be interesting to see how consistent with this
account of symbols and signs Hegel's treatment of poetry and art is.

Symbolic fantasy is an important turning point in mind's growth
to free self-determination, for "insofar as the content it derives from
itself has an imaged existence, intelligence is perfected into intuition of itself within phantasy" (§457). Previously what was present
to mind was best accounted for by reference either to the external
influences on mind (intuition) or to what prior experience the mind
had already accumulated together with the present intuition (representation in the lower stages). In symbol fantasy, however, this is
no longer true; the particular images, what is present to mind, are
now to be accounted for by reference to particular goals or interests

or to larger-scale chunks of spirit's life, such as character or projects. With the ability to symbolize, spirit becomes capable of dealing effectively, although still rudimentarily, with universals beyond the universals of sense. We can symbolize such universals as justice and thus begin to get an adequate grasp on what must otherwise remain beyond the power of sense or recollection. Spirit and thought are themselves nonsensible universals, and the symbolizing imagination marks a significant step toward the self-comprehension of spirit.

Let me summarize metaphorically the route we have watched spirit take. At the level of intuition spirit is, as it were, a mirror of its objective environment. It obeys set laws in reflecting the environment, but these are constant enough to be ignored for most purposes—the explanation of what plays across the face of the mirror is carried by the facts about the environment. But this will not do totally for two reasons, and our attention is directed to the mirror itself. There are or can be flaws in the mirror that need to be taken into account (illusion, madness), and, more important, the mirror itself is not a merely passive reflector—it is active within its reflection, reorganizing the input. At first the reorganization of the input seems merely a matter of adding depth or body to the reflection by including in the now increasingly multidimensional reflection afterimages and other perspectives of the objects reflected, but we then notice that some images now are "shadowed" with related but non-coobjectual images, and that these shadows group the images into new suborganizations. We also find some images unrelated to anything in the immediate environment. In our explanations of why the mirror's overall image is what it is, we find these shadows to be of increasing importance, and by grouping them into similarity classes we can develop theories of the character of various mirrors, what their interests are, and so on—and these theories simplify our now otherwise incredibly complex task of explaining why they reflect the images they do.

Sign-making Imagination

In that spirit only begins at the level of symbolic fantasy to determine itself, to determine its own content, it is only relatively free, for to embody the general representation it must find an image that exemplifies that property. Spirit advances to sign-making fantasy, for the sign is an arbitrary vehicle for the universal content of spirit, and in the sign spirit achieves a higher measure of freedom. But the transition from symbolic to sign-making fantasy is not clear in the *Encyclopedia*; it seems the proper move, but just how is it effected? Hegel points out several times that the symbol is subjective, and he maintains that this failing is overcome in the sign. "Subjective" is a protean word in Hegel's philosophy, and each of its occurrences demands our attention.

In using "subjective" here Hegel is clearly not pointing out the mentality of the image that serves as symbol. Insofar as we are dealing with mental images here this needs no pointing out; but if we extend our discussion to include artistic images, which Hegel seems to allow, then we are no longer limited to mental images at all. In what other sense are all these things subjective? If the ontological status of the symbols is not relevant, then I suggest that the link between symbol and symbolized is. There is a purely natural connection between the two in that they share common properties. But this does not account for the choice of a particular image as a symbol, for there are presumably many other images that share the natural link to the symbolized. There is no rule to decide what symbolizes what, and no common agreement is necessary for something to be a symbol to someone. To this extent the link between symbol and symbolized is subjective and up to the whim of the agent. In the sign, this subjectivity is supposed to be overcome, but as the sign is also an arbitrarily chosen entity that stands for another, is the sign-signified link not just as subjective? It is subjective, but this case is different in an important aspect. There is no longer a natural link between sign and signified. Whereas symbols can be varied relatively arbitrarily on the assumption that the natural link between symbol and symbolized will carry the brunt of the symbolic labor, such an assumption can no longer be made about signs. Precisely because the link between sign and signified is totally arbitrary, it must be held to consistently; the arbitrary linkage has become the essential tie.[1]

---

1. Even in a private language, if such is possible, the sign-signified relations must be held to consistently if they are to exist at all.

Any semantic relation must depend on certain uniformities. In the case of the symbol-symbolized relation, the crucial uniformities are intrinsic to the respective contents, but the existence of a particular symbol-symbolized relation is dependent on fully arbitrary choice. In the sign-signified relation the crucial uniformity is none other than the continued observance of a once-arbitrary correlation. The original correlation was fully arbitrary, but the existence of a particular sign-signified relation depends on its having become a rule, an objective fact, that the two are correlated.

If this is the sense in which a sign is a more objective embodiment of spirit's representation, why is this to be seen as an advance beyond the more subjective symbol? Because, in making a sign, spirit has broken still further from being determined and has become to an even greater extent the determining factor in its own existence. "In its use of intuition therefore, intelligence displays more willfulness and sovereignty in *designating* than it does in symbolizing (§458)." For in the sign the particular content of the intuition employed has become fully unimportant; it must, of course, have a content, but which content is fully arbitrary. In creating signs "from its own self, [intelligence] then gives its independent representation a definite determinate being, *using* the filled space and time, the intuition *as its own*, effacing its immediate and proper content, and giving it another content as significance and soul" (§458, my tr.). The sign-signified relation is higher than the symbol-symbolized relation because the activity of spirit is now fully responsible for the link. Further, because there need not be a direct sharing of properties between sign and signified, more complex, more abstract, more universal contents can be easily signified than can be symbolized, and thus spirit is able to possess these more abstract contents determinately in the sign.

The sign-making fantasy seems to mark a watershed for spirit in that, due to the markedly increased ability to deal with universals that such signs afford, a significant advance can be made in spirit's self-comprehension, and in particular in spirit's ability to give itself concrete embodiment and expression. "Intelligence *qua* reason starts by appropriating to itself the immediacy it finds within itself . . . , that is, by determining it as *universal*; from here on its activity as reason (§438) is to determine as *being* what is perfected (completed) to the concrete intuition of itself within it, that is, to

make itself into *being*, into the *subject matter* [*Sache*]" (§457, my tr.).
In earlier stages the emphasis was on unfolding the universal content of the "found" material. The emphasis now shifts, however, to
individualizing and expressing the universal, the proper content of
spirit, spirit's inner nature. "It is to be emphasized that insofar as
fantasy brings the inner content [*Gehalt*] to image and intuition and
this is expressed by [fantasy's] determining it as having being, the
expression that intelligence makes itself *be* or makes itself into a
thing should not seem peculiar, for its content [*Gehalt*] is intelligence itself, as is the determination intelligence gives the content"
(§457, my tr.).

Spirit's self-comprehension makes its first recognizable appearance here, but it is still severely limited by the mode of universality
available to sign-making fantasy, for it is confined to the abstract
universal and is therefore merely formal. "The formations of phantasy are recognized everywhere as such unifications of what is
proper and internal to spirit [the universal] with what is intuitable
[the singular]; . . . As the activity of this unification, phantasy is
reason, but insofar as the capacity [content, *Gehalt*] of phantasy as
such is a matter of indifference, it is merely *formal* reason, whereas
reason as such determines the truth of the content" (§457).

We are now on the brink of language, but we must be aware that
not all signs are linguistic signs. Hegel's first examples of signs are
cockades, flags, and gravestones. These are signs, for their link
with what they signify is fully arbitrary and conventional. Indeed,
to the extent that they lack the semantic structure we find in language, they are more adequate examples of signs than words are,
for linguistic structure looks beyond the imaginative activities we
have been discussing, anticipating the standpoint of thought, of the
understanding in particular. The ability to create signs Hegel calls
the productive memory; he reserves the term "memory" (*Gedächtnis*)[2] for sign-using mental activity, "for although in general usage
memory is often taken to be interchangeable and synonymous with
recollection, and even with representation and imagination, it is
never concerned with anything but signs" (§458).

2. Unlike *Erinnerung* (etymologically, "inwardizing"), which we translate "recollection," *Gedächtnis* seems to be derived from the past participle of "to think."
Perhaps it is for this reason that Hegel uses it for the higher activity of signification.

Although language itself is the product of the later stage, memory, Hegel devotes a good deal of time in §459 to a discussion of the nature of the linguistic sign per se, for the linguistic sign, in particular not the written sign but the spoken, exhibits the nature of being a sign most fully. As a sign, "intuition . . . acquires the essential determination of having being only as a sublatedness. . . . In its truer shape, the intuition of a sign is therefore a determinate being within *time*—determinate being which disappears in that it has being, while in accordance with its further external, psychical determinateness it is the positedness of the *tone*, which intelligence furnishes from the anthropological resources of its own naturalness, the fulfillment of the expressiveness by which inwardness makes itself known" (§459).

Spirit's being is spatial and temporal, but since space is static and time active and moving, spirit expresses itself more adequately in time than in space. The tone is "physicalized *time*" (§401, *Zusatz*), and, in the tone, space and time find a relation that parallels the abstract nature of their relation in spirit itself to a surprising degree. "For in the tone, corporeality becomes posited temporally as motion, as an internal oscillation of the body, a vibration, as a mechanical shock through which the body as a whole moves only its parts without having to alter its relative place, sublates its indifferent juxtaposition by positing its inner spatiality temporally, and by this sublation allows its pure inwardness to emerge from the superficial alteration brought about by the mechanical shock, before immediately restoring itself" (§401, *Zusatz*). In the tone, the activity of spirit is evident as activity, rather than as frozen in the spatial self-externality of the written word.

Hegel is attempting here to give a proof that spoken language is metaphysically or ontologically prior to written language, an attempt that depends both on his analysis of the nature of spirit and on certain theses of his philosophy of nature. The attempt does not succeed, for we can no longer take all his premises seriously. But from this priority Hegel derives the superiority of alphabetic over hieroglyphic writing systems, since in an alphabetic system the signs do not directly signify representations but rather signify the tones that are naturally used to signify representations. Insofar as the alphabetic system is an encoding of the phonemic system, which is both temporally and metaphysically prior to it, it is both a more adequate or proper and a more efficient expression of spirit than a hieroglyphic system. Hieroglyphic systems, for instance, tend to be tainted with symbolism rather than being pure signs. There is, however, no sudden break between symbolic and sign systems, for our spoken language has its roots in the onomatopoeic replication of natural sounds. But, as elsewhere in Hegel's thought, the fact that onomatopoeia is only the beginning of language shows that it is the lowest level, unessential (§459).

10

Memory: Language as
the Material of Thought

SIGNIFICATION AND LANGUAGE

At the level of sign-making imagination we have sign making only in its genesis. The immediate cry welling up from within, the grunt that only later comes to be attached to an object or situation—these are better illustrations of sign-making imagination than the more complex activities of highly trained language users. "The name is initially a *single* transient production, and the connection of the representation as something inner with the intuition as something external, is itself *external*" (§460, my tr.).

In the section on memory we watch this attempt of spirit to indicate and embody itself gain objectivity and independence, become stable and meaningful, and then get left behind by spirit as something still too external, atomistic, and passive to properly express spirit's nature as spirit then transcends symbols and signs to realize itself as pure thought. The word is itself something intuited, something perceived; consequently it too is subject to the generalizing activity of representation which gives rise to signs in the first place. But the recollection of a word is not the same as the recollection of the sound constituting the word, for sounds can at best be tokens of words—and even so one can hear a sound as a sound yet not hear it as a word, if, for instance, one does not know the language. So the recollection of a word is no longer the recollection of a mere intuition but the recollection of a significant intuition, one that already embeds within it a prior recollecting. To clarify this difference, let us look more closely at Hegel's conception of the signification relation before we turn to the paragraphs on memory.

The theory of meaning plays a central role in contemporary epistemology and metaphysics, so we find ourselves naturally putting great weight on the theory of meaning when we turn to the examination of a past philosophy. But to some extent the emphasis on the theory of meaning can be misleading; as crucial a role as pre-twentieth-century philosophy may have accorded language, language was not thought to be the key to resolving most epistemological and metaphysical problems.[1] Hegel was still under the influence of the (by then old) new way of ideas, according to which the primary explanandum was our *understanding* of the world, not our ability to speak correctly about it. It was taken for granted that language's connection with the world is quite indirect; words are signs or marks for ideas and gain meaning or reference to objects only because their immediate significations are ideas, mental acts, that have antecedent connection with the objects. Locke insists on this understanding of signification and claims that to try to make words signify something other than the ideas of the speaker "would be to make them signs of nothing, sounds without significance" (*An Essay Concerning Human Understanding*, bk III, pt. 2, sect. 2)

It is within this tradition that Hegel is working. When Hegel says, for instance, that a word signifies a representation, he clearly does not mean that all we can talk about is our representations. Hegel is concerned here to understand the role language plays in the economy of the individual spirit as a being that comprehends his world.

For Locke language plays no essential role in the constitution of experience or knowledge; language opens up experience in that through language we have access to the experience of others, but our basic experience of the world is not affected by language or the lack of it. According to Locke, language's role is the communication of thoughts to another, which is only a supplement to the ideational process, not an essential part of it. In Hegel's theory, on the contrary, language is essentially involved in the process of thinking.

---

1. Ian Hacking argues that Locke, Arnauld, and others working within the new way of ideas had no theory of meaning as we presently understand the term, and that to expect them to deal with our problems leads to misunderstanding and disappointment; see *Why Does Language Matter to Philosophy?*.

Hegel does not believe that one could have a full, rich cognitive life without language; indeed, language is a necessary presupposition and concomitant of thought, according to Hegel, and is therefore not a mere adjunct that conveniently allows us to communicate with others. Language plays a necessary role in the development of the richness and complexity of our mental life; it is essential for spirit's ability to instantiate reason.

Whereas Locke tends to think of the ideas words signify as images, Hegel by no means thinks of the representations signified by words as particular images. Locke, of course, founders when confronted with words like "or," "every," or "when," for it seems impossible to come up with an image they could signify. Hegel, on the other hand, has told us that the signified representations are abilities to generate images either on the occasion of external causal affection or freely, that is, determined from within. Locke talks as if the ideas are images of objects; for Hegel the representations are generals that find their being in and subsume mental individuals, namely, intuitions. He acknowledges that "the formal factor in language is, however, the work of the understanding, which informs it with its categories, and it is this logical instinct that gives rise to what is grammatical" (§459). The understanding, we shall see, is concerned with the universal articulation of experience, and the logical operators or grammatical words in a language signify, not images of objects, but the ability to structure images and representations in general in a certain way and to recognize that structure in our experience. Bluntly put, "and" signifies the ability to conjoin images and representations and the (same) ability to experience a conjunction of items as a conjunction. This is why the grammatical, structural principles of the understanding and reason must already be at work in intuition, even though they only "come to consciousness" in the higher, still more reflective stages of the Psychology.

By having words that signify our mental activities or abilities, we can invoke those abilities without having to use them. Language performs the immensely useful (indeed, necessary) task of distilling the complex abilities of mind into simple form; a general representation, "however rich a content it may include, is still for the mind simple in the name." I may have, for instance, the general representation of a democracy, which means having the ability to recognize a democracy and the ability to generate images on my own of situations that count as democratic.[2] Democracy is a general notion, and for me to have an actual thought of democracy it must be embodied in something singular, such as images. But if our images were always as complex as the phenomenon in question, it would be very difficult for our finite, limited minds to do much thinking at all. Rather than thinking about democracy by the complex *use* of my ability to intuit and imagine one, I think about a democracy through the *mention* of this ability in the simple use of a word. The connection between the word and the general representation is immediate; the word, as it were, goes proxy for the representation: "With the name lion we need neither the intuition of such an animal, nor even the image; rather, the name, in that we understand it, is the image-less, simple representation. We think in names" (§462, my tr.).

The fact that words allow one, if not totally to dispense with intuition and the sensible, at least to minimize the direct involvement of complex sensate constructions in the higher mental activities of man, is also important to Hegel, for this is yet another stage in the progressive sublation of sensation. The particularities of sensation become less and less important. It is certainly impossible for a congenitally blind man to possess a direct image of red, but he can acquire the use of the word "red" and thus an indirect ability to recognize cases of red, not on the basis of direct perception, but on the basis of descriptions, meter readings, and so forth. Thus Hegel, unlike a severe empiricist, need not deny a representation of red to a well-educated blind man. The empiricist tends to think that the ability to recognize red directly is essential to the representation of redness, but for Hegel the former ability is not essential to representing redness, to being able to reason correctly about redness. The sensation of red is something subjective, itself noncognitive, and it gives us only the nonconceptual occasion for forming the representation of red.

This analysis leaves some problems. Clearly the abilities that, on my account, constitute the representation of red can be quite different for a blind man and a sighted man; by what right do we call them representations of the same thing, and how is intersubjective communication between the two possible, given that the representations invoked by the word "red" could be disparate? We have

2. There is no reason to think that the images generated must be static, or of individual objects; an image of a democracy might be a montage of images of actions—people voting, an assembly convening, etc.

been treating having a representation of red as basically having the ability to recognize red things in a wide range of actual and possible circumstances. But the ability to recognize something cannot be simply the ability to attach a label, for that is what we are trying to explain. It rather comes down to an ability to generate in image an appropriate similarity class of situations and an ability to respond appropriately in other ways. The blind and the sighted man can agree, by and large, on which situations count as similar in this respect even if their criteria, their ways of telling, are different. There may be some minor divergence due to the vagueness of the term "red," but we do not need exact correspondence. Large-scale intersubjective agreement is sufficient at our present level.

The most important aspect of language, however, is that the complex abilities of spirit to generate images and recognize things can now be replaced by the relatively simpler ability to use words. Words are simpler elements standing for complexes, and to that extent they are something like abbreviations. They are of course more, for the intuitions that are words themselves go through the process of recollection, and the representative powers of spirit reflect on themselves, creating still higher levels.[3] This first reflection occurs at the lowest level of memory, to the examination of which we now turn.

THE STAGES OF MEMORY

The section on memory is subdivided into three subsections: they are, roughly speaking, (a) recollective or name-retaining memory, (b) reproductive or imaginative memory, and (c) mechanical memory, which is, so to speak, memory memorized.

Recollective Memory

Recollective memory is the analysis of the activity of understanding words at the level of recollection$_3$. "Making that connection,

---

3. There may be interesting analogies between the way words function in Hegel's theory and the way function names operate in a computer language such as LISP. If a large number of complex functions are defined in the computer language, an extremely complex program can be expressed very simply and elegantly, because each function is itself very complex. Furthermore, in LISP there is no distinction between program and data; everything is a function.

which the sign is, its own, intelligence raises the single connection to a universal, that is enduring connection, through this recollection, in which name and meaning are objectively combined for it, and makes the intuition, which the name initially is, to a representation, so that the content, the meaning, and the sign are identified, are one representation" (§461, my tr.).

The sound is originally a single spontaneous production of spirit which expresses or signifies spirit's representation. But, by recollecting the sound with its connection to the representation, spirit constructs a standing connection; the word as significant is now present within spirit as an abstractly preserved image that is called forth by the appropriately related intuitions. Once again, the "abstractly preserved image" is nothing more than the ability to recognize and appropriately respond to a word given the appropriate intuition. But already at this level the connection between the sign and what it signifies has become objective: "The primary thing here is that we retain the meaning of names—that we become able, with the linguistic sign, to recollect the representations objectively linked to them" (§461, *Zusatz,* my tr.). Note that Hegel is not saying here that, on hearing a word, an image of something to which the word applies comes into our heads, but rather that at this stage knowing the meaning of a word does mean that one has the ability to generate such images; the word signifies the ability, not the images. This is what is most important for Hegel, for insofar as the word goes proxy for the representation, in order for us to have an actual mental presentation of the content of a general representation we need no longer invoke the imagistic abilities involved in it. We can dispense with all actual images, for, if necessary, we can construct or generate the necessary images given the words. Things are now presented to us through words. The connection between sign and signified is now fully objective [*Objektiv*] because, having been generalized through the activity of recollection, it no longer depends on the whim or immediate urge of an individual subjective spirit.

Reproductive Memory

Insofar as the process of full appropriation of verbal signs has been accomplished, the stage of reproductive memory has been reached: "The name is the subject matter [*Sache*], as it is present in the realm of representation and has validity. The *reproductive* memory, with neither intuition nor image, possesses and recognizes the subject matter in the name, and with the subject matter the name" (§462, my tr.). A content of representation can be either an individual spatiotemporal thing or an abstractum such as justice; in either case, for actual representation there must be a determinate individual presented to mind that acts as the vehicle or embodiment of the content.[4] In the lower stages of representation we must re-present the thing itself, which makes the representation of abstracta (contents peculiar to spirit itself) impossible. At a higher level we can substitute a symbol for the thing itself, and finally an arbitrary sign serves as the representation of the thing and the content of the mental act is embodied in a foreign matter. Insofar as we recollect this matter as a sign, we create an ability that embeds another, for the recollection of the sign is an ability to represent the connection between sign and signified, which last is itself an ability.

We can set out the parallelism between stages of representation and stages of memory as follows. We have analyzed the recollection of a lion as the ability to re-present the lion, as knowing how to construct the lion from sensate material and how to respond to such intuitions. The recollection of "lion" is the ability to re-present "lion" *as a sign*—that is, to construct "lion" in its relation to the ability to represent lions. In reproductive imagination we achieve a general representation of lion, the ability to re-present not just *a* lion, or a class of similar-looking lions, but lions in general—that is, to construct lions from sensate material. The reproductive memory of "lion" is the ability to represent "lion"s,—that is, to construct "lion"s from our sensate material. In recollective memory we are still re-presenting word tokens, and in reproductive memory, I believe, we move up to the re-presentation of word types. Again there are embedded abilities in reproductive memory, for the re-presentation of "lion"s as signs involves the implicit reference to what they signify, itself an ability. But the embedded ability need exist only implicitly—to represent "lion" as a meaningful sign, I need not actually exercise the ability it signifies; and an unexercised

4. Spatiotemporal "individuals" are almost as much general things for Hegel as, for instance, properties such as redness; individuals have properties in common, and properties have individuals in common; which way one slices the pie is a matter of indifference.

ability, having nothing actually embodying it, remains a mere potency and thus is not realized in any mental act at the time.

Thus through our use of words we have eliminated the need for intuitions and images of the things we represent. The things we represent exist for us in the names themselves: "As the existence of the content within intelligence, the name is intelligence's internal self-externality, and as the intuition brought forth from intelligence, the recollection of the name is at the same time the externalization in which intelligence posits itself within its own self" (§462). This passage, so confusing in its statement, is explicated in the following passage from the *Zusatz*:

> Although the spoken word vanishes in time, and time therefore displays itself in the words as an abstract or merely destructive negativity, the truly concrete negativity of the linguistic sign is intelligence, since it is through intelligence that it is changed from an externality into an internality, and preserved in this altered form. It is thus that words become a determinate being animated by thought. This determinate being is absolutely necessary to our thoughts. We only know of our thoughts, only have thoughts which are determinate and actual, when we give them the general form of objectivity, of being different from our inwardness, i.e., the shape of externality—and moreover of an externality which at the same time bears the stamp of supreme inwardness. (§462, *Zusatz*)

Thought is general; its form and its content are general, and it is mere appearance that we can *think* the individual. But the general cannot exist without the individual; if something general is to be one of an "indefinite multitude of existents as reflected-into-themselves, which at the same time are correlative, and form a world of reciprocal dependence and of infinite interconnection between grounds and consequents" (§123), it must individualize itself and become a determinate one among many. The general contents of theoretical spirit are most adequately individualized and given a determinate being through words, for, since words are the free production of spirit, unlike intuition and even images, they are immediately presented to mind as imbued and informed with spirituality. Words have a thoroughly mundane existence as sounds, but what they are—words—is essentially the expression of the spiritual. Without such an expression spirit would remain unarticulated generality. Implicit in this view is the thesis that the individuation and identity criteria for words give us the individuation and identity criteria for thoughts, and thus, although they are not the same as words (words are in a language, for instance, whereas representations and thoughts are not), our only access to the thoughts we have is through and in words. Further discussion of this difficult topic must await our examination of thought itself in Chapters 11 and 12.

Thought and reason are essentially systematic; insofar as language considered at the level of memory has not yet attained the level of thought, and thus is not yet systematized, the individual signs are not systematically joined but simply follow one another in our heads as we experience the world and respond to it verbally. In intuition or representation we "run through series of" (§462) words internally with no particular connection between them. The move to names within grammatical structures rather than lists depends on language use being informed with thought. In the grammatical structures available in language we can do more than simply name our representations; we have the ability to think about them, to reflect on their relations and internal structure. The representations this reflection gives rise to are themselves capable of being named.

Mechanical Memory

The reproductive memory itself does no more than set the foundations for the complex activity of language use. The next stage, what Hegel calls mechanical memory, presents us with a rather surprising move in which spirit, which in the previous few stages of its activity had been trying to express itself ever more fully, now divorces itself from its product, the words, rendering them senseless. This is the last stage of representative spirit and the transition to thought itself.

Hegel's concept of mechanical memory poses many problems for us, for on Hegel's own admission, "to grasp the placing and significance of memory and to comprehend its organic connection with thought in the systematization of intelligence, is one of the hitherto wholly unconsidered and in fact one of the most difficult points in the doctrine of spirit" (§464). Mechanical memory is crucial in Hegel's account, for it constitutes the point of transition from representation to thought—even though it seems itself to be the antithesis of thinking.

Briefly and bluntly put, in mechanical memory, spirit is once again divided into a multiplicity of simple elements that "appear as something found" (§463) on the one hand and as a purely abstract container holding them together on the other. We have seen similar stages earlier in spirit's progress, for instance at the stages of feeling and habit. But as we shall see, there are significant differences, for the elements at this point are of a radically different nature.

Hegel's manner of speaking about this stage is fairly confusing. He talks of subjectivity here being the "universal space" of "senseless words" and spends a disproportionate amount of time unfolding the analogy to rote memorization, which analogy I find not particularly illuminating unless one already understands his interpretation of memory sufficiently well to see why it serves as the example. The interpretation Hegel has in mind may be briefly put as follows. In reproductive memory an important new wrinkle enters the picture of mind Hegel has been sketching: mind explicitly presents itself to itself insofar as in the general representation of a word the link between the sign and the signified is represented, for in order to do this, the signified, which is itself a general representation, something subjective that needs an objectivity in order to achieve actuality, must itself be at least implicitly represented. Thus the general representation lion is included implicitly in the general representation 'lion'. But this latter general representation can itself be named, signified—as indeed we have done with the word "lion." Any representative ability of mind can be named. We have already seen that names come to replace images and intuitions. If we take the process of naming to its extreme and abstract from the necessarily ongoing intuitions and representations in the mind, what is left? "At the same time however, this taking up [of the heart of the matter in the word] also has the further significance of intelligence making a matter [*Sache*] of itself, so that subjectivity, in that it is different from the matter, becomes something that is quite empty.—The spiritless reservoir of words that constitutes *mechanical* memory" (§462, *Zusatz*).

We certainly have a mess of names left—but what else? Any actual ability of mind to represent either intuitions, images, or names is itself named and replaced by the name. Yet we cannot say that all we have left is a large collection of names, for undoubtedly spirit itself is not identical with these names, these externalizations of itself, its products; yet it is nothing in particular over against them, for otherwise it would have been particularized in a name and replaced. Still, something must be left to account for the coexistence and occurrence of series of names. "The I, which is the abstract being, is, as subjectivity, at the same time the power of the different names, the empty bond that fixes series of them in itself and keeps them in stable order" (§463, my tr.). Another way to put this is to point out that none of the particular representative abilities of spirit exhaust spirit. The particular abilities of spirit can be named insofar as they are particular—"intelligence is however the universal, the simple truth of its particular externalizations" (§463). There can be no real name for spirit because naming particularizes, and spirit can never be reduced to a particular.

This account of the nominalization of subjectivity explains Hegel's talk of subjectivity as a space of or abstract power over words, but we still need to see how it is that words have become "meaningless" at this stage. This is particularly important, for, just as words have become meaningless in mechanical memory, Hegel claims that thought itself "no longer has a meaning" (§464). It seems at best incongruous to attribute meaninglessness to thought, so we must understand just what is involved in the denial of meaning to thought.

Having a meaning is, according to Hegel, a relational characteristic of intuitions; an intuition has meaning when it stands in the signifying relation to a general representation, which is then its meaning. But given this state of affairs, we can ask several revealing questions. What are the relations between these various products of intelligence, the words? And second, if we carry through the "nominalization" of spirit discussed above, what is left of this notion of meaning?

The answer to our first question is that the only relations that exist between words at this stage are accidental juxtapositions as spirit runs through them in series in reaction to its internal and external environment. That there are only accidental relations between any words here can be demonstrated as follows. Each general representation is different from every other, even though it is not clear just what the criteria of individuation are. Still, each general representation receives a name, which is its simple presentation to mind. That must mean that, qua name, no name admits of analysis; it is the simple presentation of a general representation. The general representation of a male sibling receives, for instance, the name "brother." But as this is its *simple* presentation to mind, it is not itself capable of analysis, and neither does subjective spirit have the conceptual tools at this stage to perform any acts of analysis. Thus in our minimal verbal reactions to our environment it may well be the case that "brother" always occurs together with "male" and "sibling" as we survey our world, but there is at this level insufficient structure for spirit to construct the assertion that brothers are male siblings. Our words at this stage are linked in parallel with the representations they express, and the representations still retain priority. In the second edition of the *Encyclopedia* (1827) this point is made adequately clear in a paragraph Hegel later replaced with the present §463: "There is a general multiplicity of words, and insofar as they are as such mutually contingent, there is nothing but ego and this multiplicity" (*PSS*, vol. 3, p. 207). To the extent that we do not yet have a language *system*, the words are meaningless (in our sense), since any kind of definition, either explicit or implicit, is impossible.

In answer to our second question, if the nominalization of spirit is carried through, then the general representations have lost distinct actuality, for they are abilities to generate images, abilities that, with the dominance of words, have become otiose. These image-generating abilities remain actual, then, only insofar as they are themselves represented in the general representation of the word that signifies them. But insofar as the word replaces the images that are the actualization of the general representation it signifies, the word replaces the general representation itself and makes it unnecessary. The word thus becomes meaningless, since it has now lost that toward which it bore the meaning relation. Clearly this never occurs so baldly in the human, for, even while we are verbalizing, we are also intuiting, recollecting, imagining, and thus invoking the abilities to image. But the point is that these activities are separable from the verbal activities we have been investigating. They are surely the presuppositions for verbal abilities in that without them verbal abilities would be impossible to acquire, but once those abilities have been acquired we can "dispense" with the lower abilities on which they are built, except insofar as the lower abilities actually constitute a part of the higher. Once we have an appropriate stock of words, we no longer need images. But then to the extent that our imagistic abilities have been rendered otiose and superfluous, the words that name those abilities have become meaningless. Becoming meaningless thus means becoming independent of the original imagistic base, and such meaninglessness becomes more and more prominent, particularly as linguistic sophistication increases and, as an activity of thought, new words are gained through definition in terms of already familiar words. In philosophy in particular it is important to divorce the words one uses from the shallow imagistic bases that may still cling to some of them, for in those abstract reaches images only confuse the matter, introducing contingent elements into a necessary discipline.

We are now finally in a position to understand why Hegel calls this stage mechanical memory and compares it so often to the phenomenon of rote memorization. Insofar as the imagistic abilities have been replaced by words, which, however, are not yet systematized by thought, the words are mere counters, series of which are produced by subjectivity with no necessary order or connection between them. This situation is similar to that of rote memorization, the perfect example of which for Hegel's purposes is, not the actor recreating a character in a scene, but a schoolboy ticking off the words of a poem expressionlessly, neither understanding what is said nor even calling up the images the poet tries to evoke. The poem has been reduced to a mere series of words, and nothing at all is "going through the child's head."

> The ability to retain by rote series of words the connectedness of which is devoid of understanding, or which by themselves are as senseless as a series of names might be, is therefore so truly remarkable on account of its being the essence of spirit to be with itself [*bei sich*], whereas here it is as it were inwardly externalized, its activity seeming to be a mechanism. Spirit is with itself only as the unity of subjectivity and objectivity however; and here in memory, after being initially external and so finding determinations in intuition, and recollecting and appropriating what is found in presentation [*Vorstellung*], it makes itself

inwardly into an externality as memory, so that what it has appropriated appears as something found. *Objectivity,* which is one of the moments of thought, is here posited within intelligence itself as a quality pertaining to it. (§463)

What we have in spirit at the level of mechanical memory is a reliable verbal responder, someone whose "language" skills are purely Skinnerian, untouched by the formal syntactic and semantic structures indigenous to real thought, someone whose references have roots but not fruits.

Hegel's account of mechanical memory is far from unproblematic. If words are, as I suggested earlier, our access to "general representations," then each person has a limited number of such general representations, and different people can have sets of general representations that diverge to a significant degree. But more important, if at this stage the structure of language is not present, what sense can we make of talking about words in any case? We are confronted with the modern dictum that words have meanings only in the context of a sentence, which seems to be precisely what Hegel is denying. There is of course ambiguity in Hegel's use of the word "meaning" and its meaning in the Fregean dictum. But even so, the problem still remains of differentiating between a word properly so called and other verbal signs such as the ejaculation "Ow!" With the machinery available to him here, it is unlikely that Hegel can make the distinction. Is this, however, a problem for him? Should he be able to make that distinction here? I see nothing in his task indicating that he should. With the machinery he has he can explain the fact that "Ow!" has a significance that is conventional but objective; the fact that it is a rather peculiar part of speech, one that does not enter normally into syntactic combination with other verbal signs to form sentences, is not yet in his purview. Hegel is setting up what he takes to be the foundation of highly sophisticated, thought-imbued, linguistic activity. The social practices necessary for such a sophisticated activity find their discussion elsewhere.[5]

In the process of replacing representations by words it is clear that, whatever level we are at, we can always go higher. But could

---

5. The best survey of the role of language in Hegel's philosophy that I know of is T. Bodammer, *Hegel's Deutung der Sprache.*

this process come to an end; could we reach a point at which there are only words, and no abilities? Clearly not; it is impossible for a mind to be a mechanical memory and nothing else and to still be a mind. But again this is not a problem for Hegel, for he takes mechanical memory to be, not a separable faculty of mind, nor a distinct stage in the growth of a thinker, but a form of activity that can be isolated within, but not separated from, the complex activities of a thinking being. One must pay careful attention to the task Hegel concerns himself with at each level of analysis; it is easy to think that he is trying to do more at each stage than he actually intends.

There is one major problem left: how does mechanical memory constitute the transition to thought? The full answer to this question requires the complete account of thought, which is the subject of Chapters 11 and 12, but we can point the way now. In thought spirit almost begins again from the beginning; as in feeling, subjectivity is the merely abstract and indeterminate unifying power that stands over against its material. But there is now a significant difference in the material. No longer mere sensations, the material of thought is loaded with implicit internal structure, for words are the material of thought. The paradigmatic activity of thought will be rational discourse, the systematization of words, although thought infects, informs, and affects every level of spiritual life.

Because its material is words, thought has broken away from any immediate dependence on intuition and sensuous experience. Furthermore, in its systematization of words, which we can view metaphorically as the construction of an ideal language, particular contingent truths are not what is sought, qua thought. Any particular unification of words, such as "The cat is on the mat," which is contingent, is a *representative* use of thought's structures; thought itself is concerned with necessary, systematic connections between words, and, insofar as it treats the words only with respect to their necessary connections, the words are raised to signs of concepts, not mere general representations.

Mechanical memory is the transition to thought because it represents the point at which thought can begin to realize itself as the pure activity of organizing and uniting words: "Reason now exists in the subject as its activity, and as such is *thought*" (§464).

11

Representing versus Thinking

In Hegel's account of the increasing generality of spirit's productions, the theory of the structure of representations may seem an attempt to solve the problem of generality by sophisticating the perception-based "new way of ideas" found in Locke and Hume. But in the long run, Hegel believes, all such approaches fall short of a full explanation of the nature of thought, for real thinking is something that differs in kind, not just in degree, from the imagistic abilities of representing. My task in this chapter is to explain Hegel's distinction between representing and thinking in preparation for our examination of his theory of the structure of thought in the following chapter.

TRADITIONAL ACCOUNTS OF THOUGHT

The Classical and Symbolist Theories of Mind

According to H. H. Price, there have been two major approaches to explaining what it is to have a concept, the classical and the symbolist theories.[1] In the classical theory, whose heritage extends at least to Plato, having a concept is a relation to a special sort of object, usually called a concept or a universal. The kind of relation the thinking mind has to this object is most often conceived as analogous to sight, a version of the classical theory which Price calls

---

1. This distinction is taken from H. H. Price, *Thinking and Experience.*

inspectivism. Opposed to this rich tradition stands the more radical approach of the symbolists. On this approach, having a concept consists of possessing a certain ability, in particular, the ability to engage in symbolic activity. "The symbolist philosophers, when *they* talk of concepts or abstract ideas, treat them not as inspectable entities ('objects of thought') but as dispositions or capacities. To possess a concept, they tell us, is just to have the acquired capacity for using one or another sort of general symbol."[2] The symbolists take the basic sense of having a concept to be dispositional—the disposition being acquired (at least in the case of simple concepts) by abstraction from an encounter with an instance of the concept through sense experience. Using the concept is a later actualization of such a disposition. Those who take images as primary and words as secondary symbols that must be understood in terms of the primary symbols (Price cites Berkeley) are called imagists; those who take words to be the primary signs or symbols with which we think Price calls nominalists.[3]

Neither classical nor symbolist accounts of the nature of thought are necessarily representational, that is, committed to the view that thought is to be understood in terms of the thinker's possession of an inner representational system that bears some semantic relation to the world. Nonrepresentational symbolism has been given a spirited defense by Gilbert Ryle. But once one says that thinking is overt symbolic activity, the move to admitting that there is also covert symbolic activity within an internal representational system seems irresistible, given the variety and richness of intelligent human activity. The pressures on the classical view to posit an internal representational system seem not nearly so strong, since the

2. Ibid., p. 309. Hegel and Price both use "symbol" and "sign," but whereas symbols for Hegel have some natural connection with what they symbolize and signs do not, it is just the reverse for Price. This terminological matter should not bother us.

3. Although lately there have been few advocates of the classical view—Kurt Gödel and Alonzo Church, perhaps—the symbolist tradition is clearly dominant, especially in the cognitive sciences. Within the contemporary debate there are none who would adopt a pure imagist position, but there is considerable controversy over the forms mental representation might take and the possible role of images and natural language words in thinking. See Ned Block, ed., *Readings in the Philosophy of Psychology*, vol. 2, or Ned Block, ed., *Imagery*, for a representative sample of positions.

relation to the universal which defines this approach can be variously interpreted and need not be thought of as a relation to an internal representation of the universal. The following table roughly sketches the possible positions and gives some putative examples in each category.[4]

Theory	Representational position	Nonrepresentational position
Classical	Possessing a concept of A = standing in some relation R to an inner representation of A (Plato, Descartes)	Possessing a concept of A = standing in some relation R' to A itself (Russell and Moore in their realist period)
Symbolist	Imagist: Possessing a concept of A = being able to image A (Berkeley) Nominalist: Possessing a concept of A = being able to use mental word "A" (Hume, Geach, Sellars)	Possessing a concept of A = being able to behave appropriately toward A's and the absence of A's (Ryle, Skinner)

The classical inspectivist and symbolist theories are too narrow to account straightforwardly for the full range of thought; each has a different area of strength. The classical theory is more suited to an account of our thought about abstracta, whereas the symbolist theory seems especially suited to our thought about concreta. It seems implausible to claim that, when I think about what I had for dinner, I am inspecting a universal or concept; it seems much closer to the truth to say that various images, visual and gustatory, or various words, such as "omelet," "potato," or "sauerkraut," are flashing through my mind, and that my thinking consists in the rehearsal and interaction of these symbols. On the other hand, the idea that mathematical thinking consists of the inspection of or insight into the nature of pure intelligible entities has long had a (perhaps surprising) power to it.

Hegel makes a studious attempt to reconcile and do justice to the truth in each of these theories by incorporating the strong points of

---

4. The examples are meant only to be suggestive; each of these thinkers is too complex to be adequately characterized in this simple chart.

each into a highly structured theory of mental activity.[5] Contrary to what one might expect, Hegel rejects the classical representational theory of Plato and Descartes and unites symbolic representationalism with classical nonrepresentationalism.

Problems with Symbolism

In symbolist theory it is maintained that thinking is *nothing but* the rule-governed manipulation of symbols or signs. But even at first blush only the knowledgeable or intelligent (though not necessarily conscious) manipulation of symbols can be plausibly identified with thought, and that seems either circular or regress-generating.[6]

Hegel's symbolist predecessors often did not fully exploit the possibilities of their position. All too often they treated simple possession of a symbol, its mere presence before the mind, as sufficient to constitute having the appropriate concept. The lure of the classical, relational picture of concept possession is evident in this tendency. This view is made plausible by the idea that there is a set of natural symbols, namely, the symbols for simple concepts, that wear their meanings on their sleeves. Simple concepts are supposed to be intelligible independent of any other concept, even in isolation from all others, and are represented in the mind by nonconventional symbols—either innate or generated by perception. If the symbolist then forgets to take the dispositional sense of concept possession as basic, the occurrence of the thought and the occurrence of the symbol seem identical, making it easy to infer that

5. I use "mental activity" here to signal that my concern is with Hegel's theory of what he calls subjective thought. Hegel distinguishes subjective thought—what goes on in the minds of individual thinkers—from objective thought—the working of reason in the world at large (see §§24–25).

6. This is a relative of what Daniel Dennett calls "Hume's Problem"; see *Brainstorms* pp. 102, 12. Symbolists give two answers to this problem. The answer given by Dennett or Jerry Fodor avoids the regress by analyzing intelligent capacities into complexes of less intelligent capacities. Ryle, on the other hand, replies by giving an adjectival analysis of intelligence: doing X intelligently or knowledgeably is not doing two things concurrently, namely, doing X and thinking about X, but is instead a matter of how one does X. Both strategies defeat the regress; the most satisfactory theory might combine them. For evidence that Hegel noticed this problem, see *Encyclopedia* §455. I find no evidence that he saw either of these ways out of the problem.

the thought and the symbol are identical. Such a view leads toward the possibility of having a concept by having a symbol present to the mind which is not connectable in any way with any other symbol. Conflating concept possession with the simple presence to mind of a symbol results in a very poor theory of thinking and one particularly inept at dealing with self-reflection, for it abandons the essential symbolist insight into the active nature of thought.

Hegel strongly attacks this weak but popular form of symbolism. Since symbol and concept are identified, mental activity seems to be decomposable into various distinct operations on symbols—thinking, remembering, imagining,—and the unity of conceptual activity as such is lost. Rather than engaging in one complex activity with many essential components, we seem only to engage in assorted simple activities. Thus, Hegel complains, thinking becomes just another faculty of mind alongside others (*EL* §20). Furthermore, the content of thought then appears to be without intrinsic connection—a set of individual, discrete universals (§20). From the weak symbolist point of view, any connection between two concepts must appear totally contingent; necessary, intrinsic connection between concepts must be impossible, for there are no necessary connections between symbols. Such a conception of thinking condemns all thought to being incapable of containing truth.[7]

Furthermore, symbolism, especially as instantiated in the classical empiricist theories of Hume, David Hartley, and James Mill, tends toward the mechanistic, and Hegel is absolutely convinced that no mechanistic theory can be adequate to the phenomenon of thought. Mechanism leaves no room for ends and purposes and thus cannot account for the teleological process of rational thought. Even a mental chemism, as John Stuart Mill liked to call his theory to contrast it with his father's, falls short in this respect. Hegel is committed to a mental organicism, which he takes to mean a teleological holism. The fact that symbolist theories of mind are particularly attractive to materialists and mechanists, however, is not much of an argument against them, even for Hegel, for it is not clear that a mental organicism must eschew symbolism. And in his theory, symbolic representations do play a central role.

7. See §25. We examine Hegel's reasons for this below, in the critique of representationalism.

Hegel in fact maintains that all subjective thought is tied to symbol and sign manipulation. We think *in* words, he says (§462); whenever we think, the thought is embodied in a sign or symbol (§462, *Zusatz*). The thought is not the sign or symbol; rather it is at work through the sign or symbol (§462, *Zusatz*). Thinking expresses itself in the *use* of a sign. When we think about thought, we think about what is at work in the symbols or signs that are presented to us.

Problems with the Classical Theory

In classical theories it is claimed that thinking consists of the mind's standing in some relation to a universal. But how, then, can we think about individuals? The answer must be that we have no such contact with individuals qua individuals.

Attempts by classical theorists to explicate the nature of the relation between mind and universal have not been very successful. The metaphor of seeing has dominated such attempts.[8] Inspectivism is a child of substantialist theories of mind, theories in which the mind itself is reified as an entity related to its objects in the way a person perceiving physical objects is related to them. Inspectivism, like symbolism, is threatened with either circularity or a regress, for, as Kant saw, perception itself involves thought and therefore relation to the universal. Hegel puzzles over how an individual mental entity can represent a universal.[9] A representational version of classical inspectivism seems to boil down to the obviously inadequate theory that there are signs the mere presence of which to mind constitutes possession and exercise of a concept, a theory Hegel rejects. Hegel does not completely reject the classical theory, however. How and why he thinks it has to be salvaged is revealed by his understanding of the problems of representationalism. The idea of a nonrepresentational symbolist theory of mind is entirely foreign to him; the existence of internal symbols in imagination and memory is obvious to him. So symbolism is considered by Hegel to

8. For a sustained critique of visual metaphors in epistemology and the philosophy of mind, see Richard Rorty, *Philosophy and the Mirror of Nature.*

9. The section of the *Philosophy of Subjective Spirit* entitled *Vorstellung* traces the stages in which our mental representations become increasingly universal in content.

be committed to representationalism. Yet he believes that representationalism entails certain consequences that condemn it as a final answer about the nature of thought.

Problems with Representationalism

Hegel is well aware of the pressures within any representational theory, pressures that tend to cut the mind off from external reality, keeping it trapped behind a veil of ideas. Whatever semantic relation is supposed to exist between our representations and their objects, its veridicality must remain forever beyond our ken. If this worry is taken seriously, even our self-knowledge is threatened.

Epistemological skepticism and the problem of the thing-in-itself are vitally linked for Hegel. Both are often motivated by entirely separating the subjective from the objective world to be cognized, by adopting a picture of the mind as an inner space populated with merely subjective representations.[10] But then, since we have access only to our representations, we cannot independently ascertain whether they are indeed veridical representations or whether there is any relation at all between our representations and any other reality. We cannot even ascertain whether they are correctly characterized as representations. The Kantian answer to such empiricist skepticism, the division of knowledge into possible phenomenal and impossible noumenal knowledge, Hegel regards as a sham. Knowledge that is not knowledge of things as they are is not knowledge at all; Kant's theory is just another form of skepticism, according to Hegel.

Purely representational theories of mind, Hegel believes, condemn one to subjective idealism, an intolerable position. Hegel does not reject representationalism wholesale, however; he believes that, as a theory of perception and the lower cognitive functions that involve sensory elements (intuition and *Vorstellung*), representationalism must be the correct answer. There needs to be a nonrepresentational anchor for our mental activity, however, one that ensures that our knowledge is of things as they are in themselves.

Hegel's rejection of representationalism in order to escape from

10. Rorty, *Philosophy and the Mirror of Nature,* also criticizes this metaphor of inner space at length.

subjective idealism depends on his other metaphysical positions. In particular, his claim that the universal, and not the individual, is the substance of the world is crucial. We cannot have other actual individuals in our minds; this is why our dealings with such individuals in perception, imagination, and so forth are representational. But the idea of having universals themselves in the mind has not seemed as impossible. Often enough it has been claimed that this is the only place they exist. It is our knowledge of the universal—the object of pure thought—that is nonrepresentational and fully objective, according to Hegel; because the universal is the in-itself of the world, we know things as they are in themselves. Hegel does admit that we *can* represent universals to ourselves (and do so in art and religion), but when we do so we have not yet achieved true thought. In true thought we stand in a nonrepresentational relation to the object of our thought, which must always be a universal. Thus we turn next to explicating the nature of the universal, the object of thought, and the nature of its relation to the thinking mind.

HEGEL'S RESPONSE TO THE TRADITIONS

Hegel's attempt to reconcile representational symbolism and nonrepresentational classicism revolves around his notion of a concrete universal. He believes that his predecessors erred in assuming an absolute distinction between individuals and universals and attempts to overcome this rigid distinction by arguing that both the individual and the universal are to be reconceived as *moments* of a more complex, articulated unity, the concrete universal, or concept. For our purposes, his technical terms "concrete universal" and "concept" can be treated as one. His basic argument for reconceiving the world in these terms is that we are otherwise incapable of reaching a fully coherent conception of the world. That argument, however, is beyond our bounds here.

The Active Concrete Universal

Hegel believes that most of his predecessors have chosen the wrong paradigm of predication. These philosophers—philosophers trapped in the "attitude of the understanding"—have taken such accidental predications as "The ball is red" as paradigmatic. In such a case there is no intrinsic connection between the universal and the individual it is predicated of—both the universal and the individual seem quite indifferent to each other. Taking this to be the paradigmatic predication relation leads, Hegel believes, to a metaphysics in which the world is seen as composed of nexus of bare particulars (in his terminology "abstract individuals") and ontologically independent universals (he would call these "abstract universals"). Hegel thinks such a metaphysics impossible; to escape being trapped in it one must reject both the abstract individual and the abstract universal.[11]

In the place of accidental predication Hegel considers a version of essential predication as an ideal to be striven toward, for in an essential predication the universal and the individual are intrinsically tied. The essence of something is also seen by Hegel to have some explanatory power; saying of what kind a thing is can be a legitimate explanatory move. But Hegel goes further than this, for an essence, something's concept, is held to be, not a *descriptive* essence, but a *prescriptive* ideal. Something's concept offers an ideal pattern that the thing strives to realize in the course of its existence, although individual things are never perfect exemplars of their essence. In this respect we can begin to see a rather strange melding of Aristotle's concept of essence with the Kantian notion of concept. Kant insisted that "a concept is always, as regards its form, something universal which serves as a rule" (*Critique of Pure Reason*, A107). Hegel seizes on three aspects of Kant's a priori concepts— their unrestricted universality, their prescriptive force, and their conceptual priority over their instances—and transfers these properties to the basically Aristotelian conception of an essence or thing-kind.

Hegel also learned from Kant that concepts are not discrete entities that exist and can be known each independent of any others; neither thinker has the notion of a *simple* concept. We can say that Hegel took over from Kant a coherence theory of concepts: even bottom-level basic ideas are to be understood through their interaction with other ideas in basic principles, in contrastive relations, and so forth. Perhaps most important, the crucial relations between concepts need not all be construed as analytic "inclusions"; Kant

11. See R. Aquila, "Predication and Hegel's Metaphysics."

inaugurated the search for nonanalytic but also nonpsychological, rational connections between concepts, and Hegel willingly followed. Thus what Hegel calls a concept is a prescriptive ideal that is part of a system of such ideals that the world is striving to realize and in terms of which we can make sense of what happens in the world. Hegel, however, takes the rule-like character and implicit systematicity of concepts so seriously that he makes a move Kant would never dream of; he insists that the being of the I is the being of a concept, for the I is the rule for the unification of all experience. The unity of apperception is the ideal governing all synthetic activity in the mind. Indeed, since the I provides the ultimate rule— all concepts must be unified under it, including the pure concepts— the I, the self, becomes a super-concept, a concept of concepts (*WdL*, vol. 2, pp. 220–21; *SL*, p. 583).

Every universal of whatever kind unifies something, but, in contrast to abstract universals like red, concrete universals not only unite various different individuals under some heading but also account for their internal unity. The model for this internal unification is the synthesis of the manifold into the unity of apperception. The manifold is unified, according to the Kantian vision, because I make it mine, constituting myself in that very process. Hegel attributes this kind of self-constituting activity to every concrete universal, to all concepts. Any unity of a manifold which is not thus actively involved in the very nature of the elements, while also constituting its own self in the activity, is to that degree a merely abstract universal. A concrete universal is therefore different from the abstract universals that previous thinkers in the classical tradition took to be the object of thought: "The universal of the concept is not a mere sum of features common to several things, confronted by a particular which enjoys an existence on its own. It is, on the contrary, self-particularizing or self-specifying, and with undimmed clearness finds itself at home in its antithesis" (*EL* §163, my tr.). An abstract universal is a tag that can be hung on things otherwise quite indifferent to it in order to sort them out; a concrete universal, on the other hand, must reach to their very hearts and afford an explanation of their being. An abstract universal is static and unchanging because it is dead, a mere sum of otherwise unrelated features. A concrete universal, however, is alive, dynamic, and dialectical; it is essentially a part of a self-developing system.

In sum, the foremost characteristic of a concrete universal is that it is *active*. The whole universe is the realization of a universal activity—and this activity *is* the concrete universal. Its mode of action is teleological, that is, it is self-realization; the concrete universal is both cause and effect, it is self-developing. Second, a concrete universal is the *truth* of those objects it characterizes and animates. It is their essence, that which explains what they are and why they behave the way they do. Third, a concrete universal is not separable from its instances; it actively manifests itself in and through them. Fourth, concrete universals, concepts, have an essence of their own, *the* concrete universal, which realizes itself in the active self-realization of its contributory moments. Concrete universals are essentially parts of a self-realizing system. What ultimately *is*, according to Hegel, is a universal self-constitutive activity that becomes self-conscious in man's knowledge of it—the Absolute.

The Rejection of Inspectivism

It is Hegel's ontology that allows him to break away from representationalism and the classical tendency toward inspectivism, for at the highest level of pure thought, he believes, the concept is not an inert entity we inspect but rather the activity we *are*. Instead of standing apart from a universal or a representation that we somehow "look" at, in pure thought we become a special realization of the concrete universal, and realizing a concrete universal is not the same as representing it.[12] Hegel ultimately transcends representationalism, abandoning a common assumption shared by most philosophers since Descartes.

Hegel takes thought to be a certain distinctive and dynamic, structured activity. He is a symbolist to the degree that he holds that this activity must be realized as symbolic activity in a subjectivity, but he refuses to identify thinking with any specific set of symbolic activities; he also refuses to say that the action on the symbols is itself symbolic. Hegel insists rather that, when we are thinking, the symbols themselves, the representations before the mind, are in-

---

12. This is one of the points of his discussion of thought in §§20–25 of the *Encyclopedia*. Only in this way can we make good sense of his distinguishing between objective and subjective thought while maintaining their identity. This also explains why philosophy or thought is the self-movement of the concept, which we, as it were, simply observe; §238, *Zusatz*. See also *WdL*, vol. 2, pp. 485–8; *SL*, pp. 824–7.

consequential. What really counts is what we do with the symbols. The activity actually operating on the symbols—for which the symbols are but "pieces in a game"—is thinking. This activity is not, of course, a kind of action performed by some homunculus on inner symbols. The activity is implicit in the symbols themselves; they are symbols for concepts by virtue of participating in a system of demands and permissions, and in this sense they are codes that directly invoke activity.[13] Although Hegel would admit that symbols are not the things they symbolize, but only representations of them, he would not say that the system of demands and permissions that govern the interactions of the symbols (in veridical thought) is only a representation of the demands and permissions that govern the interactions of the things symbolized.[14] Real thinking, which, according to Hegel, is always veridical, is achieved when our internal symbol system is governed by the *same* rule system as the world. Thinking is to be identified with the instantiation of this rule system; our ability to think true thoughts about the world is based on the fact that we instantiate the same rule system that governs the world.[15] In philosophy this rule system also becomes the object of our thought, not by our symbolizing it to ourselves, but by our self-consciously participating in the system, self-consciously playing the game. Thus Hegel rejects a representationalistic reading of thought, rejects inspectivism, and synthesizes the symbolist and classical theories through the claim that in thinking the active universal is present in our symbolic activity.

13. In Douglas R. Hofstadter's popular book *Gödel, Escher, Bach: An Eternal Golden Braid*, a distinction is drawn between inert and active symbols. Hofstadter, along with other contemporary symbolists, insists that active symbols are spatiotemporal entities and that, in the final analysis, their interaction is to be explained causally. Hegel, in effect, would deny that such symbols are physical entities (according to him, they are like mental utterances) and would probably even more strongly deny that their interaction is to be explained by the laws of physics and chemistry. The interaction of such symbols must be explained entelechially, as being the fulfillment of a telos.

14. Otherwise, he would have to deny the identity of subjective and objective thought.

15. Hegel sees the world as the interplay of concrete universals. But thinking is precisely that, an interplay of concrete universals. He distinguishes objective thought and subjective thought, the only difference between them being their venue and mode of realization. Objective thought is realized everywhere, subjective thought is realized within individual subjectivities (through their symbolic activity). But Hegel insists on the identity of the two forms of thought.

12

Thought

As central to Hegel's philosophy as the concept of thought is, it seems strange that there are only four relatively short paragraphs (§§465–68) devoted to it as the culmination of theoretical spirit. Hegel takes thinking to be the ultimate activity lying behind all worldly processes, responsible for the grand structure the world exhibits. But these paragraphs in the philosophy of subjective spirit are not an outline of that topic, to which Hegel devotes a gread deal of space, for instance, in the *Wissenschaft der Logik.* However, in the philosophy of subjective spirit Hegel is concerned, not with Thought, the active substance of the world, but merely with thought, an ability possessed and exercised by individual human beings, the relation of which to Thought is open to discussion. Hegel claims that subjective thought and objective Thought are in reality one and the same, though admittedly in different forms.

In the first section below I restate the situation at the lowest level of thought. The second section is devoted to spelling out in greater detail what Hegel thinks goes on when we think, and in the third section we briefly discuss the transition to practical spirit, which does not concern the nature of thought itself so much as the relation between thought and will.

THE IMMEDIACY OF THOUGHT

"In the first instance, however, thinking cognition is *formal*; universality and its being is the simple subjectivity of intelligence. Thus the thoughts are not determined as being in and for themselves, and the representations recollected as [or into] thought are still the given content" (§466, my tr.): thus the general situation at the end of the section on representation is stated. Spirit is taken as an abstract power standing over against a collection of words, which are the embodiment of or represent certain spiritual capacities. These words, the representations, are raised to the level of thought through a recollection. But insofar as this recollection is a kind of generalization in which we move behind the words to what is expressed in them—not subjectively (that would be a regression to an earlier stage of representation) but objectively (that is, for a hypothetical *anyone* who understood the words)—there are several things to be said about words recollected as thoughts.

First, such thoughts are merely abstract universals, not concrete universals. They are taken as sundered entities, each apart from all the others, and the individuals in which they are taken to be expressed are words, not the things themselves. They are not yet inner principles of activity, structural nodes organizing their local relatives to fit into a larger pattern. A concept can be understood itself to be a set of permissions, demands, and prohibitions on that power of unification which is thought in abstract generality. No concept can be an atomistic counter indifferent to the power of thought that manipulates it. Thought, therefore, must go beyond this initial abstract universal to develop the true concrete universal.

Second, thoughts here are in an important sense present to mind as merely given; that is, we find language already there and already cutting the world up a certain way. We do not invent the words we use, we learn them. We slowly learn the abstract connections between words and phrases as we learn to think. The creation of a new word for something previously unexpressible, when done consciously, is itself an act of highly sophisticated thought. The world generally seems to come to us prearticulated by our language, and we continue to see it in these terms unthinkingly most of our lives until we start theorizing, thinking in the strongest sense. The articulation of the world is taken to be a mere matter of fact for the most part, something given, but Hegel insists that all such articulation is ultimately generated out of the self-revealing nature of thought. Thought is active in subjectivity and in nature; it is not conscious of its own activity in nature; this activity is *for itself* only in subjectivity. "In the first instance, thought knows the unity of the subjective and objective as wholly abstract and indeterminate, as merely a certain unity, which is neither filled nor confirmed. To this unity therefore, the determinateness of the rational content is still external and therefore given,—and cognition is therefore formal. Yet since this determinateness is implicitly contained in thinking cognition, this formalism contradicts it and is the therefore sublated by thought" (§466, *Zusatz*). The thinking spirit is convinced of the adequacy of its thought to the world. But at first this is an unreflective assumption; spirit merely finds its words fitting its experience. That thought and being are one is precisely the "determinateness of the rational content" that Hegel talks of here, for the "rational is the actual and the actual is the rational" (preface to the *Philosophy of Right*). But although at the opening level of spirit, spirit has this conviction, it is nothing but a conviction; spirit cannot back it up. Spirit's original conviction that its thoughts capture the world successfully does not result from its own thinking about thought and the world, and to this extent its claim to knowledge of the world is merely formal, awaiting fuller justification. The conviction that thought and being are one and that thought is adequate to the world is, according to Hegel, both the necessary assumption of the attitude of thought—its working hypothesis, as it were—and its ultimate result.

THE NATURE OF THOUGHT

Hegel compresses his theory of the essential structure of thinking activity into one paragraph, §467. In this culmination of the entire discussion of theoretical spirit, we find two lists of three levels within thought. What is the relation between these lists? They duplicate each other; there is one set of levels described with two different aspects highlighted. In the first list the distinction between form and content is retained; taking for granted thoughts as the "content" of thought as discussed in his previous paragraph, Hegel describes the increasingly adequate form into which these contents can be cast. Thus the first list gives us a description of the formal structure of thought. The second list is, I believe, a slightly more adequate statement, for it leaves the rather static and artificial distinction of form and content behind, even as heuristic, and brings out more fully the activity that thought is.

The Formal Structure of Thought

Concepts

> In respect of this content [*An diesem Inhalte*] thought is (1) formally identical *understanding*, which transforms the recollected representations into genera, kinds, laws, forces, etc., in general into the Categories, in the sense that the material first has its truth in these forms of thought. As negativity infinite in itself, thought is (2) essentially *diremption—judgment* [*Urtheil*], which however no longer dissolves the concept into the previous opposition of universality and being but rather distinguishes it [or divides it] according to the connections peculiar to the concept, and (3) thought sublates the form-determinations and at the same time posits the identity of the differences;— formal reason, syllogizing understanding. (§467, my tr.)

We start with "recollected representations," which I have maintained to be abstract universals, each isolated from all others. Through thought these representations are "processed" or "transformed" [*verarbeitet*] into genera, kinds, laws, and forces. What does this mean exactly? Three questions arise: (a) How are they transformed, what happens to them in this transformation? (b) what exactly is it they are transformed or worked up into? (c) What is the common element of genera, laws, and so forth which makes this transformation one process rather than many?

We have seen that the recollected representations are generalizations of a range of sophisticated capacities of spirit, the capacities to call up certain images and words. They are generalized in the sense that the particular idiosyncrasies of individuals have been discounted. In other terms, the representations are unities within certain activities and potentialities of individual subjective spirits. The recollected representations that are thoughts, however, are unities of such activities and potentialities within subjective spirit in general, that is, intersubjectively and objectively. The capacities of spirit embodied in thought are not all entirely separated from one another. They exhibit certain interconnections, although spirit has not yet become aware of these interconnections. There are patterns of cooccurrence, or permissible association, for instance, and the transformation undergone in understanding is our coming to awareness of these patterns in consciousness. As we then seek to explain and, more important, to justify these patterns, the associations are no longer mere instances of a pattern but become examples of explicit rule following. This appears first in the imposition of structured connections on the formerly discrete units in thought. One such structure is the partial ordering of genus and species. Thought now sees all its objects as essentially participating in such ordering structures. This is the first step in the overcoming of the atomism of the standpoint of abstract, formal thought, but it is only the first step, and the relations focused on tend to be highly abstract and are thought of as affecting the relata only minimally.

We have already before us most of the material for answering our second question, namely, what kind of thing the representations are transformed into. Today we think of genera and kinds as very different from laws and forces, categorically different. But Hegel did not think this, for he focused on their common character as modally laden relations of a one over a many. The one, the genus, kind, law, necessitates certain characteristics in the manifold that falls under it. The application of one of these concepts necessitates applying certain other concepts, and thus these concepts can be seen as structuring the conceptual realm, unifying our concepts into a coherent scheme. Concepts are no longer merely contingently associated with each other; they are now seen as modally related. This systematization and unification of our concepts are the activity of the concept of a concept in one of its manifestations, the essential activity of spirit.

Judgments

From the systematic classification of concepts by the understanding it is not far to progress to their explicitly asserted interconnection in a judgment, although Hegel would complain that many philosophers before him misunderstood the nature of such assertion. Judgment in Hegel's eyes is not merely the assertion of a relation between two independent and indifferent things; this is precisely the view of the nature of judgment which must be overcome, which is mired too deeply in the theory of the abstract universal.

Hegel emphasizes that judgment is a kind of distinguishing by playing on the etymological structure of the German *Urteil*—"original or primordial division or partition."[1] Hegel does not believe that judgmental structure applies only to certain subjective acts of mind:

> The judgment is usually taken in a subjective sense as an operation and a form occurring merely in self-conscious thought. This distinction, however, is not present in Logic, and judgment is taken in the quite universal signification that all things are a judgment. That is to say, they are individuals, which are a universality or inner nature in themselves—a universal that is individualized. Their universality and individuality are distinguished, but the one is at the same time identical with the other. (*El* §167, my tr.)

The self-individualization of the concrete universal is a judgment. Since it is the very nature of the concrete universal to have its being in individual existents, it is of the essence of the concrete universal to develop itself in judgments. Individuals possess judgmental structure in that they realize a universal. There are no bare particulars in the world. Indeed, individuals always realize a multitude of universals, so there is no such thing as a purely simple thing in the world. Not only are individuals complex, but even their complexity is complex, with different aspects contributing to the complex in different ways. Thus a plant may be of a particular kind, say a rose, and its being both plant and rose is one kind of complexity. The plant may also have certain parts, such as roots, flowers, and leaves, and this is another sort of complexity. The flowers may be of a certain color, say red, and this is still another sort of complexity. The individual realizes different universals, but not all of the universals it realizes are equal. Some are essentially abstract, others are concrete; the judgments through which the individual and the universal are distinguished in each case are different. Hegel's theory of judgment is a theory of the different ways the individual and the universal are distinguished and unified.

It is easy to forget that according to Hegel judgment is as much a feature or structure of objective reality as of the subjective. Individ-

---

1. This approach seems to have come from Fichte and Hölderlin. J. G. Fichte, *Sämtliche Werke*, vol. 1, pp. 102–3, and F. Hölderlin, "Urtheil und Seyn," in *Materialien zu Schellings Philosophischen Anfängen*, ed. M. Frank und G. Kurz, pp. 108–9.

uals and universals are essentially related in both realms. To forget that everything objective is a judgment is to fall into the metaphysical error of believing in bare particulars, platonic universals, and so forth. To separate the subjective concept from the judgmental contexts in which it can occur is to fall into the theory of the abstract universal, which renders all judgmental structure arbitrary.[2]

There is no room here for a treatment of Hegel's full theory of judgment as it appears in his *Logics*, but its outlines emerge relatively easily from what we have said already. We have already noted that judgment can be viewed as the unfolding of the necessary complexity of a concrete universal, and that even this complexity is complex. Hegel's theory of judgment is an attempt to regiment the kinds of complexity in the individualization of a concrete universal, ranking them in accordance with their ability to express the original structural unity of the concept.

There are two different contrasts involved in Hegel's ranking of judgments. First, not everything propositional qualifies as a judgment, for Hegel distinguishes between judgments and propositions:

> A judgment [*Urteil*] is however distinguished from a proposition [*Satz*]. The latter contains a statement about the subject, which does not stand to it in any universal relationship but expresses some single action, or some state, or the like. Thus "Caesar was born at Rome in such and such a year, waged war in Gaul for ten years, crossed the Rubicon, etc." are propositions but not judgments. Again it is absurd to say that such statements as "I slept well last night" or "Present arms!" may be turned into the forms of a judgment. "A carriage is passing by" would be a judgment, and a subjective one at best, only if it were doubtful whether the passing object was a carriage or whether it and not rather the point of observation was in motion:—in short, only if it were desired to specify a representation which was still short of appropriate specification. (*EL* §167)

Hegel says something similar about the distinction in the *Wissenschaft der Logik*, adding that a judgment "requires that the predicate

---

2. The empiricists are particularly subject to this danger. Although they all leave some room for trivial knowledge or relations of ideas, any nonanalytic judgment tends to be conceived by them as a mere association of ideas, which, as Kant saw, dooms their attempt to understand human knowledge or human mental activity.

be related to the subject as one concept determination to another, and therefore as a universal to a particular or individual" (*SL*, p. 626; *WdL*, vol. 2, p. 267). He adds that there is "something of a judgment in a proposition" when the fact expressed by the proposition is placed in doubt (repeating here a remark in the *Encyclopedia*) and the proposition is "asserted on the strength of some reason or other."

It seems that this distinction is one of degree, not kind [see also *SL*, p. 683; *WdL*, vol. 2, p. 330], although perhaps Hegel thought that there was some break dividing the sentences into genuinely different kinds. Whether a sentence is a judgment or a proposition is not solely dependent on its grammatical form but also on the job it performs in its context. A mere statement of contingent fact is only a proposition; an attempt to theorize or explain is a judgment. Some sentences appear more naturally in theorizing contexts and carry with them, as it were, a lot of theoretical machinery because of their content; these are most clearly judgments, better realizations of judgment per se. And statements that might easily be immediate statements of fact, made in a context in which they are results of inferences, approximate judgments because of their theoretical content. The raising of a representation to thought and the raising of a proposition to a judgment are quite similar in nature, I believe. Although informed with the grammatical structures of thinking, propositions are at the level of representation and share with that level the concern with individuality per se; yet, because they use the grammatical structure of judgment (by using the copula), they give evidence of the presence even in representation of the power of the Concept. Insofar as the representer has gone beyond the occurrence of mere lists of names within its mind—and without seeing through to the inner connection of the particular things it represents to itself still wants to assert the existence of a particularly close tie or bond between them—it uses the grammatical structure of the judgment. The awareness that there are associations of representations and then that some are of a different sort from others is already the first step toward thought, and widely different strata all find some accommodation, more or less adequate to the level of the content, in the grammatical forms of judgment.

Hegel also draws a distinction between truth, or adequacy to the Idea, and correctness. A judgment is correct when it is an idealization of what is exemplified in a particular individual thing or state of affairs.

Truth, on the contrary, lies in the coincidence of the object with itself, that is, with its concept. That a person is sick, or that someone has committed a theft, may certainly be correct. But the content is untrue. A sick body is not in harmony with the concept of body, and there is a want of congruity between theft and the concept of human conduct. These instances may show that an immediate judgment, in which an abstract quality is predicated of an immediately individual thing, however correct it may be, cannot contain truth. The subject and predicate of it do not stand to each other in the relation of reality and concept. (§EL172, *Zusatz*)

A judgment is true according to Hegel, we may say, when it is an idealization of the concept. He would find our use of "true" in the phrase "a true friend" a perfect illustration of his intent.

At the lowest end of the judgmental spectrum we find qualitative judgments, by which Hegel means judgments in which some abstract universal is predicated of an individual:

To say "This rose is red" involves (in virtue of the copula "is") the coincidence of subject and predicate. The rose however is a concrete thing, and so is not red only; it has an odour, a specific form, and many other features not implied in the predicate red. The predicate on its part is an abstract universal, and does not apply to the rose alone. There are other flowers and other objects which are red too. The subject and predicate in the immediate judgment touch as it were, only in a single point, but do not cover each other. (§172, *Zusatz*)

Hegel admits that such simple judgments may be *correct*; he does not consider them *true*. But insofar as in the judgmental form the universal and the individual are, though sundered, still connected, we have not simply "dissolved . . . the concept into the previous opposition of universality and being" (§467). The articulation of the concept in accordance with its own natural internal structure increases as we progress through the ranked forms of judgment.

According to Hegel, the judgmental relation, through its development, starts to approach a *consequence* relation, for we unfold a concept by seeing what follows from its use and from what other concepts it follows. Concepts are determined by their logical relations with other concepts, so the self-determining of a concept in judgment must take place through the specification of such logical relations. But although some logical relation is stated in the judgment, it is not *supported* within the judgment but simply given by or in the judgment. To this extent the relation given in a judgment is external and appears as a merely given necessity. These modes of relation are what is expressed in the copula. Hegel says that the copula expresses the *identity* of the subject and the predicate, but this is misleading to us, for he means not numerical identity but identity within the concept; the subject and the predicate are themselves but moments of one (self-identical) concept. The development of the judgment is not only from correctness-incorrectness to truth but also from the copula as the merely implicit identity of subject and predicate to the explicit identity of the two in a unifying third. Identity statements are not Hegel's ideal judgments; correct, justified attributions of essences are.

Unity in a third is a necessary condition for the judgment's being an "objective connectedness." In his attempt to answer Hume within the limits of an atomistic psychology, Kant developed the analytic-synthetic distinction to isolate the problem of *combination*, for this is where Hume's focus also lay. Analytic judgments were uninteresting to Kant in general because there was no *new* combination; the predicate was supposedly already contained in the subject. But Hegel considers the separation as important as the combination, perhaps even more so.

Kant focused on the need for a third thing X to ground the combination of representations in a true, objective synthetic judgment. Hegel seizes this insight and generalizes it, maintaining that the copula is the representative for an implicit third that grounds both the combination and the separation in any judgment. According to Kant, in any a priori synthetic judgment the third that grounds the combination is the transcendental unity of apperception. Hegel reinterprets the transcendental unity of apperception as his Concept, and therefore a judgment is, according to Hegel, something in which the concepts are combined and separated "in virtue of the necessary unity" of the Concept (to paraphrase Kant; *Critique of Pure Reason*, B142). A judgment combines concepts according to the structure of the Concept, the concrete universal, and, to the extent to which the judgment adequately reflects that structure, it is true. Hegel goes further than Kant by insisting that *all* judgments be combinations grounded in a third thing. Those that are not, such as "A lion is a lion," are not really judgments (§173). Take, for example, what Hegel calls judgments of necessity (§177), such as "Man is an animal," which might well be thought analytic. Hegel would point out that man and animal are not immediately and emptily identical, but rather that man is a mammal and mammals are animals, and that neither of these two links is an immediate link itself. The concept of man may in some sense contain that of animal, but only mediately, because men are mammals. The concept of mammal not only ties the other two together but also separates them, for not all animals are mammals.

Every judgment leaves itself open to question, as do all things that appear merely given, and this question is answered by showing that the judgment is grounded. This ground is a third thing that mediates the relation of the subject and the predicate. Only in the ultimate stage of judgment is this third thing made explicit, but it is implicitly present throughout. Abstractly taken, this third is the Concept itself, as we have seen, but according to its own nature this must particularize itself and appear as a determinate unifying concept: "What has been really made explicit is the oneness of subject and predicate, is the concept itself, filling up the empty 'is' of the copula. While its constituent elements are at the same time distinguished as subject and predicate, the concept is put as their unity, as the connection which serves to intermediate them: in short, as the syllogism" (§180, Wallace tr., adapted). Ideally, two concepts are objectively linked in a judgment, according to Hegel, not when one is contained in another, but when both are moments of a third; this is the structure we should expect to find in philosophical propositions. Two concepts are objectively linked in a judgment when they are brought to unity in a third concept.

According to Hegel's notion of judgmental connection, any judgment implies a whole systematic network of concepts behind it and supporting it; full knowledge of a concept is a knowledge of all its conceptual relations.

The final level of judgment Hegel calls the judgment of the concept, a judgment in which the individual is assessed relative to its kind. The highest form within this level Hegel calls the apodictic judgment, although it is certainly not what was normally so called. In it the ground or reason for the assessment is also made explicit.[3]

3. Perhaps he calls it apodictic because "apodictic" literally means "shown" or "demonstrated."

Thus "This rose, as fulfilling criteria (X, Y, Z), is beautiful" would count as such a judgment. "*All things* are a *genus* (their determination and end) in an *individual* actuality of a *particular* constitution. And they are finite, because the particular in them may and also may not conform to the universal" (§179). This apodictic judgment is the highest form of judgment, for it is the fullest realization of the judgmental structure implicit in the concept. The three moments of the concept, individuality, particularity, and universality, are all explicitly stated in their relations to one another. The apodictic judgment can be both correct and true, for it gets to the very heart of the matter, articulating the very essence of the thing.

Hegel believes it fully possible, indeed necessary, that in general things do not ideally embody their essences or concepts. Thus, when confronted with the booming, buzzing confusion and complexity of nature, he does not infer that the order characterized by our theorizing activity is merely imposed from without, or that the recalcitrant examples that do not fit our theoretical categories are always indications of a failure in our theory. At some point he is willing to assign the fault to nature itself; it is the "impotence" of nature that it cannot adequately embody the Concept and is prey to contingency. Thus each individual thing, although a realization of some concept or other, and thus determined through the activity of the concept, is also subject to an indeterminate range of other external influences and thus is not determined solely by its concept. Only in pure thought does a concept determine itself alone, and in pure thought a concept is an ideal.

This seems a very peculiar doctrine, for we immediately want to say that the last thing an inquirer has a right to do is toss off troublesome cases as bad or untrue simply because they do not fit a theory. But there is more to Hegel's move than blunder. It is precisely this doctrine of the imperfection of nature that allows Hegel to maintain the ideal of a rational system of the world without falling into the trap of thinking that therefore every aspect of the world (including Krug's pen) should be a priori deducible on the basis of purely a priori rational considerations.

When confronted with the extreme and recalcitrant confusion in nature, there seem to be several possible attitudes we can take. (a) There is no order in nature; all is chaos. This seems unacceptable, for then nothing is understandable, especially the fact that we do understand much about nature. (b) There is no order in nature; an order is imputed to nature by us. But then, Hegel would argue, our "knowledge" of nature is only appearance, and not knowledge; this is too Kantian a solution for Hegel and smacks of the thing-in-itself. (c) There is a complete order in nature, but it is deeply hidden. This still does not account for our present knowledge of nature, and it allows the deduction of Krug's pen if we ever gain knowledge of the order of nature. Finally, (d) there is an order in nature, but order only imperfectly realized. Thus we can have real knowledge of nature, yet certainly we cannot deduce Krug's pen. "Perfection" here has teleological underpinnings, and if we rid our concept of nature of all vestiges of teleology, this alternative becomes senseless to us (as it probably has).

From another point of view we can note that, if one has a very good theory about some range of phenomena, one often throws away or otherwise dismisses some conflicting or recalcitrant data as spurious. Hegel is, in effect, elevating such a pragmatic methodological maxim into a constitutive principle, for he is ready to accept the possibility that in the long run the ideal theory could be developed and yet not account for *everything* natural, that a classification scheme could be ideal, for instance, even though there were anomalies. Hegel wants us to take the fact that there will always be a discrepancy between theory and nature as a necessary truth, and he attributes the shortcoming to nature, not to theory. It is the mark of nature and the natural to be less than ideal.

Is there not a danger in this Hegelian view? It seems all too easy to relax one's scientific vigilance. At what point in our investigation of nature are we justified in claiming that further attempts at a new theory are neither necessary nor sensible—not merely for economic or pragmatic reasons but for intrinsic theoretical reasons? Perhaps Hegel would reply that the natural (and social?) sciences could not reach such a point, and that this is itself an example of a *bad infinite*, a going on endlessly. This response would make sense within his system, for one of the imperfections of nature is that the true infinity of the concept, the infinite return into self, is never fully realized in nature. There we find only bad infinites. It would, then, be fully appropriate that the sciences of nature be subject themselves to infinite progression toward adequacy.

It is crucial to remember that the sciences of nature are not the highest forms of knowledge for Hegel. The highest forms of knowledge, religion and philosophy, are in principle and in fact perfectable, and it is from the point of view of philosophy, not science, that we evaluate nature as imperfect. This position still diverges widely from philosophical beliefs held today, and again it is Hegel's acceptance of a teleological worldview that is the foundation of the difference. Empirical science is not, however, dispensable according to Hegel. Empirical science tries to build a theory of the world from the bottom up and is doomed to be caught in the infinite detail and complexity of nature. Philosophy constructs a theory of the whole from the top down, but it can never reach the individual per se. The complete enquirer must follow both paths.

Whatever we think of the doctrine of the necessarily imperfect realization of concepts in nature, its counterpoint is played by the doctrine of the possibility of perfect "realization" of concepts in mind—the doctrine of the self-determination of the concept in thought. Natural things are imperfect because what they are does not depend on or is not explainable solely on the basis of their concept. Men are different because they have different heritages, live in different environments; these differences are all indifferent to the concept of man and account for the contingent variation in men and the impossibility of a perfect exemplar of the species. But a concept in a subjectivity is in a slightly different position from the concept as realized in nature. A concept is realized in nature by an individual that simultaneously realizes an infinite number of other concepts, even if ultimately subordinated to the most essential concept. Some of the concepts may not be compatible with the others, thus forcing change and ultimately finiteness and destruction on the thing.

In mind each concept is individualized abstractly. It is the great contribution of the abstractive powers of representation and understanding to thus isolate the individuality of concepts. Working with these "given" concepts as material, intelligence as pure thought is the activity of reconstituting the purely conceptual links and relations between them. Since they are purely conceptual and determined by the concepts themselves, the relations discovered (or reconstructed) in thought are modalized.

Since in pure thought concepts appear in their abstract individuality rather than their concrete and complex individuality, they need no longer be involved in contingent, arbitrary relations, as they are often in nature or in Vorstellung. Pure thought perceives only those relations between concepts which are intrinsically involved in the concepts.[4] Thus removed from the imperfection and recalcitrance of nature and representation, the concepts are realized as ideals. We have realized the true concept of man when we know what the ideal man is.

Inferences

The mediated relation of one concept to another is a syllogism according to Hegel, and just as a concept has its "truth" in judgment, so does judgment have its "truth" in the syllogism, which makes explicit what is the implicit nature of the judgment. We turn to the role of the syllogism, of formal inference, in Hegel's theory of mental activity.

As much as Hegel may have disliked the traditional Aristotelian logic, he was still mightily under its sway in his consideration of the formal aspect of thought, and this is particularly evident in his discussion of the syllogism. It seems that what Hegel really has in mind is a general theory of our forms of inference; the German *schluß* can as well mean "inference" pure and simple as "syllogism," and under this rubric Hegel discusses inductive and analogical reasoning as well as the deductive, three-termed syllogism. Working within the confines of the rather narrow understanding of formal logic available at the time, Hegel constructs an interpretation of the significance of inference and a rank ordering of kinds of syllogisms which we must find quite strained. Yet it is masterfully woven into his philosophical system and reflects the structures and themes dominant in the system in a rather natural way.

What Hegel would have to say in reaction to the richness of contemporary logic—not just the logic of Russell and Whitehead's *Principia Mathematica* but also modal logics, many-valued logics, logics of relevance and entailment, intuitionistic logic, paraconsistent logics—we shall never know. Hegel's mind was certainly keen

---

4. When we talk here of an intrinsic relation between concepts we do not have in mind the Leibnizian ideal of analysis into simple natures. The picture that seems to me best to capture Hegel's vision here is rather that of a set of nodes in a net, each of which is identified solely by its relations to the other nodes.

enough for him to have realized that these developments would motivate a fundamental rethinking of much of his system. Perhaps the most significant difference between the logic that Hegel knew and contemporary logic is that, whereas Aristotelian logic is through and through a logic of terms, the fundamental level of virtually every branch of contemporary logic is propositional. Today terms are always introduced in a more complex logic on a propositional base. What Hegel would have thought of this change we can only guess. Would he take our systems as expressing more adequately the relations between concept, judgment, and inference, or less? But such speculation is not to the point here; rather, by pointing out this difference we can bring to the fore a feature of Hegel's interpretation of the syllogism that might otherwise confuse us. We think of inferential relations as obtaining between propositions (or sentences, or statements, or what have you). Due to his confinement to a logic of terms, Hegel thinks of the inferential relation as obtaining at the basic level between terms, as being a more complex connection between terms than the judgmental relation. The term is the all important piece in the logical puzzle, and finding the right term, the right concept, is like finding the passkey that will unlock the nature of the world by permitting inferential access from every part of it to the whole in terms of which it can be understood.

The syllogism is, then, seen by Hegel as an interrelation of concepts. In judgment in general we also find an interrelation of concepts, but this is, Hegel claims, quite a rigid relation, each term of the judgment seemingly independent in its own right of the other and possessed of certain formal characteristics that distinguished it unfailingly from the other term. Thus one term, say the subject, is formally determined as a universal or a particular, and therefore as formally of a distinct kind from the first. In the syllogism, however, "thought sublates the determination of form and at the same time posits the identity of differences" (§467). This is best exemplified by the middle term of a syllogism, which occupies (standardly) both the subject and the predicate positions in different premises. The form determinations of the concepts are sublated still further in that the premises in which the middle term occurs can also be premises or conclusions in further syllogisms, where the former middle term has become an extreme, that is, a major or minor term.

In the syllogism, the full systematicity of our conceptual net comes to the fore explicitly, and the lesson Hegel draws from his understanding of syllogistic is about the nature of concepts. Concepts are individual, differentiated among themselves, excluding one another; they are particulars, that is, specifications of a higher universal; and they are universals, having species and ultimately individuals under them. These are the moments of the Concept, and in the syllogism they are all brought to a unity, the unity of the Concept. A concept starts its unfolding in judgment but completes it and shows its true structure in syllogisms.

> The syllogism has been taken comformably to the distinctions which it contains; and the general result of the course of their evolution has been to show that these differences work out their own abolition and destroy the concept's outwardness to its own self. And, as we see, in the first place, 1) each of the moments has proved itself the systematic whole of these elements, in short a whole syllogism,—they are consequently implicitly identical. In the second place 2) the negation of their distinctions and of the mediation of one through another constitutes independency [*Fürsichsein*]; so that it is one and the same universal which is in these forms, and which is in this way also explicitly put as their identity. In this ideality of its moments, the syllogistic process may be described as essentially involving the negation of the characters through which its course runs, as being a mediative process through the suspension of mediation,—as coupling the subject not with another, but with a suspended other, in one word, with itself. (*EL* §192, Wallace tr.)

The syllogism shows that every concept is implicitly a system of conceptual relations; the concept comes to its truth in the syllogism. In the syllogism, in our abilities to infer, we idealize most adequately the complex structures exemplified in the world: "Everything is a syllogism. Everything is a concept, the existence of which is the differentiation of its members or functions, so that the universal nature of the concept gives itself external reality by means of particularity, and thereby, and as negative reflection-into-self, makes itself an individual. Or, conversely; the actual thing is an individual, which by means of particularity rises to universality and makes itself identical with itself" (*EL* §181, Wallace tr., adapted).

In the syllogism, concepts are brought to an articulated unity. But the unity given in any one syllogism presupposes other such unities. This sequence of pro-syllogisms could go on and on, but Hegel would call such an infinite progression a bad infinite (not a vicious regress, which it clearly is not). Reason refuses to remain content with the bad infinite and conceives instead the true infinite, the totality of conditions which is itself unconditioned. There must be, according to reason, an overarching unity, for reason, the great unifier, is self-reflective. The ideal lying behind the syllogism, then, is that of the articulated totality, the ultimate unity of all things in one system. This, the totality of conditions, is the unconditioned, the absolute. Here, obviously, Hegel joins battle with Kant. Kant saw that reason, the syllogizing faculty, has an innate urge to push onward to the unconditioned, the totality of conditions. But, he claimed, since such a totality can never possibly be given to our sense experience, and since knowledge is possible only through the conjoining of sense experience and thought, we can never claim *knowledge* of the totality of conditions. Kant is willing to grant the idea of the unconditioned totality of conditions (of which he thought there were three subspecies) a *regulative* role in the *use* of our reason.

The status of the unconditioned, together with the problem of the thing-in-itself, forms the major point of contention between Hegel and Kant, but the issues in this debate are so complex that we cannot hope to do them justice here. Kant, following his empiricist bent, rejects all ontological claims of the Ideas of reason because the Ideas transcend possible experience; Hegel, with his opposing rationalist bent, considers their transcendence of possible subjective experience to be a strength ontologically. Perhaps the most straightforward way to state the disagreement is as follows. As regulative principles, the Kantian Ideas are maxims for action, prescriptions, oughts. But they are not constitutive, and they represent ideals that can never be fulfilled, maxims that prescribe an impossible task. But, as Kant himself so strikingly pointed out, ought implies can. Kant seems stuck with a dilemma, an internal inconsistency, one that he escapes by saying that what is commanded is striving for the ideal, not achieving it. But this seems hollow to Hegel, like telling a midget to strive for a professional basketball career. According to Hegel such infinite striving is simply empty; an end without end is no end at all. Hegel's proposed solution is clear: ought does imply can, and the Ideas of reason (which Hegel unifies in his own one

Idea) as the *in principle* achievable task or object of rational thought are not merely regulative, they are what is in and for itself, what is real.

For Hegel, to think is to transcend sensation toward universality and necessity. The fact that through reason we pose ourselves an object that transcends all possible sense experience shows that here we have finally freed ourselves from the immediacy of sensation— finally begun to think purely: "The rise of thought beyond the world of sense, its passage from the finite to the infinite, the leap into the super-sensible which it takes when it snaps asunder the chain of sense, all this transition is thought and nothing but thought. Say there must be no such passage, and you say there is to be no thinking" (*EL* §50, Wallace tr.). This does not mean that Hegel thinks we can achieve the ideal scientific theory of natural phenomena; for reasons we have already discussed, the theory of nature is open to infinite refinement on Hegel's view. But philosophy studies thought itself, the universal and necessary structure of the world, and furthermore comprehends the ideal of thought, which is knowledge of the absolute, the unconditioned, itself none other than thought. Hegel's system, as has been noted before, seems to pull itself up by its own bootstraps. But since thought is not itself an item in our sensory experience, it is necessary to transcend sense experience if thought is to comprehend itself, if it is to be thought at all.

There is another way we can put this dispute. C. D. Broad suggests that there are two fundamental principles in Kant's discussion of the proofs for the existence of God, the Ideal of Pure Reason.[5] First, if anything exists, something must exist in its own right; or, not everything derives its existence from something else. This principle has found acceptance among philosophers since Parmenides. Second, it is not possible that the existence of anything should be a necessary consequence of its nature or definition. Kant's resolution of the conflict is to make both principles regulative (although, as Broad points out, he need only have made one regulative). Hegel rejects that solution and instead accepts the first principle and denies the second outright. His reason for doing so is that, whereas the second holds of natures and definitions abstractly conceived,

5. C. D. Broad, *Kant: An Introduction*, pp. 298–300.

that is, conceived as abstract universals, it is simply false of the concrete universal (see *SL*, pp. 705–8; *WdL*, vol. 2, pp. 353–57).[6]

The Nature of Thinking Activity

I have discussed the first list given in §467 in some detail, so the discussion of the second list can be shorter. As I have said, the second list focuses on the *activity* of theoretical spirit. It is thus a more adequate description of the actuality of thinking, yet we have covered most of the ground already in our extensive discussion of the first list.

> Intelligence cognizes as thinking. Indeed, a) if the understanding explains the singular from its own universalities (the categories), it is called self-comprehending; b) if the understanding explains it [the singular] as a universal (genus, kind) in a judgment, then the content appears in this form as given. c) However, in a syllogism the understanding determines the content from itself in that it sublates the distinction of forms. The last immediacy that remains attached to formal thinking disappears with the insight into necessity. (§467, my tr.)

What first strikes our attention is that Hegel consistently uses the word "explain" (*erklären*) to describe the activity involved in thought. Hegel adopts a rather Aristotelian view of explanation, recognizing different "why" questions in answer to which explanations can be given. But he gives pride of place to teleological explanation, for it is a form of explanation grounded in the concept of the thing explained; it alone relies on intrinsic necessities. The philosophical theory of the world is a teleological theory, and only such a theory, according to Hegel, could count as a philosophical explanation of the nature of the world.[7]

Some parts of this second list seem confusing. If the understanding tries to get at something's concept, to explain the singular thing

---

6. Applied to the ontological argument, though, Hegel's position begs the question, for he has not demonstrated the correctness of his theory of the concrete universal.

7. See deVries, "The Dialectic of Teleology," Proceedings, Hegel Society of America, 1980.

by means of "its own [the understanding's] universalities (the categories)," what is it doing, and why does this count as "comprehending itself"? First, Hegel seems to reserve the term "categories" for the concepts of the objective logic, Being and Essence, so he is here talking of explaining something in terms of its qualities, quantities, relations, and so forth. This certainly seems straightforward enough; but how does this result in understanding's comprehending itself? We have already seen that Hegel's theory is a version of the macrocosm-microcosm view; intelligence has reconstructed the world within itself, and understanding any part of the world, it is also in part understanding its own activity in reconstruction. The categories are generic rules by which it operates, and knowing how to apply them is a form of understanding, just as knowing how to use the tools properly is a form of understanding construction work. And, of course, the categories are themselves the product of intelligence; to understand them, understanding must understand itself in its product. The formulation Hegel gives the last part of this paragraph in the 1827 edition of the *Encyclopedia* bears this out: "In that it comprehends, intelligence has the determinedness which in its sensation is at first sight an immediate material, in itself as simply its own. In the insight into the necessity of the content first given to thought itself, the course of its own activity is, for intelligence, identical with the implicit being of the determinedness of the content, intelligence being for itself as determining" (*PSS*, vol. 3, pp. 221–23).

This passage also brings out the important fact that Hegel believes that, in thinking, the activity of the mind is "identical" with the "implicit being" of the determinateness [*an sich seyenden Bestimmtseyn*] of what is thought about. Hegel takes it to be the case that the structure of thought is the structure of the world. All things are judgments; all things are syllogisms, according to Hegel. The structural relations discernible in the activity of thought are the same as the ontological structures of the world. There is, however, no argument here for this position; such an "argument" is the burden of the *Logik* and of the system as a whole.

In §467 Hegel encapsulates a vision of the nature of man's theoretical activity. We begin with a confrontation with the individual facts and entities of the world, yet this is not a mute acceptance, for they have been raised to exemplars of the universal, they belong to kinds. This point is made explicit in the second stage of thought, judgment. The content of thought still *appears* to be *given* here, insofar as we are still making explicit the interconnections between the universals, which universals appear otherwise independent of each other. An example of this kind of approach might be taking "mass" to be an independent concept that can enter into different theories, such as the Newtonian or Einsteinian, without being intrinsically affected in any way.

This point of view is superseded at the highest level of thought, where our awareness of the importance of the inferential connections among our concepts is explicit. Even the universals through which we first grasped the individual facts and entitites are now seen to be specifications of the one universal activity of thinking. Thought is to this extent a closed system, adapting itself to itself, giving itself its own structure. By dealing thus only with itself, building within itself a pure system of relations, thought has transcended all particular content and all immediacy, achieving "insight into necessity."

This final stage is not, one must realize, a form of a special science; it is not an empirical scientific theory of an aspect of nature, nor of nature as a whole. It is the unitary, philosophical theory of how things in the broadest sense hang together. A scientific theory, which must have some particular subject matter, never achieves this exalted status, for it always depends on some form of given, something that spirit merely finds before it. Only in the theory that unifies not only the particular phenomena of nature but also religious, ethical, and aesthetic phenomena and, perhaps most important, philosophical theorizing itself into one complete picture of the world-whole is all particular content transcended. By transcending all particular content, philosophical theorizing is left with only the universal content: thought. Philosophy, like the absolute, thinks thought. The goal of pure thought is the comprehensive knowledge of itself, of the conceptual articulation of the world, of which it is itself an aspect and of which it is the goal. Its method is pure inference, taking everything offered to it and following out all its consequences (where deductive inferences are the most trivial and least important form of reaching consequences).

The universal is known here as self-particularizing and as collecting itself together from the particularization into singularity—or, which is the same—as the particular reduced from its independence to being a

moment of the concept. Accordingly, the universal is no longer external to the content here, but is rather the veritable form that produces
the content out of itself—the self-developing concept of the subject-
matter [*Sache*]. Thinking, therefore, has at this point no other content
than itself, than its own determinations, which constitute the immanent content of the form. Thinking seeks and finds in the object
[*Gegenstand*] only itself. The object is therefore distinguished from
thinking only in that it has the form of being, of subsisting for itself.
Thus thinking stands here in a perfectly free relationship to the object
[*Objekt*]. (§467, *Zusatz*, my tr.)

The goal of thought is the construction of a completely self-contained, self-explanatory conceptual system, one identical with the
conceptual articulation of the world itself. The explanations that
this system will afford, however, are not deductive arguments in
which a particular event, property, or object is shown to be necessary; they are teleological, interpretive "makings sense of" particular aspects of the world. Philosophy will never allow us to predict
the course of the world or its individual events, but it should enable
us to understand in retrospect how it all hangs together. Through
philosophy we gain a vision of the whole through which the individual parts make sense. But this vision metaphor must be handled
gingerly, for the perceiver is normally distinct from the perceived.
The "vision" of the whole gained through philosophy can only be
achieved by identifying with that whole; our "vision" is better
called a re-creation: "In this thinking that is identical to its object
[*Gegenstand*] intelligence achieves its completion, its goal, for it is
then in fact what, in its immediacy, it was only supposed to be—
self-knowing truth, self-recognizing reason. This mutual self-pen-
etration of thinking subjectivity and objective reason is the result of
the development of theoretical spirit through the stages of intuition
and representation that precede pure thinking" (§467, *Zusatz*, my
tr.).

THE TRANSITION TO PRACTICAL SPIRIT

Although the internal re-creation of the structure of the whole is
the culmination of theoretical spirit, it is of course not the final end

to the story, for theoretical spirit develops into practical spirit, which transition is the topic of §468: "Intelligence, knowing itself to be the determinant of the content, which is determined as its own no less than as being, is *will*." Concepts are ideals, and the theorizing activity of spirit produces knowledge of ideals. In particular, spirit's self-knowledge is a knowledge of its *own* ideal nature. Intrinsic to the notion of an ideal, however, is that it is a goal to be pursued, and the knowledge of its ideal which results from spirit's theoretical activity necessarily culminates in *practical* activity.

> Pure thinking is, to begin with, a disinterested (*unbefangenes*) activity in which it is absorbed in the object. But this action necessarily also becomes objective to itself. Since objective cognition is absolutely at home with itself in the object, it must recognize that its determinations are determinations of the object, and that, conversely, the objectively valid determinations immediately present in the object are its determinations. By this recollection, this withdrawal into itself of intelligence, the latter becomes will. (§468, *Zusatz*, Miller tr.)

It is part of our nature to be knowers, and we therefore strive to achieve the ideal theory of the world. But we are not, and could not be, *only* knowers. The task of the lower levels of theoretical spirit is to idealize that which is realized in the world; as it progresses and develops, spirit develops its content from within itself through its theorizing. There is a certain amount of practical activity here, of course—creating words, making judgments and inferences. Hegel does not intend us to think that theoretical and practical activity can be divorced from one another; the relation between them is only that levels of practical activity conceptually presuppose levels of theoretical activity. In fact, however, they cannot be disjoined. When Hegel turns to the analysis of practical spirit, he has to backtrack quite a bit, to a conception of "practical feeling." In actuality the theoretical and the practical are simultaneous aspects of the activity of spirit, but as we all know, exposition is always linear, even if the subject matter is not.

In emerging into the sphere of practical spirit, spirit testifies to its freedom and its self-certainty. It is now sure of itself as the moving power of the world, sure that its own products must be realized in the world. To the extent that nature does not exemplify the ideals of spirit, nature falls short, and spirit must undertake to work its will on nature. This process is itself subject to a complex dialectical progression, but that lies beyond the bounds of this essay.

CONCLUSION

Hegel maintains that, in thinking, concepts are active within me, and I am their vehicle, as it were. These are one and the same concepts that are active in the world, and they constitute the true substance of the world. The problem of a divorce between my concepts and the natures of things as they are in themselves therefore does not arise. But although the problem of a thing-in-itself may not arise for Hegel, it would be more than naive to think that no other problems arise.

The notion of a creative, self-structuring activity is awesome, fascinating, and powerful—but also quite hard for us to accept. It is hard to tell, of course, whether we fully understand Hegel's concept of spirit and reject it because of lingering suspicions about its coherence, or whether we have not yet succeeded in comprehending the concept—a concept, supposedly, in which comprehension breeds credence. Neither our suspicions nor our lack of insight can count as a refutation of such a notion, but the notion is so vague that more exacting criticism of it is equally elusive. We do know that self-reflection often generates paradoxes in otherwise straightforward matters, especially where all-inclusive self-reflective totalities are concerned. The set-theoretical paradoxes are the best examples of this. But how would one even begin to construct an argument that Hegel's notion of a self-reflective totality, the Absolute, is as barren as the notion of the set of all sets? One tends to avoid self-reflective totalities whenever possible, because of their extreme complexity, yet, in Hegel's defense, it is not clear that we can avoid them altogether. We certainly cannot rule out limited self-reflection—it is too obviously a feature of the world we live in and of our own being.

Someone of naturalistic bent might easily point out that there seems to be no particular problem involved in one part of the world "mapping" another part, even if it is an element of what is mapped. There need only be restrictions on the detail of the map. I have much sympathy with such an approach, but working out the details, we also know, is an extremely difficult task. Hegel did not adopt such an approach for a reason the strength of which I am still uncertain. The world as he saw it was too obviously teleological.

Standard physical theory tells us that the world ought to run down, approaching a random distribution of energy. Organic and mental phenomena seem to gainsay this result (remember that Hegel wrote well before Darwin). Explaining organic and mental phenomena on the basis of the principles adequate for the explanation of the inorganic, material world did not look feasible. The only alternative, if the world was not to be bifurcated into alien realms, was to explain the material, inorganic, and mechanical somehow on the basis of the teleological principles used in the explanation of the organic and the mental. This is the route Hegel took. But the attempt to fit the material and mechanical into an organic framework, when it concerns the world-whole, raises its own problems, for there are major disanalogies between the world-whole and organisms or minds. Organisms and minds have environments with which they interact causally, for instance. Even if we accept the idea that organisms and minds are to be explained through teleological principles, an idea Hegel never doubted, deep puzzles arise when we try to apply these principles, as vague as most of them are, to the world-whole. As we learn more about what kind of thing teleology is, we may well find that Hegel's route looks even less plausible.

But even if most of us find it hard today to accept Hegel's notion of the Absolute and much of the attendant metaphysics that accompanies it, his system is still worth our attention. I have often been asked what profit there is in studying Hegel's philosophy of mind, and the subtext of the question is whether there are insights there that would transform current philosophy of mind, insights unrepresented in the current debate. Perhaps regrettably, the answer must be that there is nothing strikingly new in Hegel's philosophy of mind. Fifty years ago, however, the question would have been answered with a resounding yes! Against the atomism and reductionism of the positivists, Hegel would have been a welcome antidote. As it happened, Hegel's own primary inspiration in philosophical psychology, Aristotle, provided much of the inspiration to those who battled positivism within the Anglo-American tradition. But positivism was not simply overthrown in a movement to restore past philosophical glories; its own adherents rigorously investigated its assumptions and its arguments, and its own internal dialectic gradually led to a repudiation of the atomism and reductionism characteristic of positivist thought. Hegel has little *new* to offer us because, after much hard work, we have finally caught up with him.

The purely historical interest in comprehending a great philosophy for its own sake is quite sufficient justification for reading Hegel, particularly when there are interesting resonances with current work in the field. Surely we understand our own assumptions better by seeing them employed or rejected by others, particularly those who have been major figures in our own history. An ahistorical philosophy is an unreflective philosophy—and that is a contradiction in terms.

References

Ameriks, Karl. *Kant's Theory of Mind.* Oxford: Oxford University Press, 1982.

Anscombe, G. E. M. "The First Person." In *Mind and Language,* edited by S. Guttenplan. Oxford: Oxford University Press, 1975.

Aquila, Richard. "Predication and Hegel's Metaphysics." In *Hegel,* edited by M. J. Inwood. Oxford Readings in Philosophy. Oxford: Oxford University Press, 1985.

Aristotle. *The Basic Works of Aristotle.* Edited by Richard McKeon. New York: Random House, 1941.

Artelt, Walter. *Der Mesmerismus in Berlin.* Abhandlungen der Geistes- und Sozialwissenschaftlichen Klasse, 1965, no. 6. Mainz: Akademie der Wissenschaften und der Literatur, 1965.

Block, Ned, ed. *Imagery.* Cambridge: M.I.T. Press, 1981.

——, ed. *Readings in the Philosophy of Psychology.* Cambridge: Harvard University Press, 1981.

Bodammer, T. *Hegel's Deutung der Sprache.* Hamburg: F. Meiner, 1969.

Broad, C. D. *Kant: An Introduction.* Cambridge: Cambridge University Press, 1978.

Burge, Tyler. "Individualism and the Mental." *Midwest Studies in Philosophy* 4 (1979):73–121.

——. "Other Bodies." In *Thought and Object,* edited by A. Woodfield. Oxford: Oxford University Press, 1982.

Davidson, Donald. "Mental Events." In *Experience and Theory,* edited by L. Foster and J. W. Swanson. Amherst: University of Massachusetts Press, 1970.

Dennett, Daniel. *Brainstorms.* Montgomery, Vt.: Bradford Books, 1978.

Descartes, René. *The Philosophical Works of Descartes.* 2 vols. Translated by

E. S. Haldane and G. R. T. Ross. Cambridge: Cambridge University Press, 1931.

deVries, Willem. "The Dialectic of Teleology." *Proceedings, Hegel Society of America,* 1980.

——. "Hegel on Reference and Knowledge." *Journal of the History of Philosophy* 26 (1988):297–307.

——. Review of *Appropriating Hegel* by Crawford Elder. *Owl of Minerva* 14 (December 1982):5–8 and 14 (March 1983):4–8.

Elder, Crawford. *Appropriating Hegel.* Aberdeen: Aberdeen University Press, 1980.

Fichte, J. G. *Sämtliche Werke,* vol. 1. Berlin: Veit, 1845.

Fodor, Jerry A. *The Language of Thought.* Cambridge: Harvard University Press, 1980.

——. *The Modularity of Mind.* Cambridge: M.I.T. Press, 1983.

Foster, K., and Humphries, S., trans. *Aristotle's "De Anima" in the Version of William of Moerbeke and the Commentary of St. Thomas Aquinas.* New Haven: Yale University Press, 1951.

Fulda, Hans Friedrich. *Das Problem einer Einleitung in Hegels Wissenschaft der Logik.* Frankfurt am Main: Klostermann, 1965.

Gardeil, H. P. *Psychology.* Vol. 3 of *Introduction to the Philosophy of St. Thomas Aquinas.* Translated by J. Otto. St. Louis: B. Herder, 1956.

Garfield, Jay. "Propositional Attitudes and the Ontology of the Mental." *Cognition and Brain Theory* 6 (3) (1983):319–331.

Hacking, Ian. *Why Does Language Matter to Philosophy?* Cambridge: Cambridge University Press, 1975.

Hamlyn, D. W. *Sensation and Perception: A History of the Philosophy of Perception.* New York: Humanities Press, 1961.

Hartmann, Eduard. *Body, Soul, and Substance.* Princeton: Princeton University Press, 1977.

Hartmann, N. "Aristoteles und Hegel." In *Kleinere Schriften II.* Berlin: deGruyter, 1957.

Haugeland, John. "Weak Supervenience." *American Philosophical Quarterly* 19 (January 1982):93–104.

Hegel, G. W. F. *Enzyklopedie der philosophischen Wissenschaften.* Edited by F. Nicolin and O. Pöggeler. Hamburg: F. Meiner, 1959.

——. *Enzyklopedie der philosophischen Wissenschaften.* Werke, edited by Eva Moldenhauer and Karl Markus Michel, vols. 8–10. Frankfurt am Main: Suhrkamp, 1970.

——. *Hegel's Phenomenology of Spirit.* Translated by A. V. Miller. New York: Oxford University Press, 1977.

——. *Hegel's Philosophy of Mind.* Translated by W. Wallace and A. V. Miller. New York: Oxford University Press, 1971.

——. *Hegel's Philosophy of Nature.* 3 vols. Translated and edited by M. J. Petry. London: George Allen & Unwin, 1970.

——. *Hegel's Philosophy of Nature.* Translated by W. Wallace and A. V. Miller. New York: Oxford University Press, 1970.

——. *Hegel's Philosophy of Subjective Spirit.* 3 vols. Edited and translated by M. J. Petry. Boston: D. Reidel, 1978

——. *Hegel's Science of Logic.* Translated by A. V. Miller. London: George Allen & Unwin, 1969.

——. *The Logic of Hegel.* Translated by W. Wallace. New York: Oxford University Press, 1892.

——. *Phänomenologie des Geistes.* Edited by J. Hoffmeister. 6th ed. Hamburg: F. Meiner, 1952.

——. *Vorlesungen über die Geschichte der Philosophie.* Bd. 2. Frankfurt am Main: Suhrkamp, 1971.

——. *Werke in 20 Bänden.* Edited by Eva Moldenhauer and Karl Markus Michel. Frankfurt am Main: Suhrkamp, 1970.

——. *Wissenschaft der Logik.* Edited by G. Lasson. Hamburg: F. Meiner, 1934.

Heintel, Erich. "Aristotelismus und Transzendentalismus in 'Begriff' bei Hegel." In *Die Welt des Menschen-Die Welt der Philosophie.* Edited by Walter Biemel. Den Haag: Martinus Nijhoff, 1976.

Henrich, Dieter. "Hegels Theorie über den Zufall." In *Hegel im Context.* Frankfurt am Main: Suhrkamp, 1967.

Hofstadter, Douglas R. *Gödel, Escher, Bach: An Eternal Golden Braid.* New York: Basic Books, 1979.

Hölderlin, F. "Urtheil und Seyn." In *Materialien zu Schellings Philosophischen Anfängen,* edited by M. Frank und G. Kurz. Frankfurt am Main: Suhrkamp, 1975.

Hume, David. *A Treatise of Human Nature.* Edited by L. A. Selby-Bigge. 2d ed. edited by P. H. Nidditch. Oxford: Clarendon Press, 1978.

Inwood, M. J. *Hegel.* London: Routledge & Kegan Paul, 1983.

Kant, Immanuel. *Critique of Judgment.* Translated by J. H. Bernard. New York: Hafner Press, 1951.

——. *Critique of Pure Reason.* Translated by Norman Kemp Smith. London: Macmillan, 1929.

——. *Kritik der Urteilskraft.* Kants gesammelte Schriften, edited by the Königlich Preußischen Akademie der Wissenschaften, vol. V. Berlin: Walter de Gruyter, 1968.

Kemeny, John G., and Oppenheim, Paul. "On Reduction." In *Readings in the Philosophy of Science,* edited by Baruch Brody. Englewood Cliffs, N.J.: Prentice-Hall, 1970.

Kim, Jaegwon. "Supervenience and Nomological Incommensurables." *American Philosophical Quarterly* 15 (April 1978):149–156.

Kitcher, Patricia. "Kant's Real Self." In *Self and Nature in Kant's Philosophy*, edited by Allan Wood. Ithaca: Cornell University Press, 1984.

Litt, Theodor. *Hegel: Versuch einer kritischen Erneuerung*. Heidelberg: Quelle & Meyer, 1953.

Locke, John. *An Essay Concerning Human Understanding*. Edited by P. H. Nidditch. Oxford: Clarendon Press, 1975.

McTaggart, J. M. E. *Studies in Hegelian Cosmology*. Cambridge: Cambridge University Press, 1901.

Nagel, Ernest. *The Structure of Science: Problems in the Logic of Scientific Explanation*. London: Routledge & Kegan Paul, 1961.

Nagel, Thomas. *The View from Nowhere*. Oxford: Oxford University Press, 1986.

Plumer, Gilbert. "Hegel on Singular Demonstrative Reference." *Southwestern Journal of Philosophy* (1980):71–84.

Pöggeler, Otto. *Hegels Idee einer Phänomenologie des Geistes*. Freiburg and Munich: Alber, 1973.

Price, H. H. *Thinking and Experience*. London: Hutchinson University Library, 1953.

Putnam, Hilary. *Philosophical Papers*, vol. 2: *Mind, Language, and Reality*. Cambridge: Cambridge University Press, 1975.

Rorty, Richard. *Philosophy and the Mirror of Nature*. Princeton: Princeton University Press, 1979.

Royce, Josiah. *Lectures on Modern Idealism*. New Haven: Yale University Press, 1919.

Sellars, Wilfrid. "Philosophy and the Scientific Image of Man." In *Science, Perception, and Reality*. London: Routledge & Kegan Paul, 1963.

——. *Science and Metaphysics*. New York: Humanities Press, 1968.

Soll, Ivan. *An Introduction to Hegel's Metaphysics*. Chicago: University of Chicago Press, 1969.

Solomon, Robert C. "Hegel's Concept of *Geist*." In *Hegel, A Collection of Critical Essays*, edited by A. MacIntyre. Garden City, N.Y.: Anchor Doubleday, 1972.

Spinoza, B. *Ethics*. Edited by J. Gutmann. New York: Hafner, 1949.

Stace, W. T. *The Philosophy of Hegel*. New York: Dover, 1955.

Strawson, P. F. *The Bounds of Sense*. London: Methuen, 1966.

Taylor, Charles. *Hegel*. Cambridge: Cambridge University Press, 1975.

Vendler, Zeno. "A Note to the Paralogisms." In *Contemporary Aspects of Philosophy*, edited by G. Ryle. Boston: Oriel Press, 1976.

Index

Absolute, self-realization of, 3, 13–14, 45–46, 50, 105–7
Abstraction, 126–28, 132, 137–39
Ameriks, Karl, 18n
Animals, 47–48, 55–57
  distinguished from humans, 102, 116
  and feeling, 72–73
Anscombe, G. E. M., 91n
Aquila, Richard, 22n, 95n, 172n
Aquinas, St. Thomas, 65, 72–73
Aristotle, 44–45, 55n, 64–67, 172, 201
Artelt, Walter, 28n
Associationism, 1, 137–41
Attention, 111–16

Behaviorism, 1
Bodammer, T., 162n
Broad, C. D., 194
Burge, Tyler, 41n, 81n

Chisholm, Roderick, 103n
Church, Alonzo, 165n
Concept:
  Hegel's understanding of, 2, 67, 105–7, 137, 171–75, 179–80, 184–86, 189–92
  and representations. See Representational theory of mind
  and words, 163, 175, 177, 183
Concrete universal, 137, 171–74, 175n, 177, 181–82
Connectionism, 130
Content, 70
  vs. form, 65, 105, 178
  and functional role, 65–66
  and sensation, 60–63, 65–70
Copula, 31n, 183, 185–86

Davidson, Donald, 40n
Dennett, Daniel, 167n
Descartes, René, 2, 32, 36, 89, 166–67
Dualism, 3, 36

Ego. See I
Elder, Crawford, 42n
Eliminative materialism, 37
Emotions, 62
Empirical sensitivity, 14, 27–28, 31–35
Empiricism, 18, 22–24
Eschenmayer, A. C. A., 28–29
Existence, concept of, 106

Faculty psychology, 23–24, 59–60
Feeling, 56–57, 71–85
  vs. intuition, 108–10
  vs. sensation, 71–72
Fichte, J. G., 181n
Fodor, Jerry, 36n, 59n, 167n
Form. See Content
Fulda, Hans Friedrich, 87n
Functionalism, 1, 63, 65, 101, 107, 122, 141, 175, 183, 201

Gardeil, H. P., 73
Garfield, Jay, 41n, 81n
Gödel, Kurt, 165n
Goethe, Johann von, 11

Habit, 84–86, 102
Hacking, Ian, 150n
Hamlyn, D. W., 53n, 68n, 90n
Hartley, David, 139, 168
Hartmann, N., 45n
Haugeland, John, 41n
Heintel, E., 56n

Hofstadter, Douglas, 175n
Hölderlin, F., 181n
Hume, David, 1, 2, 19, 32, 89, 127, 138–40, 166, 168, 185
Hypnotism, 27–28, 79, 81, 83

I, 85–107
  as concept of concepts, 173, 185
  not soul, body, or transcendental ego, 97–99
  as power of names, 159–61
  as self-relation, 100–4
  as such, 94–96
  as system of pure concepts, 104–7
"Ideal," 49, 58
Image:
  abstracted from spatiotemporal context, 126–27, 132
  association of, 136–41
  generality of, 131–33, 136–37
  vs. intuition, 126
  and language, 151–54, 156, 161
  preservation of, 128–30
  as symbol, 141–43
Imagination, 134–48
  and intuition, 135–36
Inspectivism, 165–66, 169–70, 174–75
Interpretation, 16–17
Intuition, 108–18
  vs. feeling, 108–10
  and imagination, 135–36
  vs. representation, 119–25, 127–28
  and sensation, 109
  as singular, 108
Inwood, M. J., 90n, 104

Judgment, 180–90
  vs. proposition, 182–83

Kant, Immanuel, 9, 17–19, 31–32, 34n, 49, 55n, 67, 89, 95n, 97–99, 102, 105, 108, 114, 169–70, 172–73, 185, 193–94
Kemeny, John G., 36n
Kim, Jaegwon, 41n
Kitcher, Patricia, 95n, 98n, 99n
Krug, Wilhelm Traugott, 14n

Language, 146–63, 177
  and grammar, 151, 162, 183
  and nominalization of spirit, 158–63
  spoken vs. written, 147–48
  and theory of meaning, 149–53, 159–62
  thought and, 149–53, 163
Lewis, David, 103n

Litt, T., 52n
Locke, John, 129, 132, 139, 150–51
Logic, 33–34, 190–91

McTaggart, J. M. E., 19
Meaning. *See* Language
Memory, 146, 149–63
  mechanical, 157–63
Mental illness, 77–79
Mill, James, 168
Mill, John Stuart, 168
Modularity in psychology, 59–60
Monad, soul as, 80–83
Mure, G. R. G., 45n

Nagel, Thomas, 7
Names, 92, 152–56
  replacing images, 158–61
Natural kind, 9, 11–17
Nature:
  imperfection of, 187–89
  practical relation to, 4–10
  and spirit, 33–49
  theoretical relation to, 4–7, 10–13
Noneliminative materialism. *See* Token identity theory

Oppenheim, Paul, 36n

Petry, M. J., 27, 76n
Phenomenology of Spirit, 53, 68n, 87–89, 93
Philosophy, 13–17, 197–98
Physicalism, 2–3
Plumer, Gilbert, 90n, 91n
Pöggeler, Otto, 87n
Predication, 22, 171–72, 180–87
Price, H. H., 164–65
Psychology:
  faculty, 23–24, 59–60
  modularity in, 59–60
  pure, 29–31
Purpose:
  objective, 7–10
  universal, 10–13
  See also Teleology
Putnam, Hilary, 36n

Qualia, absent or inverted, 66

Rationalism, 18–22, 97
Recognition, 132–33
Recollection, 125–34
  vs. imagination, 135–37
  nonatomistic, 128
  of words, 149–50, 153–55, 177–80

Reductionism, 36–37, 42
Reference, linguistic, 90–93, 97–99,
  103n
Representation:
  explanations of, 122–23
  generality of, 131–34, 136–37, 142,
    151–53, 155, 160–62, 164
  vs. intuition, 119–25, 127–28
  and memory, 155–56
  problem of individuating, 128
  See also Image; Language; Signs;
    Symbols
Representational theory of mind, 165–
  66, 170–71, 174–75
Rorty, Richard, 169n, 170n
Royce, Josiah, 51n
Russell, Bertrand, 91n, 166
Ryle, Gilbert, 165–67

Self:
  bundle theory of, 79–80
  emergence of, 85–86, 101
  See also I
Self-feeling, 74–78
Sellars, Wilfrid, 7, 109n, 114, 166
Sensation, 48, 53–70, 100–1
  vs. feeling, 71–72, 110n
  vs. intuition, 108–9
  object of, 60–67
  organized in feeling, 75
  sublation of, through language, 152
Sense, inner vs. outer, 61–63

Sentience vs. nonsentience, 54–60
Signs, 143–48
  and things signified, 145, 154
Simple ideas or concepts, 129, 172–73,
  192
Solomon, R. C., 25n, 51n, 53n
Soul, 18–26, 97, 101
  immateriality of, 20–21
  vs. spirit, 25
Space, 69–70, 79, 112–15
Spinoza, Baruch, 64n
Spirit, Hegel's characterization of, 25–
  26, 46–52
Strawson, P. F., 99n
Supervenience, 40–46, 81–84
  and expression, 83
Syllogism, 63, 103n
  theory of, 190–96
Symbols, 141–43
  inert and active, 175n
  and things symbolized, 144

Taylor, Charles, 51n, 53n
Teleology, 4, 7–17, 26, 45, 195, 201
Thought, subjective vs. objective, 104–
  7, 171–78, 196–97
Time, 111–15
Token identity theory, 38–39, 42
Truth vs. correctness, 183–84

Vendler, Zeno, 98–99n

Library of Congress Cataloging-in-Publication Data

DeVries, Willem A., 1950–
   Hegel's theory of mental activity: an introduction to theoretical spirit/Willem A.
deVries.
       p.   cm.
   Bibliography: p.
   Includes index.
   ISBN 0–8014–2133–0 (alk. paper)
     1. Mind and body—Philosophy—History—19th century. 2. Hegel, Georg Wil-
helm Friedrich, 1770–1831—Contributions in philosophy of mind. 3. Psychology—
Philosophy—History—19th century. 4. Hegel, Georg Wilhelm Friedrich, 1770–
1831. Philosophie des Geistes. I. Title.
BF161.D46 1988   88–47723   128′.2—dc19